MW01122019

2009 03 30

Henri-Georges Clouzot

MANCHESTER
1824

Manchester University Press

FRENCH FILM DIRECTORS

DIANA HOLMES and ROBERT INGRAM *series editors*
DUDLEY ANDREW *series consultant*

Jean-Jacques Beineix PHIL POWRIE

Luc Besson SUSAN HAYWARD

Bertrand Blier SUE HARRIS

Robert Bresson KEITH READER

Leos Carax GARIN DOWD AND FERGUS DALEY

Claude Chabrol GUY AUSTIN

Jean Cocteau JAMES WILLIAMS

Claire Denis MARTINE BEUGNET

Marguerite Duras RENATE GÜNTHER

Georges Franju KATE INCE

Jean-Luc Godard DOUGLAS MORREY

Diane Kurys CARRIE TARR

Patrice Leconte LISA DOWNING

Louis Malle HUGO FREY

Georges Méliès ELIZABETH EZRA

Jean Renoir MARTIN O'SHAUGHNESSY

Alain Resnais EMMA WILSON

Coline Serreau BRIGITTE ROLLET

François Truffaut DIANA HOLMES AND ROBERT INGRAM

Agnès Varda ALISON SMITH

Jean Vigo MICHAEL TEMPLE

Henri-Georges Clouzot

CHRISTOPHER LLOYD

165101

Manchester University Press
MANCHESTER AND NEW YORK

distributed exclusively in the USA by Palgrave

Published by Manchester University Press
Oxford Road, Manchester M13 9NR, UK
and Room 400, 175 Fifth Avenue, New York, NY 10010, USA
www.manchesteruniversitypress.co.uk

Distributed exclusively in the USA by
Palgrave, 175 Fifth Avenue, New York, NY 10010, USA

Distributed exclusively in Canada by
UBC Press, University of British Columbia, 2029 West Mall, Vancouver,
BC, Canada V6T 1Z2

British Library Cataloguing-in-Publication Data
A catalogue record for this book is available from the British Library

Library of Congress Cataloging-in-Publication Data applied for

ISBN 978 0 7190 7014 3 *hardback*

First published 2007

16 15 14 13 12 11 10 09 08 07   10 9 8 7 6 5 4 3 2 1

Typeset in Scala with Meta display
by Koinonia, Manchester
Printed in Great Britain
by Biddles Ltd, King's Lynn

Contents

List of plates

All illustrations reproduced by kind permission of Mme Inès Clouzot.

Series editors' foreword

To an anglophone audience, the combination of the words 'French' and 'cinema' evokes a particular kind of film: elegant and wordy, sexy but serious – an image as dependent on national stereotypes as is that of the crudely commercial Hollywood blockbuster, which is not to say that either image is without foundation. Over the past two decades, this generalised sense of a significant relationship between French identity and film has been explored in scholarly books and articles, and has entered the curriculum at university level and, in Britain, at A-level. The study of film as an art-form and (to a lesser extent) as industry, has become a popular and widespread element of French Studies, and French cinema has acquired an important place within Film Studies. Meanwhile, the growth in multi-screen and 'art-house' cinemas, together with the development of the video industry, has led to the greater availability of foreign-language films to an English-speaking audience. Responding to these developments, this series is designed for students and teachers seeking information and accessible but rigorous critical study of French cinema, and for the enthusiastic filmgoer who wants to know more.

The adoption of a director-based approach raises questions about auteurism. A series that categorises films not according to period or to genre (for example), but to the person who directed them, runs the risk of espousing a romantic view of film as the product of solitary inspiration. On this model, the critic's role might seem to be that of discovering continuities, revealing a necessarily coherent set of themes and motifs which correspond to the particular genius of the individual. This is not our aim: the auteur perspective on film, itself most clearly articulated in France in the early 1950s, will be interrogated in certain volumes of the series, and, throughout, the director will be treated as one highly significant element in a complex process of film production and reception which includes socio-economic and political determinants, the work of a large and highly skilled team of artists and technicians, the mechanisms of production and distribution, and the complex and multiply determined responses of spectators.

The work of some of the directors in the series is already known outside France, that of others is less so – the aim is both to provide informative and original English-language studies of established figures, and to extend the range of French directors known to anglophone students of cinema. We intend the series to contribute to the promotion of the informal and formal study of French films, and to the pleasure of those who watch them.

DIANA HOLMES
ROBERT INGRAM

Acknowledgements

For offering helpful advice, ideas and access to sources, I would like to thank staff at the Bibliothèque du Film, the archives of the Cinémathèque Française, the British Film Institute and the Bibliothèque Nationale, as well as Margaret Atack, Susan Hayward, Phil Powrie, Keith Reader, the editors of this series, and other colleagues and students with whom I have discussed Clouzot's work in lectures and seminars over many years. I am most grateful to Durham University for offering research leave and funding, and to Mme Inès Clouzot for agreeing to answer questions about her husband's work and to the reproduction of images from his films in this book.

Clouzot and the cinema

Before studying Clouzot's films in detail, we need to situate him in the wider context of French history and cinema in the mid-twentieth century. Issues such as the following will be addressed in this introductory chapter. What forces, personal, political and social, shaped his career as a film-maker? To what extent do his films propose a consistent, personal vision, and how do they reflect the important social and aesthetic changes of his time? Does Clouzot qualify as an *auteur*, as an original and innovative creator, or was he essentially a technically brilliant craftsman, a skilled manipulator of audiences, who produced a series of arresting genre films? If he was as much an entertainer as an artist, why in that case did he direct so few films? And finally, were his films influenced in any way by the rise of the New Wave of French directors and critics from the late 1950s, or did they remain rooted in what some hostile commentators saw as a conventional and stultifying classicism?

Although Clouzot's output as a director spanned a period of twenty-six years, in this time he released only ten full-length feature films (from *L'Assassin habite au 21* in 1942 to *La Prisonnière* in 1968), as well as one short and six documentaries (including *Le Mystère Picasso*, 1956). In the 1930s Clouzot served a lengthy and rather obscure apprenticeship (effectively the first third of his career) in France and Germany as a writer and assistant director; he was in fact more productive as a screenwriter and adapter, having the script, dialogue or occasionally lyrics of at least twenty films credited to his name (ranging from *Un soir de rafle*, directed by Carmine Gallone in 1931, to *L'Enfer*, finally directed by Claude Chabrol and released in 1994, thirty years after Clouzot was forced by a heart attack to abandon the

project). As this last example suggests, one reason for the long inter-
vals between Clouzot's major films was poor health, which afflicted
both the director and some of his closest associates, with devastating
personal, professional and financial consequences. Hence the gap of
eight years between his last two feature films, *La Vérité* (1960) and
La Prisonnière. During this time Vera, his first wife, who had taken a
starring role in three of his films, died in December 1960 at the age of
forty-seven after suffering from chronic heart disease for several years;
his mother died in June 1964, when filming of *L'Enfer* was due to start;
the leading actor Serge Reggiani fell ill one week after shooting began
and had to be replaced. The director's own ailment after *L'Enfer* ceased
production made it virtually impossible for him to finance and obtain
insurance coverage for a large-budget film.

At the start of Clouzot's career, the onset of pulmonary tubercu-
losis and the need to retreat for nearly four years to sanatoria between
1935 and 1938 had brutally cut short his slowly rising trajectory. Paul
Meurisse (1979) records that, as he struggled to rebuild his career in
show business in 1939, Clouzot was reduced to peddling the lyrics
of songs to Edith Piaf (which she declined to purchase). The Second
World War proved to be his making and his unmaking, as circumstances turned in his favour and then against him. The military and
political catastrophe of France's defeat and subsequent occupation
by Germany in 1940 allowed Clouzot, thanks to his pre-war connec-
tions with the Berlin film industry, to achieve a certain prominence as
head of the script department for the German production company
Continental, which was established by the occupying powers in Paris
to produce films for French audiences and to achieve cultural and
economic hegemony over the French market. Having scripted two
films produced by Continental in 1941 (Georges Lacombe's *Le Dernier
des six* and Henri Decoin's *Les Inconnus dans la maison*), Clouzot was
finally allowed to direct *L'Assassin habite au 21* and *Le Corbeau* for the
company. Although he resigned from Continental in October 1943
(a few days after *Le Corbeau* was released), Clouzot's three years of
collaboration with the Germans and the caustic satirical message
of *Le Corbeau* led to a further significant setback in his career, since
his supposedly anti-patriotic behaviour was held to account by the
purging tribunals of the liberation and he was effectively barred from
film-making for four years. His reputation as a film-maker was firmly
established, however, and the controversy aroused by the banning of

Le Corbeau and its director meant that neither of them returned to obscurity. (For a fuller discussion, see the end of this chapter and the next two chapters.)

French audiences during the occupation were unaware that Clouzot's films were produced by a German company (references to Continental were also removed from the credits of most copies of their films when they were eventually reissued after the war) and they were extremely popular. *Le Corbeau* was seen by nearly 250,000 people in the first months of its initial release, and set the pattern for the reception of many of his subsequent films, by achieving commercial success, and attracting large audiences and a mixture of critical acclaim and controversy. Only three films were financial failures: *Miquette et sa mère* (1950), an adaptation of a boulevard comedy which he made reluctantly to fulfil a contractual obligation; *Le Mystère Picasso*, which despite (or more probably because of) its impressive formal innovations and the award of a special jury prize at the Cannes festival was seen by only 37,000 cinema-goers during its first run in 1956 (Marie 2003: 86); and the convoluted thriller *Les Espions* (1957). The perfectionism and urge to control all aspects of the film-making process which characterise Clouzot's mature works (and which also explain his slow output) had with this particular film degenerated into self-defeating stubbornness and a manic attention to detail, at the expense of the bigger picture. According to Tony Thomas (1971: 115), Clouzot held a 51 per cent controlling interest in the production company set up to film *Les Espions*, representing an investment of $1,000,000 of his own money. When he refused to cut a rambling scene with Vera playing a mute psychiatric patient, he failed to gain US distribution and lost $300,000. (*Le Salaire de la peur* had been distributed in the US only after supposedly anti-American sequences had been cut.)

Usually, however, Clouzot's dominating mastery paid off, both at the box office and with French and foreign critics. For example, *Quai des Orfèvres* was the fourth most popular film in France in 1947, drawing some 5.5 million spectators, as was *Manon* in 1949, winning 3.4 million spectators and a golden lion at the Venice festival. *Le Salaire de la peur* was the second most popular film in France in 1953, with nearly 7 million spectators (and it remains among the top thirty most popular films in France); it won awards for best film and best actor (for Charles Vanel) at Cannes. *Les Diaboliques* won the prix

Louis Delluc in 1954 and the New York critics' circle award for best foreign film; *La Vérité* was the second most popular film in France in 1960 (5.7 million viewers) and was Brigitte Bardot's highest grossing film (figures cited from Powrie and Reader 2002). Unsurprisingly, Clouzot's notoriety and bankability also provoked hostile reviews, which generally objected on moral grounds to the bleak pessimism of his films or to his allegedly cynical manipulation of spectators. More specifically, avant-garde critics associated with what would be called the New Wave of French directors complained that Clouzot was hidebound by outmoded conventions; thus, writing in *Cahiers du cinéma* in May 1957, Jacques Rivette asserted that middle-aged established directors like Clément, Autant-Lara and Clouzot were 'afraid to take risks and ... corrupted by money' (quoted by Marie 2003: 56).

The jibe may seem unjust, given that Clouzot's most recent films (*Le Mystère Picasso* and *Les Espions*) actually deviated quite intentionally from the usual conventions of the documentary or thriller and lost money as a result. The target, however, was more probably *Les Diaboliques*, about which J.-L. Tallenay had observed somewhat dismissively in *Cahiers du cinéma* 'It is a pity to waste so much talent on a puzzle' (quoted in *L'Avant-Scène Cinéma* 1997: 106). Clouzot evidently took this rebuke to heart, since he remarked in an interview with *Lui* in 1965 that, along with *Miquette*, he no longer considered *Les Diaboliques* important or interesting. (Both Clouzot and his critics seem to underestimate the technical brilliance of this film, as we shall see.) In any case, far from being unchallenging entertainments, all the films he made after *Les Diaboliques* can be seen as questioning conventional norms of behaviour or the nature of artistic expression. While the courtroom drama *La Vérité* is in no sense aesthetically innovative, its ostensible theme is the failure of the legal system and bourgeois morality when the truth about human relations is at stake. The documentary films made with Picasso and the conductor Herbert von Karajan are about the mysteries of artistic creation (although both Picasso and Karajan are shown as performers, practical craftsmen rather than aesthetic theoreticians). *La Prisonnière*, which was the only feature film which Clouzot made in colour, is about sexual obsession and voyeurism (familiar themes, though now treated more explicitly in the permissive era which had dawned by 1968), but also foregrounds the expressive, formal elements of film (colour, patterns, shapes, movement) far more aggressively and continuously than in his previous films.

Before pursuing this exploration of Clouzot's vision, working methods, and the wider historical and cinematic context which shaped his films, it would be useful briefly to fill in some details about his career and biography. Henri Georges Léon Clouzot was born in Niort on 20 November 1907, where his father ran a book shop, before financial difficulties obliged him to move the family to Brest and work as an auctioneer. After poor eyesight prevented him from training as a naval cadet and following a brief period as a political secretary, Clouzot began writing sketches and lyrics for cabaret artistes and joined Adolphe Osso's film production company as a script editor (assisted by his younger brother Jean, who was to pursue a successful career as a screenwriter under the pseudonym Jérôme Geronimi). In 1931, Clouzot was able to make a short film, *La Terreur des Batignolles*, from a script by Jacques de Baroncelli. The film is a fifteen-minute comic sketch, with three actors. The ironically named terror of the title is a cowardly Parisian burglar who hides behind a curtain when the owners of the apartment he is burgling return unexpectedly. They spot his feet and confiscate his loot; he realises belatedly that the couple, despite their evening dress, were not the owners at all but a bolder pair of thieves. None of the film archives which I contacted in Brussels, London and Paris possesses a copy of this film. Claude Beylie (1991) saw a copy lent by a private collector and reported that the film was surprisingly well made, with expressive use of shadows and lighting contrasts, effects which Clouzot would exploit in the full-length features he made ten years later (although Mme Inès Clouzot assured me in March 2004 that this short added nothing to her husband's reputation).

In 1932, Clouzot moved to Berlin to work for the German production and distribution company UFA, adapting scripts and supervising the French versions of their films. Like many other French people launching their careers in the movie business, Clouzot's move to the Neubabelsberg studios was triggered by the fragile state of the French industry in the early 1930s (which showed a deficit in up to 40 per cent of productions annually and where French-language versions of films imported from Germany took over 10 per cent of the market: Crisp 1997: 24). Clouzot returned to Paris in 1934, claiming he had been sacked because of his friendship with a Jewish producer, which would have been highly undesirable as UFA fell under the control

of Goebbels' propaganda ministry. In the late 1930s Clouzot met the
singer and aspiring actress Suzy Delair, who became his partner for
the next decade and starred in *L'Assassin habite au 21* and *Quai des
Orfèvres*. He also met Pierre Fresnay in 1939, who was already an established star (having played Marius in Pagnol's celebrated trilogy and a
leading role as Captain de Boëldieu in Renoir's *La Grande Illusion*).
Fresnay appeared in ten films during the occupation (four of them
made with Continental, three of which were either scripted or directed
by Clouzot). Clouzot also wrote the script of *Le Duel*, which Fresnay
directed in 1939, and two plays for him, *On prend les mêmes*, performed
in December 1940, and *Comédie en trois actes*, performed in March
1942.

If Fresnay effectively acted as Clouzot's patron, Clouzot repaid
the favour by giving him one of his greatest roles in *Le Corbeau*.
After Clouzot quarrelled with Fresnay's wife Yvonne Printemps,
relations were broken off. The pattern was set for Clouzot's tumul-
tuous dealings with the major actors and actresses who appeared
in his films. He would attract performers (sometimes rising or
waning stars, like Yves Montand or Charles Vanel) from a variety of
backgrounds (from stage actors like Louis Jouvet, Paul Meurisse and
Laurent Terzieff, to a cabaret singer like Montand, to popular film
actresses like Ginette Leclerc, Simone Signoret and Brigitte Bardot),
extract a compelling performance from them, but usually at the cost
of turning an initially amicable relationship into violent confrontation
or icy hostility. Brigitte Bardot presents Clouzot in her memoirs as a
repellent, bullying gnome, 'un être négatif, en conflit perpétuel avec
lui-même et le monde qui l'entourait', while acknowledging that *La
Vérité* was her favourite film and made her an 'actrice reconnue, enfin
la consécration de ma carrière' (Bardot 1996: 242, 237).[1] Louis Jouvet
had already achieved such recognition when he took the leading male
role in three films (*Quai des Orfèvres*, *Miquette et sa mère* and the short
Le Retour de Jean), and began work with Clouzot on an adaptation
of Graham Greene's *The Power and the Glory*. They parted company
in February 1951 after Clouzot tactlessly criticised Jouvet at a read-
through, and the script was passed on to Pierre Bost. There was no
reconciliation: Jouvet died six months later.

1 'A negative being, for ever at odds with himself and the world around him.'
  'Recognised as an actress, the ultimate consecration of my career.' Unless
  otherwise stated, all translations are the author's.

Clouzot's humiliating exclusion from this project is recounted with a certain relish by Jouvet's secretary, the actor Léo Lapara, who had minor parts in *Quai des Orfèvres* and *Le Retour de Jean*. In 1938, Lapara had married Vera Gibson Amado, the daughter of a Brazilian diplomat. When Jouvet's acting company returned to France in 1945 (having spent the previous four years on tour in South America), Lapara and Vera lived with Jouvet in his spacious Paris apartment for several years, an arrangement which led Vera to accuse her husband of being married to Jouvet (who was himself separated from his wife and family: Lapara 1975: 263). She met Clouzot when working as a continuity assistant on *Miquette*; after she divorced Lapara, they were married in January 1950. The couple undertook a seven-month visit to Brazil from April 1950, with the intention of making a documentary film about their voyage. When this proved impossible, for technical and financial reasons, Clouzot recorded his experiences in a book, *Le Cheval des dieux* (1951); apart from purely anecdotal aspects, this deals notably with fetishist sects which practise the ritual sacrifice of animals (slaughter witnessed and described in explicit detail, showing by contrast how restrained and stylised the violent scenes are in his films).

The nearest Clouzot got to filming in South America was when directing *Le Salaire de la peur* in 1951 and 1952 on an exterior set built in the Camargue, which stood in for the town of Las Piedras (while the scenes showing the lorries on the road were shot in the Cévennes). In order to retain as much independence as possible (one reason he was reluctant to work in the USA, which he visited only as a tourist), Clouzot had created his own production company, Vera Films, through which he co-produced this and most of his subsequent feature films. Unseasonal torrential rain delayed filming of *Le Salaire* and caused costs to overrun; shooting finally resumed after a lengthy delay needed to allow refinancing. Clouzot's last five features were expensive ventures. *La Vérité* had a budget of $1.5 million (five times the cost of the average French film in 1959: Marie 2003: 49), with Brigitte Bardot taking a fee of $250,000, according to Clouzot's biographers Bocquet and Godin (1993: 120). Writing in *Le Nouvel Observateur* in November 1964, Clouzot argued that cinema needed to let the public touch 'the details of the truth' by showing material space on a large scale; hence very lavish and costly spectacles were most likely to attract the mass audiences needed to defray costs and to compete with television (quoted by Bocquet and Godin 1993: 137).

Following Vera's untimely death in December 1960, Clouzot retreated to Tahiti, returning to Paris in January 1962. He married Inès de Gonzalez (herself a widow) in December 1963. After the debacle of *L'Enfer*, the five documentary films which he made for television with Herbert von Karajan between 1965 and 1967 allowed Clouzot to finance filming of his final feature film. Shooting of *La Prisonnière* began in September 1967, but the director fell ill again and was hospitalised until April 1968. Filming recommenced in August 1968, following a further interruption caused by the events of May 1968, when nation-wide protests and strikes brought de Gaulle's regime near to collapse. Though no radical, Clouzot joined in the campaign demanding the reinstatement of Henri Langlois, the celebrated director of the Paris Cinémathèque, who had been summarily dismissed in February. But when Clouzot put in an appearance at the 'Etats généraux du cinéma', he was insulted by cinema students, the younger generation taking the view they had nothing to learn from this particular 'vieux con' ('old fart'). Clouzot's final decade was not a productive time, as his health continued to decline and projects came to nothing; for example, a film planned about Indochina was dropped when timorous producers gave in to threats of censorship (Gauteur, 1997: 105). Hence his apt if gloomy aphoristic remark, 'On meurt par morceaux' ('one dies bit by bit': quoted by Bocquet and Godin 1993: 151). Following open-heart surgery in November 1976, he died aged sixty-nine on 12 January 1977.

Clouzot unfortunately experienced a protracted demise, creatively and professionally speaking, as his poor health increasingly isolated him from the film-making community, and his well-crafted, big-budget, star-driven films seemed alien to the cheaper, more improvised style popularised by New Wave directors. The least one can say is that his films aroused strong reactions, and have continued to divide critical opinion. Typically, critics who adopt an avant-garde position are hostile and dismissive, while those who think popular genre films deserve taking seriously are more positive (although, as this outline of his career suggests, Clouzot's energy and talent make him far more than a director of popular genre films). Thus, writing twenty years after Clouzot's death in the highbrow journal *Positif*, Noël Herpe (1996:

105) asserts: '*Les Diaboliques* (de même que *Les Espions* et *La Vérité*) témoignent d'une surenchère stérilisante dans l'expérimentation des pouvoirs mystificateurs de la fiction'.[2] Although experimental work usually finds favour with critics, its value is cancelled out, it seems, because it is devoted to fiction and fiction's power to mystify; the implication is that thrillers, or possibly all films which practise narrative deceit, are worthless. Yet mystification (which in this case means illusion masquerading as melodramatic realism) was a basic, guiding principle for Clouzot, who argued, for instance, that 'Ce qui est intéressant pour un auteur de films, c'est arriver à faire croire qu'une chose est vraie alors qu'elle ne l'est pas' (quoted in Jeancolas 1992: 92).[3] The same objection about sterile mystification could of course be levelled at Hitchcock (whose status in the French critical pantheon rose higher than Clouzot's when he was consecrated by the New Wave directors Truffaut, Chabrol and Rohmer). Hence Philippe Pilard's wry observation: 'Il ne fait pas de doute que, si Clouzot avait travaillé pour Hollywood en appliquant les recettes des studios US, il serait aujourd'hui encensé par la même critique qui, aujourd'hui [*sic*], veut l'ignorer' (quoted in *La Revue du cinéma* 1978: 213).[4]

While Clouzot enjoyed an uneasy, at times hostile relationship with critics and many of the major actors and actresses who appeared in his films, if we look more closely at the process of his film-making, we discover that he also surrounded himself with a group of producers, writers, cinematographers, technicians and second-rank actors who remained loyal to him, often for an extended period. In this sense, he was much like other celebrated French and European directors (such as Renoir, Truffaut or Bergman) who achieved a high degree of creative independence partly by surrounding themselves with a reliable team, a sort of professional family. While Hitchcock's career was marked by his struggle against domineering studio bosses and producers like David O. Selznick, as well as his attempts to circumvent the timid and prudish censorship which Hollywood imposed on matters either ideological or sexual, Clouzot enjoyed a remarkable

2 '*Les Diaboliques* (just like *Les Espions* and *La Vérité*) reveals a sterile and increasingly exaggerated urge to experiment with the mystifying powers of fiction.'

3 'What is interesting for a film-maker is to manage to make people believe something is true when it is not.'

4 'There is no doubt that, had Clouzot worked for Hollywood and applied the formulas of US studios, today he would be lauded by the very critics who prefer to ignore him.'

degree of independence in what he was able to film and get screened (the production of the scathing satire *Le Corbeau* during the occupation being the most striking example).[5]

Although most spectators and students of films focus their attention only on their most visible creators, namely stars and directors (we are far more aware of the product, rather than the process, of film-making, in other words), commercial films are of course made by large teams of people, most of them technical experts working under the industrial and economic constraints imposed by the need to develop and manufacture a marketable product. It is worth acknowledging their contribution to Clouzot's filmic universe, before describing its characteristics in more detail. For example, the sound engineer William-Robert Sivel worked on nearly all Clouzot's films, from *L'Assassin habite au 21* to *La Prisonnière*, following the director throughout his career. Similarly, the cinematographer Armand Thirard worked with him on seven of his major films (apart from *Le Corbeau*, shot by Nicolas Hayer, *Le Mystère Picasso* by Claude Renoir, *Les Espions* by Christian Matras, and *La Prisonnière* by Andréas Winding). Jean Ferry assisted Clouzot with the script of four films in the late 1940s, while his brother Jérôme Geronimi did the same for the four features produced in the following decade. Georges Lourau produced the four films made in the mid-1950s. A dozen or so actors whose physique or reputation limit them mainly to secondary parts also recur in Clouzot's films, usually playing strongly defined characters who contribute a certain depth and satirical insight to the social world portrayed. Pierre Larquey (who played supporting parts in over 150 films) appears no fewer than five times, gaining promotion from the role of seedy serial killer in *L'Assassin habite au 21* to that of the principal antagonist, the duplicitous psychiatrist Vorzet, in *Le Corbeau*, before being demoted to play downtrodden taxi drivers in *Quai des Orfèvres* and *Les Espions* and a bibulous schoolteacher called M. Drain in *Les Diaboliques* (along with Michel Serrault, whose second film this was). Similarly, Noël Roquevert (who specialised in playing comic parts as 'l'éternel rouspéteur' ('the eternal grumbler') in 180 films: Floc'hlay 1987), appeared in four films, as did Louis Seigner.

As we have seen, Clouzot was an *auteur* in the most literal sense

5 Although Clouzot disliked the comparison with Hitchcock (perhaps because by the end of his career, it was rarely to his advantage), it seems inevitable and will be pursued in more detail at a later stage.

that he wrote or co-wrote the scripts of all his features (even if most derived from work previously published by other authors), as well as lyrics, plays and a travel book. But unlike other celebrated contemporaries or younger directors (such as Renoir, Truffaut or Godard), he did not produce a body of critical, autobiographical, still less theoretical writing on which one can draw in attempting to offer a general perspective on his films. His views on the cinema are scattered across a fairly small number of interviews and articles. One reason his reputation suffered an eclipse in the 1960s and 1970s, at a time when polemical theorising was much in fashion, may well have been the absence of a forthright attempt at self-justification. Martin O'Shaughnessy (2000: 231–2) observes in his book on Jean Renoir in this series that his subject is 'the most valuable prize in the French cinematic pantheon'; he devotes a thirty-page chapter entirely to Renoir's 'other career' as an 'object of critical analysis'. Clouzot may be a lesser prize, but he merits recapturing, though few critics have attempted to do so other than fleetingly, particularly since his death. As far as I am aware, no book-length study in English has ever been published about him, and none in French or Italian since his death, apart from an informative biography by José-Louis Bocquet and Marc Godin (1993), on which I have drawn for some of the information in this chapter (correcting a few minor factual errors). In other words, there is little purpose in offering here a systematic review of previous critical writing, which is more usefully cited when dealing with specific topics and films. Certain critics have, however, offered a succinct and helpful encapsulation of Clouzot's vision and aesthetics which merits more immediate attention.

In his short book on Clouzot, Philippe Pilard (1969b: 44) trenchantly summed up his achievement as an 'Auteur noir, remarquable technicien'. The director's universe is a bleak one, but engages the spectator thanks to the remarkable plausibility with which he endows it. Every single one of his feature films involves deception, betrayal and violent death in varying but usually lurid and melodramatic forms (with the possible exception of the comedy *Miquette et sa mère*, although even here the same themes are enacted on stage by the troupe of actors in their performances). Pilard observes too that many films take place in enclosed spaces, oppressive environments where individuals nurse guilty secrets and are constantly under surveillance. Certain recurrent motifs reinforce this claustrophobic atmosphere.

Three films begin, for example, with shots of gates blocking the entrance to sinister communities through which the camera then takes us: the gates that appear to open without human intervention and show us the graveyard of Saint-Robin in *Le Corbeau* (just as the mysterious 'Corbeau' appears to have unlimited access to the household secrets of his fellow citizens, with potentially deadly consequences); the boarding school in *Les Diaboliques* and its murderous denizens; the run-down psychiatric clinic and its proliferating, duplicitous inmates and staff in *Les Espions*. Spying through keyholes, a more comic variant on the theme of domestic surveillance, similarly features in five films (*L'Assassin habite au 21*, *Le Corbeau*, *Miquette*, *Les Espions* and *La Vérité*), while voyeurism and entrapment are the central subjects of *La Prisonnière*, as its Proustian title suggests.

On the other hand, open, natural spaces are equally dangerous in Clouzot's films (the sea and desert in *Manon*, the road and mountains in *Le Salaire de la peur*). Such environmental pressures lend weight to Pilard's argument (1969b: 33) that décor and objects are often as important as human actors and that Clouzot's characters are mainly 'des fonctions dramatiques'. They are not purely schematic or two-dimensional, since most are dissemblers and their concealed past gives them a sort of depth. René Prédal (1991: 76–7) goes further, asserting that Clouzot

> dénonce la bassesse, la profonde laideur humaine ... démolit consciencieusement l'individu lui-même ... Sa vision naturaliste s'encombre paradoxalement d'une esthétique à mi-chemin entre le baroque (les décors) et l'expressionnisme (les éclairages), mais son extraordinaire talent technique donne à l'ensemble une élégance glacée qui enrobe ces éléments disparates dans l'attrait pervers d'une expression souveraine. Clouzot ne se sert pas du studio pour recréer le monde réel. Il joue de la magie du cinéma pour fabriquer un univers imaginaire infernal où son pessimisme se donne libre cours.[6]

Prédal is certainly right to stress the stylised nature of Clouzot's world;

6 'Denounces the baseness and profound ugliness of humanity ... conscientiously demolishes the individual himself ... Paradoxically, his naturalist vision is burdened with an aesthetics halfway between the baroque (sets) and expressionism (lighting), but his extraordinary technical talent gives the whole thing an icy/glossy elegance which cloaks these disparate elements in the perverse appeal of masterly expression. Clouzot does not use the studio to re-create the real world. He plays with the magic of cinema to make an imaginary, infernal universe in which his pessimism knows no bounds.'

for all his use of conventional narrative, continuity editing and meticulously realistic settings, the motivation of characters, plot and dénouement of most of his films prove on closer investigation to contain
numerous gaps and compressed elements. Clouzot's 'naturalism'
involves grafting a dramatically compelling, but often contrived story
on to a plausible background which corresponds only superficially to
everyday reality: it would be fatuous to consider *L'Assassin habite au 21*
as a serious documentary account of serial killers or *Les Diaboliques*
as telling us much about real school teachers. Clouzot also makes his
characters suffer in rather degrading ways: his habit of killing off not
merely secondary characters but the hero or heroine who has been the
main focus of the audience's interest and involvement (for example
in *Les Diaboliques*, *Le Salaire de la peur* and *La Vérité*) certainly deviates
from the conventional happy ending associated with classic Hollywood movies.

But *audiences* do not suffer watching Clouzot; they are more
likely to be exhilarated than depressed by his style of film-making,
which engages them emotionally and intellectually (even if they may
feel surprised or cheated by the way in which a character's fate or
an enigma is resolved). In this sense, his expressive mastery is far
more important than the misanthropic pessimism to which Prédal
claims it is paradoxically yoked.[7] The dialogue of most films also
reveals a stylised naturalism: it is invariably carefully composed to
allow characters to express themselves with apparently spontaneous
wit or slangy repartee. Characters' verbal exchanges, as a result, do
not convey tragic resignation or doleful gloom, but a sense of verve
and resourcefulness. Ironically, Clouzot agreed with his brother Jean,
who explained the failure of *Miquette* on the grounds that the director
'n'avait pas le goût du comique' ('had no feeling for comedy': quoted
by Bocquet and Godin, 1993: 59), unlike Billy Wilder or Hitchcock.
While this is undoubtedly true as far as this boulevard comedy is
concerned, and the mugging of Bourvil, the preening of Jouvet and
the simpering of Danièle Delorme all seem desperately overstated
attempts to enliven the most puerile jokes and gags, Clouzot's other

7 Watching violent or tragic events in a feature film, however realistic, is obviously
 a quite different experience from enduring or witnessing them in normal life.
 As Dudley Andrew observes (1984: 42): 'The cinema fascinates because we
 alternately take it as real and unreal, that is, as participating in the familiar
 world of our ordinary experience yet then slipping into its own quite different
 screen world.'

films often contain a great deal of incidental humour, often of the blackest variety. Comedy works best for Clouzot when it is oblique or stylised, rather than the main object of the exercise. Thus as Robin Buss observes (1994: 16), *L'Assassin habite au 21* is a comedy thriller with 'elements of the American 1930s series [produced by MGM], *The Thin Man*, but filmed in an expressionist style that foreshadows Clouzot's subsequent films'.

Roland Lacourbe (1977: 96) notes that one of Clouzot's essential characteristics is to take the spectator by surprise, a point reinforced by the director himself when he stated that antithesis and contrast were central to his conception of cinematic narrative. Images presented with graphic clarity prove nonetheless to be deceptive, just as generic conventions are put in place only to be overturned, as we shall see with *Les Diaboliques*. This raises two related questions: how far does such playful subversion represent genuine innovation, and in any case do genre films allow more than a minimal amount of thematic subversion or formal experimentation? Dudley Andrew (1984: 110) crisply defines genres as 'specific networks of formulas which deliver a certified product to the waiting customer', while Rick Altman (1999: 25) likewise suggests that 'The pleasure of genre film spectatorship ... derives more from reaffirmation than novelty'. Altman also remarks, however, that film studios sell films by stressing their individuality rather than genre affiliation, and that

> Even though genre films commonly conclude by a return to cultural norms, genre spectators typically seek (and find) in genre films some sort of counter-cultural pleasure. (Altman 1999: 165)

Clouzot drew the screenplays of six of his films from popular novels, but while he clearly needed recognised genres like the thriller or romance for inspiration and marketing purposes, their formulas are heavily re-branded in his adaptations. This led to furious or resigned protests from the original authors about the alleged betrayal of their works. Thus S.-A. Steeman complained that Clouzot 'ne peut construire qu'après avoir démoli au mépris de la plus élémentaire vraisemblance et par goût de l'effet'[8] (quoted by Lacourbe 1977: 101). In fact, Clouzot eliminated many of the absurdities which strike the British reader of Steeman's original novel *L'Assassin habite au 21*, which is set in London

8 '[C]an only construct after having demolished regardless of the most elementary plausibility and for the sake of effects.'

and full of linguistic and cultural howlers, by transferring the action to Paris. As for *Quai des Orfèvres*, Clouzot and Ferry allegedly did not even have a copy of the original text, entitled *Légitime Défense*, when they wrote the screenplay from memory, entirely re-inventing most of the setting and action. What no doubt angered Steeman and subsequently Arnaud with *Le Salaire de la peur* and Boileau-Narcejac with *Les Diaboliques* was that they were dispossessed of their original stories by Clouzot's more powerful and imaginative films; they are read or remembered mostly because they inspired Clouzot (and Hitchcock's *Vertigo* in the case of Boileau-Narcejac). Thus most recent editions of *Légitime Défense* have been published under the title *Quai des Orfèvres*, even though the novel barely mentions this place (the headquarters of the Paris *police judiciaire*) and appears to be set in Belgium.

In his study of *French Film Noir*, Robin Buss includes five Clouzot films in a filmography of 101 items (namely, *Le Corbeau* and the four films cited in the last paragraph). Michael Walker suggests that film noir is not a genre but a 'generic field' (quoted by Buss 1994: 13), that is, a looser and broader category that allows us to relate Clouzot's work to styles and conventions established by other American and European film-makers in the 1940s and 1950s. Though Buss's book contains some perceptive comments on individual films, the director and screenwriter Paul Schrader and the critic Steve Neale have produced a more persuasive and systematic account of the features that actually define a typical film noir. These are determined more by 'subtle qualities of tone and mood' than by specific settings, and reflected by a literal and figurative darkening. Influences include a pervasive sense of post-war disillusion, the expressionist lighting favoured by expatriate German directors and cinematographers, and the cynical, corrupt world portrayed by hard-boiled novelists who often provide source texts. Typical stylistic features include the following: many scenes are lit for night; oblique and vertical lines are preferred to horizontal planes, with space being 'cut into ribbons of light'; actors and settings are given equal lighting emphasis, so that actors' faces are often semi-hidden (reinforcing a sense of oppressive fatalism); compositional tension is preferred to physical action; 'there seems to be an almost Freudian attachment to water', with scenes often taking place in streets and alleys lashed by rain, or at docks and piers. The characteristic moods are paranoia and claustrophobia (Schrader 1997: 214–20), with narratives turning on 'issues of reliability, duplicity and deception' and 'a distinctive array of male and female character types' (Neale 2000: 168, 160).

As we shall see, many of the above features can be easily identified as highly characteristic of Clouzot's films: the expressive use of light and shadow and distorted camera angles in *Le Corbeau*; the scenes involving baths and the stagnant swimming pool in *Les Diaboliques*, water no longer connoting healthy cleanliness but loss of life and identity; the sense of urban menace evoked in *L'Assassin habite au 21* and *Quai des Orfèvres*, where darkened streets are patrolled by sinister figures and the innocent and guilty are barely distinguishable. Schrader (1997: 223) also argues that films noirs of the 1950s derive their dark vision from a broader awareness of social and political corruption, 'the loss of public honor, heroic conventions, personal integrity, and, finally, psychic stability'. This sums up the social world portrayed both in *Le Corbeau* (behind which we might descry the political and moral betrayal committed by the Vichy regime) and in *Les Espions* (where cold-war paranoia destroys all trust and certainty). Although *Le Salaire de la peur* also evokes a fatalistic, inescapable destiny and shows human relations to be driven largely by greed, bravado and fear, it does not really fit the stylistic and formal criteria just outlined: for example, the film escapes from the confines of urban darkness and bourgeois respectability to a brighter, more exotic, though equally oppressive landscape, in which characters survive only if they are capable of more primitive physical action and resourcefulness.

Clouzot's vision is undoubtedly misanthropic and, according to the critics Burch and Sellier in their study of gender relations in classic French film, 'd'une misogynie sans faille!' (1996: 194). Such unfailing misogyny is however a vice they detect in many post-liberation films; in fact, in analysing films like *Le Corbeau* and *Quai des Orfèvres* they are driven (somewhat grudgingly) to retract this initial judgement that Clouzot blindly follows the prejudices of his generation and to admit that female characters are often shown far more positively than male ones. What redeems Clouzot's bleakness is his recognition and representation of the complexity and intricacy of human relations; the wit and satirical verve with which they are observed; his mastery of narrative; and the technical skill with which all this is put on film.

Clouzot's technical brilliance has again divided commentators, for whom it can either reveal painstaking mastery or, alternatively, a bullying and ultimately self-defeating obsession with trivia. Meticulous preparation and control over most aspects of the production process were clearly essential to him, while improvisation and cutting corners were alien. Thus, with *Quai des Orfèvres*, he spent some months developing the screenplay with Jean Ferry, a further two months working on a storyboard with the art director Max Douy, as well as some weeks observing detectives at work in their offices at the Quai des Orfèvres. He told Claire Clouzot (1965) that he never improvised in films, because careful planning avoided pointless waste of costly time and resources. The actor's job was to fall in with the master plan, 'qu'il entre dans l'état physique du personnage au moment donné' ('to enter the physical state of the character at the right moment'), although Clouzot also claimed that, provided actors followed his instructions for initial takes, he would sometimes let them record another take with a different interpretation (quoted by Bocquet and Godin, 1993: 29, 52–3). When actors proved unable spontaneously to produce the emotional and physical state required by a scene, the director would encourage them, sometimes by demonstrating a movement or position himself, sometimes by more vigorous persuasion and coaxing, which some people found domineering and intimidating (although their hostile or fearful reaction usually got Clouzot the shot he wanted). Dany Carrel (who has a small part in *La Prisonnière* as a nude model) found Clouzot

> un homme excessif, exclusif, envahissant, qui voulait chaque acteur totalement sous sa coupe, qui exigeait de lui plus qu'il n'avait jamais donné. Mais quel résultat! (Carrel 1991: 245)[9]

She also noted that he preferred actors to offer some resistance; hence Charles Vanel's remark, 'si on lui tenait tête, c'est lui qui s'écrasait. Dans le cas contraire, il faisait son numéro de torture' (quoted by Cartier 1989: 407).[10]

Nevertheless, it seems that Clouzot's all-controlling rigour became counter-productive in his later films. Laurent Terzieff, evoking the débâcle of *L'Enfer* which almost ended the director's career, claims that 'Clouzot vivait à l'époque dans un véritable délire narcissique pour ne

9 'An excessive, exclusive and invasive man, who wanted every actor to be totally under his control, who demanded more of them than they had ever given before. But what results!'

10 'If you stood up to him, he would back down. If not, he put on his torturer's act.'

pas dire mégalomaniaque. Le fait de disposer de moyens démesurés lui a tourné la tête'.[11] Practical considerations or safety ceased to count. For instance, when shooting *La Prisonnière*, Clouzot insisted on filming on a rocky promontory where people had often drowned; Terzieff and Elisabeth Wiener spent hours over three days perched on an exposed rock while 'des cathédrales d'eau nous engloutissaient'.[12] After months of such treatment, Elisabeth Wiener eventually came to blows with Clouzot, while Mme Clouzot attempted to separate them (quoted by Mauriac 1980: 176, 181, 183). Terzieff observed too that Clouzot had become increasingly indecisive about the simplest tasks, like shortening a scene, and needed drama and hysterics to sustain the business of filming.

The most detailed (and arguably least biased) account of Clouzot at work is provided by the book entitled *Le Premier Spectateur*, which Michel Cournot wrote after observing the director during the shooting of *Les Espions* in 1957. Ostensibly, Cournot provides a lively and sympathetic account of film-making as a practical business, which makes it clear to readers (who as consumers of films have no first-hand knowledge of film production) what actually happens on a film set. The director is almost entirely dependent on the good will and technical competence of his crew and willingness of actors tirelessly to repeat segments of a performance. He is in fact 'the first spectator', in Clouzot's words, as much an observer who sees his vision taking shape as an active agent in its construction. Others do the work for him. Most of the time is taken up by the cinematographer, production designer and sound director (Matras, Renoux and Sivel) and their teams setting up lighting and camera, finishing sets, positioning props and microphones, and overcoming unexpected hitches (for example, the Joinville studios where they are filming are poorly sound-proofed and ambient noise is hard to eliminate). Clouzot is rarely satisfied by the actors' performance and insists on endless takes and changes of camera set-ups. Consequently, it takes a day to shoot part of a scene that runs for about fifteen seconds on screen.

Though Cournot himself makes no disparaging comments about Clouzot, his lengthy descriptions of the tedious repetitions and innumerable and probably pointless minor changes which the

11 'Clouzot was living at that time in a real state of narcissistic or even megalomaniac delirium. Having unlimited resources turned his head.'

12 '[C]athedrals of water engulfed us.'

director demands certainly lead one to wonder whether such methods are not likely to stifle spontaneity and freshness. François Truffaut took advantage of this account to launch a vituperative attack on Clouzot in *Cahiers du cinéma* in December 1957, denouncing him as one of the outmoded 'Intouchables' of French cinema, bereft of inspiration and mired in sordid details, at least in *Les Espions*:

> Clouzot sacrifie toujours au réalisme extérieur, celui des apparences; partout la gadoue, les murs sales, les vêtements fripés; mais la vérité des gestes et des sentiments, où est-elle?

He adds for good measure that 'Si Clouzot raffine sur la médiocrité, le sordide, c'est pour mettre le public à l'aise' (Truffaut 2000: 345).[13] In fact, since the film was neither a critical nor a commercial success, this alleged stratagem of conniving with the public's taste for the sordid did not pay off. Spectators were discomforted by the film's apparent incoherence; whereas the overwhelming physical degradation of characters and environment in *Le Salaire de la peur* is thematically motivated (both by the narrative and the underlying ideological message), a key part of a terrifying but exhilarating odyssey, in *Les Espions* both *mise en scène* and narrative often seem gratuitous and alienating.

Truffaut's strictures, however, reveal not only his own ambivalence towards Clouzot, but also the latter's uncertain position in his final decade as a film-maker, as the new wave of younger directors swept over him. By calling Clouzot 'untouchable' (like Clair and Clément), Truffaut means primarily that such directors are (undeservedly) held to be beyond reproach; however, in another sense the word denotes a pariah or outcast. As Philippe Pilard (1969a: 70) wittily remarks, for his detractors Clouzot was 'le pape du cinéma de papa' (literally, 'the pope of poppa's cinema'), in other words an ageing pontiff ruling an archaic but still powerful branch of cinema. Clouzot's efforts to adapt to the changing culture, thematically and formally (for example by investigating youth culture and generational conflict in *La Vérité* or by emphasising purely expressive devices in *La Prisonnière*) likewise invited derision from opponents, who saw him as an 'Agaçant grand-

13 'Clouzot always prioritises external realism and appearances; everywhere, we have filth, dirty walls, crumpled clothes; but where is the truth of gestures and feelings?' 'If Clouzot overdoes the mediocre and sordid, it's to make the public feel comfortable.'

père qui prétend danser le jerk' (Gaston Haustrate, quoted in *La Revue du cinéma* 1978: 206).[14]

After he had progressed from frustrated (albeit highly perceptive) film critic to successful director, Truffaut clearly regretted his Oedipal onslaughts on patriarchal figures like Clouzot, writing sympathetically to him in September 1964 to make amends and to express admiration for *Le Corbeau, Quai des Orfèvres* and *Le Salaire de la peur* (praise which he repeated in 1975, when Clouzot's career was over). The fact remains, however, that Clouzot is one of his targets in the celebrated polemical essay 'Une certaine tendance du cinéma français', which he published in *Cahiers du cinéma* in January 1954. The tendency which Truffaut deplores is the rather platitudinous psychological realism found in so-called quality cinema, which is dominated by 'literary' scriptwriters like the famous team of Aurenche and Bost and their imitators (who include Jean Ferry and his adaptations of *Manon* and *Miquette*):

> Sous le couvert de la littérature – et bien sûr de la qualité – on donne au public sa dose habituelle de noirceur, de non-conformisme, de facile audace.

Such spurious audacity includes 'les rapports pédérastiques des personnages du *Salaire de la peur*' (Truffaut 2000: 304, 310).[15] While Clouzot's treatment of homosexuality, gender relations and social taboos demands more substantial discussion in subsequent chapters, the charge of banal commercialism and phoney radicalism masquerading as highbrow art merits more sustained investigation by way of concluding this introductory overview. Does Clouzot's style of filmmaking seem ossified and outmoded, when compared with the work of New Wave directors? And are his films essentially reactionary, in form and ideology?

There can be little doubt that most of Clouzot's major films belong to an (erstwhile) despised tradition of classic French cinema, what Truffaut derided as 'the tradition of quality'. In a recent reappraisal of New Wave cinema, Richard Neupert points out that the label 'tradition of quality' was originally an upbeat catch-phrase invented shortly after the Second World War by the Centre National de la Cinématographie. The CNC was the regulatory body that replaced the state-run organism

14 'Irritating grandfather trying to dance the jerk.'
15 'Under the pretence of literature – and of course of quality – they give the public its usual dose of bleakness, non-conformity, of facile audacity.' 'The pederastic relationships between the characters in *Le Salaire de la peur*.'

originally set up during the occupation, with the dual purpose of controlling and supporting the French film industry (whose fragile financial state in the inter-war years has already been mentioned).[16] Its aim was to reconstruct the best traditions of pre-war cinema, but by the mid-1950s the 'quality' which it promoted was often derided as meaning in practice 'old-fashioned costume epics out of touch with modern life' (Neupert 2002: xxiv). While none of Clouzot's films corresponds to this caricature, they do generally conform to the classic movie style defined by Pierre Sorlin:

> Good, sharp pictures, a sound-track which helps the spectator to follow the plot-line without ever encroaching upon her or his pleasure, audible dialogue, good actors and, more importantly, a well-defined story, with a situation revealed at the outset, developed logically, and unambiguously closed or solved at the end. (Sorlin 1994: 1–2)

We should add that this narrative cohesion is facilitated by generally unobtrusive editing and camera work (even if Clouzot sometimes diverges from unambiguous closure), with the clarity of picture and sound typically being achieved by filming with large crews on elaborate, carefully lit studio sets.

On the other hand, Michel Marie (2003) proposes the following criteria as characterising the New Wave films which were released in France in the late 1950s and early 1960s: the director's dominant creative role as 'auteur' means that he (occasionally she) is usually the author (or co-author) of the screenplay; there is improvisation during shooting, with a minimal crew; natural locations replace studio sets; direct sound recording is preferred to post-synchronisation; fast film stock and reduced lighting are used; non-professional actors may be used, or if professional actors are used they are directed in a freer style; and the distinction between professional and amateur cinema, fiction and documentary film is blurred. To this list it again needs to be added that editing styles often break the established conventions of seamless narrative continuity. While in practice New Wave films fulfil only some of these criteria (for example New Wave directors sometimes used scriptwriters who rarely became directors themselves), Clouzot really only fulfils the first.

16 Attempts at vertical integration of production, distribution and exhibition in the 1930s failed, with one in three films failing to break even, and one third of active production companies annually going out of business (including the largest companies, Pathé and Gaumont). See Crisp (1997) for details.

When we move from general criteria to particular films, however, the distinction between a classic director like Clouzot and New Wave directors (and the thesis that Clouzot was limited by adherence to outmoded conventions) becomes considerably harder to sustain. A lot depends on which films and directors one chooses to develop any stylistic and thematic comparison.[17] One could load the dice against Clouzot by contrasting *Les Espions* with Godard's *A bout de souffle* (1959), both of which are notionally films noirs, even if they have little else in common. Whereas Godard makes no attempt to establish clear narrative continuity or coherent motivation of characters (for example by presenting apparently key scenes in an incomplete way, while devoting more time to less obviously significant events), and the amateurish look and sound of his film are usually seen as deriving from a positive aesthetic choice (to convey an impression of stylish spontaneity),[18] the narrative incoherence of *Les Espions* is not linked to any such formalist project to dispense with the 'well-made' film. Had Clouzot not enjoyed a large budget and shot under elaborately controlled studio conditions, perhaps he too would have produced something rougher and fresher.

Nevertheless, film historians have noted that expressive devices sometimes considered to typify New Wave films are in fact found in their predecessors. Thus Barry Salt (1992: 250) points out that Pierre Lamorisse was one of the first French directors to use jump cuts[19] in *Le Ballon rouge* (1956), a film which Truffaut excoriated for its maudlin sentimentality. Moreover, once New Wave directors like Truffaut and Chabrol became established figures, their films became far more conventional and subject to the same commercial imperatives as Clouzot's work. One could indeed argue that, unlike Truffaut or Chabrol, Clouzot became more willing to experiment and take risks at

17 Hence Colin Crisp's assertion that 'the New Wave constituted little more than the emphatic foregrounding of the art-film end of existing production practices' (Crisp 1997: 416).

18 Raymond Borde observed sourly in *Positif* that Godard 'had salvaged the unwatchable *Breathless* by convincing the public that badly made movies were now in style' (quoted by Neupert 2002: 34).

19 That is, a break in the continuity of a shot or between shots caused by removing a section of a shot, thereby creating an awkward transition whereby, for example, an actor's or object's spatial position seems to jump significantly. These shots were much used in *A bout de souffle*. (Definition based on Blandford, Grant and Hillier 2001: 134.)

the end of his career rather than the beginning, even if he was inspired to do so by the more radical approaches of such younger directors. In this respect, it is interesting to compare Clouzot's planned version of *L'Enfer* with Chabrol's eventual adaptation, made when the latter was sixty-three.

In an interview which accompanies the DVD of *L'Enfer* released by MK2 (2002), Chabrol notes that the three versions of Clouzot's screenplay became progressively more 'hyperesthétique' and 'cinétique': as the central character descended into the hell of jealous obsession, his hallucinatory fantasies were expressed by inserted montages of subliminal shots in colour (while the objective reality of the other characters was shot in black and white). In Chabrol's view, this very marked formal distinction between hallucination and normality weakened the dramatic impact of the narrative, since it foregrounded technique at the expense of psychological plausibility. It was far more effective not to signal the transition between madness and sanity so blatantly, by adopting a more uniform style that would sustain a teasing ambiguity about how far the character's suspicions were justified and how far towards insanity he had drifted. Similarly, the fact that Clouzot's film was narrated in flashback from the character's perspective created the problem of whether all his memories were false. Chabrol preferred to restore a linear chronology, but to decelerate the rhythm of the narrative, as madness took over and time is dilated into eternity in the final sequence, which ends with the words 'sans fin' appearing on the screen in place of the usual 'fin'. While Chabrol's argument is perfectly justifiable, the key point here is that he clearly regards narrative coherence and plausible motivation as far more important than stylistic experimentation, which is effectively seen as a self-indulgent distraction. His version of *L'Enfer* is a skilful psychological melodrama about a family's destruction (a variation on a theme which defines so many of his films); Clouzot aspired to a more avant-garde film which set aside coherent narrative and motivation (and nearly destroyed himself in the process).

Such comparisons might reasonably lead one to conclude that Clouzot was more versatile and open-minded than his detractors sometimes allow.[20] If at the peak of his career he clearly knew what

20 Susan Hayward (2005: 8) states, for example, that in the last phase of his career Clouzot is often perceived as 'Old-fashioned, stuck in his practices and uninventive'.

the public wanted, he was also willing to respond to criticism and to move towards a more aestheticised style in his final films. Commercial success and highbrow aspirations rarely fit together, however. It is worth noting that Clouzot's greatest successes (from *Quai des Orfèvres* in 1947 to *La Vérité* in 1960) coincide almost exactly with the post-war boom in cinema attendance in France. Numbers of spectators rose from an average of 220 million a year in the 1930s to a peak of over 400 million in 1947, 1948 and 1957, before showing a steady decline throughout the 1960s (which also overlaps with the emergence of the New Wave and has continued to the present day). By 1963, they were below 300 million, and by 1969 under 200 million (see Powrie and Reader 2002: 196 for complete statistics). Nonetheless, it would be otiose to suggest a direct causal link between the changing style of films and the rise and fall in audience numbers, particularly since low-budget, experimental film-makers usually seek artistic recognition rather than commercial success (the most popular films in France have always been highly conventional comedies, adventure stories and costume dramas). The decline of cinema as public spectacle or collective entertainment reflects a more complex shift in leisure activities and expenditure, with economic prosperity giving people a far wider range of competing choices within the private, domestic sphere; as a consequence, nowadays twenty times more people watch films on television than in cinemas.

Michel Marie (2003: 18–19) sums up the late 1940s and 1950s as a period of 'Aesthetic sclerosis and good economic health' in French cinema, noting that 20 per cent of film production was the work of only nine directors, whose names are barely remembered nowadays and who produced on average eighteen films each in the twelve years between 1945 and 1957. In contrast, Clouzot produced only six feature films in this period, all of them meticulously crafted (only *Miquette* might be dismissed as bland entertainment) and marked with a recognisable personal vision. While his subsequent attempts to extend his subject matter and expressive techniques merit acknowledgement and sympathetic investigation in later chapters, we should return in conclusion to the question as to how provocative or audacious his treatment of controversial and taboo subjects in many films really was.

Clouzot lived through many of the events that significantly changed twentieth-century France (most notably, the appalling slaughter and destruction during two world wars, followed by further violent conflicts as France was forced to grant independence to colonised nations in Indochina and North Africa), as well as the prosperity and consumerist culture stimulated by post-war reconstruction and economic growth. Yet whereas film directors like Renoir and Godard have reflected directly on political and historical issues in some of their films, aligning themselves (at least for periods of their career) with leftist or anti-establishment causes (and getting their films banned in consequence), it is difficult to discern any such overt political or ideological commitment in Clouzot's films, which deal with private rather than national dramas. As far as I know, he never made any public pronouncement about politics and his political affili-ations, if any, remain unknown, although it seems highly unlikely he supported either communism or Gaullism, the two forces which shaped Resistance during the war and were pushed into opposition during the subsequent political reconstruction of the Fourth French Republic. This has not prevented some commentators from ascribing a political position (on the far right) to Clouzot, though the evidence adduced to support this is minimal.

For example, Gregory Sims (1999: 744 n.4) asserts that Le Corbeau is 'unambiguously fascistic', although he buries this controversial assertion in a footnote and makes little attempt to substantiate it in his lengthy article on the film. Burch and Sellier (1996: 191), on the other hand, claim that Le Corbeau reflects both sympathy for some of the Vichy government's policies and more generally 'l'anarchisme de droite des intellectuels collaborationnistes'. Again, this comment (at least if meant to be a specific political judgement, rather than a vague expression of the distaste which these authors apparently feel towards Clouzot) presupposes that Clouzot actually favoured right-wing anarchism and intellectual collaboration with the Germans. Here, the only evidence that seems relevant or available is found in the record of Clouzot's interrogation by the purging committee of the Comité de libération du cinéma français on 17 October 1944. The main charge against Clouzot was his employment by the German production company Continental and alleged Nazi sympathies:

> Clouzot répond qu'il est touché par le côté social du national-social-isme parce qu'il est, avant tout, anti-capitaliste et qu'il y voit une solution possible de lutte contre le capitalisme. (Quoted by Bertin-Maghit 1984: 137)[21]

21 'Clouzot replies that he is sympathetic towards the social side of national

Although it may seem odd to us that Clouzot expresses any sympathy at all for Nazism, we should note that by stressing his hostility towards capitalism, he is picking an area likely to find favour with jury members of left-wing persuasions, and carefully dodging more sensitive issues such as persecution of the Resistance and mass deportations.

While Clouzot's collaboration with Continental clearly put him in a very awkward position when accounts were settled at the liberation, how this affects our interpretation of *Le Corbeau* demands much fuller investigation in the next chapter. The point to be made here, to conclude this overview of Clouzot's career in the cinema, is that in practice his films deal with political or historical issues obliquely: *Le Corbeau* is not about the occupation and its dilemmas, even if it may invite interpretation as an allegory about occupation. Similarly, *Le Salaire de la peur* is not an anti-capitalist or anti-colonialist tract, even if the damage done to third-world countries by international corporations was a visible enough theme for US distributors to censor parts of the film. Clouzot's films broke taboos not because they expounded or implied politically unsavoury opinions on matters related to governance, economics or class and national identity, but in their treatment of more personal or private issues to do with human relations and sexual politics. But as this last term suggests, the private domain is ultimately determined by social norms and laws (for example, the sexual freedom apparently enjoyed by the heroine of *La Vérité* brings her to a court room charged with murder). Clouzot also revealed more about human duplicity, physical suffering or sexual obsession and voyeurism than was customary in most mainstream films in the 1950s and 1960s. Although we have become inured to spectacles of grotesque violence and explicit sexual acts in countless films produced in the thirty years since his death, and are thus unlikely to be shocked by what some contemporary viewers of Clouzot's films considered excessive, it is worth noting that we are still likely to be engaged with Clouzot's protagonists and moved by their suffering, whereas the carnage and mechanical copulation found in some post-permissive films rapidly estrange most adult spectators.

The following chapters of this study will examine Clouzot's major films in chronological order, since this allows us to relate them

---

socialism because he is above all anti-capitalist and can see in it a possible solution to the struggle against capitalism.'

coherently both to his evolving career and to wider developments in French society and the cinema. However, I have found it more convenient to consider his documentary films together in a single chapter. His relatively small output has the advantage that it permits reasonably detailed analysis of individual films within the confines of this series. In the first instance, then, we turn to Clouzot's emergence as a controversial film-maker during the bleak years of France's defeat and occupation by Germany during the Second World War.

Bibliography

Altman, Rick (1999), *Film/Genre*, London, BFI Publishing

Andrew, Dudley (1984), *Concepts in Film Theory*, New York, Oxford University Press

L'Avant-Scène Cinéma (1997), 463, June (script and reviews of *Les Diaboliques*)

Bardot, Brigitte (1996), *Initiales B.B.: mémoires*, Paris, Le Grand Livre du Mois

Baroncelli, Jacques de, 'La Terreur des Batignolles', script résumé, BIFI archives

Bertin-Maghit, Jean-Pierre (1984), '1945, l'épuration du cinéma français: mythe ou réalité?', in Marc Ferro, ed., *Film et histoire*, Paris, Editions de l'Ecole des Hautes Etudes en Sciences Sociales, 131–42

Beylie, Claude (1991), '*La Terreur des Batignolles* sort de l'ombre', *Cinéma*, 478, June, 59–60

Blandford, Steve, Barry Keith Grant and Jim Hillier (2001), *The Film Studies Dictionary*, London, Arnold

Bocquet, José-Louis and Marc Godin (1993), *Henri-Georges Clouzot cinéaste*, Paris, La Sirène

Burch, Noël and Geneviève Sellier (1996), *La Drôle de guerre des sexes du cinéma français 1930–1956*, Paris, Nathan

Buss, Robin (1994), *French Film Noir*, London/New York, Boyars

Carrel, Dany (1991), *L'Annamite*, Paris, Laffont

Cartier, Jacqueline (1989), *Monsieur Vanel*, Paris, Laffont

Clouzot, Claire (1965), 'Voix off: Henri-Georges Clouzot', *Cinéma 65*, 96, May, 58–64

Cournot, Michel (2003), *Le Premier Spectateur*, Paris, Gallimard

Crisp, Colin (1997), *The Classic French Cinema*, Bloomington, Indiana University Press/London, Tauris

Floc'hlay, Yvon (1987), *Noël Roquevert, l'éternel rouspéteur*, Paris, Editions France-Empire

Gauteur, Claude (1997), 'Le Mystère Clouzot', *L'Avant-Scène Cinéma*, 463, June, 100–8

Hayward, Susan (1993), *French National Cinema*, London, Routledge

Hayward, Susan (2005), *Les Diaboliques*, London, Tauris

Herpe, Noël (1996), 'Les Films criminels de Clouzot', *Positif*, 419, January, 103–5

Holmes, Diana and Robert Ingram (1998), *François Truffaut*, Manchester, Manchester University Press

Jeancolas, Jean-Pierre (1992), 'Clouzot en 1991', *Positif*, 374, April, 92–5

Lacassin, Francis and Raymond Bellour (1964), *Le Procès Clouzot*, Paris, Le Terrain Vague

Lacour, José-André, Jean Ferry and Henri-Georges Clouzot, 'L'Enfer', script, BIFI archives

Lacourbe, Roland (1977), 'Henri-Georges Clouzot', *L'Avant-Scène Cinéma*, 186, 94–124

Lapara, Léo (1975), *Dix ans avec Louis Jouvet*, Paris, Editions France-Empire

Marie, Michel (2003), *The French New Wave: An Artistic School*, trans. R. Neupert, Oxford, Blackwell

Mauriac, Claude (1980), *Laurent Terzieff*, Paris, Stock

Meurisse, Paul (1979), *Les Eperons de la liberté*, Paris, Laffont

Neale, Steve (2000), *Genre and Hollywood*, London, Routledge

Neupert, Richard (2002), *A History of the French New Wave Cinema*, Madison, University of Wisconsin Press

O'Shaughnessy, Martin (2000), *Jean Renoir*, Manchester, Manchester University Press

Pilard, Philippe (1969a), 'A propos d'Henri-Georges Clouzot', *La Revue du cinéma*, 232, November, 69–77

Pilard, Philippe (1969b), *Henri-Georges Clouzot*, Paris, Seghers

Powrie, Phil and Keith Reader (2002), *French Cinema: A Student's Guide*, London, Arnold

Prédal, René (1991), *Le Cinéma français depuis 1945*, Paris, Nathan

La Revue du cinéma (1978), 331b, September, 205–14 (various authors on Clouzot)

Salt, Barry (1992), *Film Style and Technology: History and Analysis*, London, Starword

Schrader, Paul (1997), 'Notes on Film Noir', in Barry Keith Grant, ed., *Film Genre Reader II*, Austin, University of Texas Press, 213–26

Sims, Gregory (1999), 'Henri-Georges Clouzot's *Le Corbeau 1943*: the Work of Art as Will to Power', *MLN*, 114, 4, 743–79

Sorlin, Pierre (1994), *European Cinemas, European Societies 1939–1990*, London, Routledge

Steeman, Stanislas-André (1985), *Quai des Orfèvres*, Paris, Librairie des Champs-Élysées (published in 1942 as *Légitime Défense*)

Thomas, Tony (1971), *Ustinov in Focus*, London, Zwemmer/New York, Barnes

Truffaut, François (2000), *Le Plaisir des yeux. Ecrits sur le cinéma*, ed. Jean Narboni and Serge Toubiana, Paris, Petite Bibliothèque des Cahiers du cinéma

Occupation and its discontents

The military defeat and subsequent occupation of France in 1940 by the Germans represent the greatest national disaster to affect the country in modern times. The devastation, chaos and loss of life caused as the French armies were ignominiously routed by the invading German forces in May and June, and the government abandoned the capital and took refuge in Bordeaux, were followed by the signing of an armistice which effectively left the Germans in control of two-thirds of the country and fully able to exploit its economic resources. The parliamentary democracy of the Third Republic was abolished and replaced by a puppet regime with direct control of only the remaining third of the country. Based in the spa town of Vichy and headed by the aged Marshal Pétain, the new French state embarked on a policy of collaboration with the Germans, a relationship which in reality amounted to subservience rather than partnership. Far from acting as a protective buffer against German depredations and restoring national unity and morale, their ostensible objectives, Pétain's government and its agencies in practice assisted the exploitation of French industry and manpower for the benefit of the German war effort (for example, by imposing compulsory labour conscription), while gaining no visible concessions in return. They also assisted the Germans in crushing resistance and in anti-Semitic persecution. By the end of 1942, when the Germans occupied the whole country in order to forestall a possible allied invasion from North Africa, Pétain and his regime had little real political autonomy. In the remaining eighteen months of occupation, France became a virtual police state, where mass arrests, detention without trial, summary execution of hostages, and deportation to concentration camps were routine occurrences, in addition to the material hardships caused by the shortages of food and other commodities needed for daily living. Liberation from the Germans came from the summer and autumn of 1944, but at the cost of turning many regions once again into devastated war zones. Finally, as part of the lengthy process of reconstruction, those French citizens who were considered to have abetted the Germans were brought to account. Pétain was sentenced to life imprisonment, while his prime minister Laval was executed; thousands of other people were detained and punished in varying degrees for crimes and acts related to collaboration.

The Germans' aims in occupying France extended far beyond the purely military and political to include economic, ideological and cultural objectives. Since 'For any totalitarian regime, the control of the principal systems of signification and representation seems a logical and inevitable step in the sanitizing of social consciousness', monitoring and controlling cinematic production was an important concern (Crisp 1997: 45). The French cinema during the occupation was effectively regulated by two bodies: in the unoccupied zone, by the corporatist Comité d'organisation de l'industrie cinématographique set up by the Vichy government under Raoul Ploquin (formerly head of production for the German company Tobis's French language films); in the occupied zone, by the Propaganda Abteilung, under the control of Goebbels' propaganda ministry. In October 1940, the production company Continental Films (an affiliate of UFA, again answerable to Goebbels) was established in Paris, moving to a prestigious address on the Champs-Elysées in March 1941. Its director was Alfred Greven, a former director of production at UFA. Though legally French, Continental was financed by German capital (much of which in fact derived from the punitive 'occupation costs' charged to the French state under the armistice agreement). Continental was intended to relaunch and then dominate the French film industry. In practice, Continental produced thirty feature films (all with French directors) from 1941 to 1944, amounting to about 14 per cent of production during the occupation. However, though it failed to monopolise production, its influence was pervasive, extending to distribution and exhibition (for example, it was able to appropriate Jewish-owned cinemas and obtain exclusive rights to certain studios, like those at Billancourt).

Continental also favoured quality and commercial success, aiming to produce entertainment that would replace American films (now banned from exhibition), rather than Nazi propaganda. Most ordinary spectators were unaware that it was controlled by the Germans and that it was therefore exempt from censorship by Vichy. In fact, Ploquin resigned from the COIC in May 1942, after failing to impose regulation on Continental, and Goebbels criticised Greven for allowing the production of Christian-Jaque's *La Symphonie fantastique* (1942), which he considered aroused unwanted patriotic sentiments in French viewers. The banning of foreign films (other than German and Italian) had the effect of increasing receipts for French-made films to 85 per cent of total revenue, while the smaller market also made them considerably more profitable. Since about 50 per cent of pre-war directors and 80 per cent of producers ceased work in France from 1940, and Jews and avowed opponents of collaboration were banned from working (about 9,000 people out of 60,000 in the film industry were thereby excluded), career opportunities for those prepared to work under German control were arguably better than in the precarious financial situation of the 1930s. Many of those associated with Continental had already worked in the Berlin industry; among them was Henri-Georges Clouzot.

Since the archives of Continental and the COIC vanished during the liberation, very little detailed information is available about their organisation or the precise activities of individuals like Clouzot who held influential positions. Clouzot was in charge of Continental's script department between January 1941 and October 1943; he wrote at least two scripts for their productions (*Le Dernier des six*, directed by Georges Lacombe, and *Les Inconnus dans la maison*, directed by Henri Decoin, both in 1941), and himself directed two films for Continental: *L'Assassin habite au 21* (1942) and *Le Corbeau* (1943). Clouzot was associated with two of the three Continental films which were attacked and banned at the liberation (*Les Inconnus dans la maison* and *Le Corbeau*); the third was Valentin's *La Vie de plaisir* (released in May 1944). All three films have in common that they are inquisitorial satires which deride 'sacrosanct icons of Vichy ideology (Church, family, youth)'; they escaped Vichy censorship, but not the censure of the Resistance press, which perceived them as 'anti-French propaganda' (Ehrlich 1985: 52). The paradox of Clouzot's early career as a director was that he was able to make an iconoclastic film such as *Le Corbeau* under the Germans, only to be banned from the film industry when liberty was restored in 1944. The reason, of course, is that he was deemed to be a collaborator.

Collaboration in its most extreme form was legally defined as a form of treason involving intelligence with a foreign power, with the most prominent political collaborators being tried by the High Court of Justice and their acolytes by local courts of justice. While both these courts were able to impose death sentences and lengthy prison sentences, lesser offences were dealt with by civic chambers, which imposed punishments for 'national indignity', usually involving the loss of civil rights. In addition, professional purging committees were empowered to impose limited sanctions on individuals who were deemed to have disgraced their profession by associating with the Germans. The Commission d'épuration du comité de libération du cinéma français listed eight banned directors in September 1944 (including Clouzot, Decoin and Valentin). Cinema purging committees investigated about 1,000 people, and imposed minor sanctions (that is, suspensions or reprimands) in 50 per cent of cases. Following the hearing held on 17 October 1944 (described in the previous chapter), the committee confirmed the ban on Clouzot, concluding that

> Il paraît bien résulter que Clouzot, employé important de la Continental est vraiment l'homme de cette firme, qu'il en défendait soigneusement les intérêts et il est bien difficile d'admettre qu'un homme qui n'aurait pas eu des sentiments progermaniques eût pu continuer à avoir des relations aussi étroites et aussi intimes avec une femme qui, comme Mlle Delair, affichait si nettement et ostensiblement ses sentiments. (Quoted in Bertin-Maghit 1984: 137)[1]

In other words, by working as an executive for Continental, rather than simply as a writer and director, Clouzot was undoubtedly guilty of a form of economic collaboration. The reference to Suzy Delair implies guilt by association, since she was one of the group of French actors who notoriously undertook a two-week publicity tour in Germany in March 1942 (though she herself was not actually held to account for this escapade). Pierre Darmon (1997: 95) claims that Clouzot and Delair enjoyed carousing with Greven and his mistresses, although

---

1 It seems clearly to follow that Clouzot, as an important employee of Continental, was truly the firm's man and carefully defended their interests; it is difficult to admit that a man who did not have pro-German feelings could have continued to enjoy such close and intimate relations with a woman like Mlle Delair, who displayed her feelings so clearly and blatantly.

this did not stop Greven from summarily sacking Delair from a film when she refused to reshoot a scene.

While many directors and actors produced self-justifying memoirs after the occupation, Clouzot himself never subsequently referred to his association with Continental films, a career option which retrospectively seems rather discreditable; yet without the support of this firm, he would never have launched his career as a director. It should also be noted that anyone employed in the film industry during the occupation ultimately depended on the approval of the Germans (although some Continental directors, like Christian-Jaque, escaped censure by establishing Resistance contacts). Clouzot became a target for retribution partly because of the success of his films. As Evelyn Ehrlich remarks (1985: 176), 'Of all the crimes committed by the film industry during the occupation, seemingly the most serious was having worked on *Le Corbeau*'. While Clouzot and his fellow script writer Chavance were originally banned 'in perpetuity', the actors Pierre Fresnay and Ginette Leclerc were imprisoned (the latter spending nearly a year in detention before she was released without charge).

Having now sketched in the historical context, the main purpose of this chapter is to investigate the controversy surrounding *Le Corbeau* by concentrating on issues of interpretation and thematic and formal features. In the first instance, however, a brief account is needed of the other films which Clouzot wrote or directed for Continental. A decade of writing scripts had convinced Clouzot that the director was the real creative force behind any film, as he observed in an interview published in *Arts* in 1957 (quoted by Gauteur 1997: 101):

On ne peut pas laisser à un autre le soin de réaliser ce qu'on a imaginé, pas plus qu'il n'est possible dans un scénario d'expliquer l'image, sinon on n'aurait plus besoin de tourner un film. Il suffirait de le publier.[2]

He was unimpressed by Lacombe's filming of his script of *Le Dernier des six* and thought he could have done better; in 1942, he was finally able to direct a full-length feature which he had also scripted, *L'Assassin habite au 21*. Both films are comedy thrillers, based on novels by the prolific Belgian writer Stanislas-André Steeman, who assisted Clouzot

2 'You cannot leave it to someone else to direct what you have imagined, any more than it is possible in a script to explain the images; otherwise there would be no need to make a film. It would suffice to publish it.'

in adapting *L'Assassin habite au 21*. *Le Dernier des six* derives from *Six hommes morts* (1931), updated to 1939, and offers an enigma all too familiar from classic detective stories. Six men make a pact to seek their fortune and meet in five years' time to share the proceeds; but when they return, four of them are murdered in turn, apparently by a one-eyed stranger. The two survivors each suspect the other of being the killer, until Commissaire Wenceslas Vorobeïtchik (shortened to Wens and played by Pierre Fresnay), assisted by his girlfriend, the aspiring singer Mila Malou (Suzy Delair), exposes the real killer as another member of the group who had faked his own murder (hence the title of the film). The killer drowns while trying to escape arrest, and Mila Malou is finally hired by one of the survivors, who runs a music hall. Apart from its implausible plot (how will the killer get his hands on the group's fortune if he's supposed to be dead?), *Le Dernier des six* suffers from the fact that the six victims are barely distinguishable from one another, and the killer is even more forgettable. What redeems the film and gives it comedy value is the repartee between the suave Wens, the ebullient Mila Malou and other characters, as well as the incidental music-hall scenes, which contain some impressive trick photography (for example, a shot of a miniaturised nude dancer vanishing into a wine glass). Ironically, Lacombe objected to this elaborate dance sequence, which was filmed by Jean Dréville (Ehrlich 1985: 48–9). The film thus reveals Clouzot's undoubted talent as a practised screenwriter, although as a rather conventional entertainment it hardly merits more sustained analysis.

Henri Decoin's *Les Inconnus dans la maison*, which Clouzot adapted from a novel by Simenon, treats violent death in a much more sombre and melodramatic fashion. The setting is introduced by a portentous voice-over (from Pierre Fresnay): it is a provincial town and the household of a lawyer, played by the ever charismatic Raimu, who has lapsed into drunken misanthropy after the failure of his marriage. When a dead body is discovered in his attic, it transpires that this unwelcome visitor was a blackmailer who has been killed by one of his daughter's suitors to prevent him from exposing their delinquent activities. The supposed killer, Manu, is brought to trial, and at first lethargically defended by Maître Loursat; finally, the advocate arouses himself from his torpor to deliver a magnificent if highly implausible tirade, in which he denounces the real culprits: these are the general moral failings caused by parental indifference, bourgeois hypocrisy, brothels, cafés and even the cinema, and, more particularly, the real killer, Manu's jealous rival, the weaselly Ephraïm Luska (played by Marcel Mouloudji), who obligingly then betrays his guilt. As with *Le Corbeau*, it is tempting to read this satirical account of a small town, run by notables motivated by the basest self-interest and willing to sacrifice the most vulnerable individuals when a crime or crisis occurs, as an allegorical representation of French society and the failure of its élites (who could be held responsible both for the débâcle of 1940 and the subsequent betrayals of the Vichy regime). Hence the banning of both *Le Corbeau* and *Les Inconnus dans la maison* during the equally authoritarian period of the liberation, when anti-establishment jibes were no more welcome. There is also a problematic racial element in *Les Inconnus dans la maison*, in that the real murderer has a Jewish name and is played by an actor of Algerian origins. François Garçon (1984) points out that, unlike Simenon's novel, Decoin and Clouzot avoided explicit anti-Semitic touches, although Alan Williams (1992: 421) argues that, by concluding with a 'Pétainesque diatribe' and implying the criminal is Jewish, the film nonetheless offers a loaded (and objectionable) ideological commentary on the decadence of French society.

L'Assassin habite au 21, by contrast, is a more innocent and stylish entertainment, filmed with a wit and panache that continue to impress. Since Clouzot re-introduced Wens and Mila Milou (who do not feature in Steeman's original novel) and transferred the setting from London to Paris, the film is effectively a sequel to *Le Dernier des six* (probably modelled on the series of *Thin Man* comedy thrillers starring William Powell and Myrna Loy produced by MGM in the USA in the 1930s and 1940s). Wens's opening words ('Patient mais circonspect') in fact repeat the motto he utters, with appropriate variations, throughout *Le Dernier des six*; he is revealed hiding circumspectly behind the door of his office, in order to avoid a reprimand from his boss Monet for not catching the serial killer known as M. Durand, who is stalking Paris and leaving his calling card on his victims' bodies. Monet has just been upbraided by his superior, and so on up to the Prefect of Police. Such comic repetitions and variations in fact define the shape of the film, with for instance the sequence of murders (predictable in their occurrence but ingeniously varied) and the successive arrest of the three principal suspects, all of whom have to be released when another killing occurs while they are in custody. Thanks to an informer, Wens learns that the killer is living at a Montmartre boarding house, the Pension Mimosas at no 21 Avenue Junot.[3] Disguised as a Protestant pastor, he takes a room there with the aim of identifying the killer. Meanwhile, Mila Malou is still trying to get an engagement as a singer. After being told she needs to get her name in the papers to attract an audience, she also moves into the boarding house in order to share Wens's glory. At a musical party held in the house, Wens realises that the three main suspects, who play in a trio, are also acting in concert as the killer; they corner him in a nearby building site, but he is rescued by Mila Malou after she draws the same conclusion and brings the police to arrest the killers.

What makes the film memorable and engaging (and shows *Le Dernier des six* to be a rather humdrum piece in comparison) are the skilful delineation of a large range of eccentric characters, witty dialogue, and a succession of carefully managed visual gags and clues to the killers' identity revealed (on a second viewing at least) by skilful use of camera movements and *mise en scène*. Thus the camera adopts the killer's point of view, in the only two murders to be enacted on screen, as first he pursues a drunken tramp who has won the lottery down a dark street and impales him with a sword stick; a second point-of-view shot shows a hand lighting a cigarette, which then produces a gun and shoots the clerk guarding the wages in a building site office. The inhabitants of the Pension Mimosas include the pipe-smoking landlady Mme Point, a blind ex-boxer and his amorous nurse, a servant whose hobby is imitating bird songs and whistles (while he is noisily rehearsing for a competition, the caged bird in the house remains stubbornly mute), and an elderly spinster, Mlle Cuq, 'une vraie jeune fille', whose hobby is writing novels which are rejected by all publishers. When Mlle Cuq, coaxed by Mila Malou, decides to write a thriller based on M. Durand's exploits and set it in a boarding house, she is effectively sealing her fate: she is found in the bath stabbed with a scalpel, either to deter her from further prying or as a punishment for commandeering the bathroom.

The scalpel belongs to Dr Linz (Noël Roquevert), a retired colonial doctor and suspected abortionist; in a vaguely fascistic tirade, he praises M. Durand's enterprise in exterminating contemptible specimens of humanity. Another principal suspect is Colin (Pierre

---

3 The name of this guest house pays homage to Jacques Feyder's film *Pension Mimosas* (1934).

Larquey), whose only occupation appears to be making faceless dolls which re-enact M. Durand's crimes. The third is Lalah-Poor (Jean Tissier), a stage conjuror and knife thrower. When Colin is arrested, Durand's next victim is found outside Wens's door. When Linz is arrested and confesses to being the killer, we see Lalah-Poor about to kill a nosy reporter (whose body then appears on stage in the trunk he uses in his performance). The conjuror is arrested in turn, but then a woman is killed, so that each suspect apparently has a solid alibi. That there are actually three killers is suggested (retrospectively at least) when they are seen grouped together at a table just before Wens arrives at the pension, and as he confronts them individually, revealing their sinister characteristics. Much of the comic business depends on mixing predictable repetition with unexpected reversal. A keyhole shot (the first of many in Clouzot's films, with their constant emphasis on voyeurism and spying) shows Wens looking into Lalah-Poor's room, which he then begins to search, only to be caught by the conjuror who was hidden by one of his props; in retaliation, the conjuror steals Wens's wallet, only to find Wens has already stolen his. The situation is reversed when Wens returns to his own room to find Linz searching his suitcase; Linz repeats Wens's ludicrous excuse that he has gone in by mistake. Mila Malou embarrasses Wens by getting herself arrested for carrying his gun, and then by knocking him unconscious with a vase; in her final intervention as an amateur detective, however, she saves him from the killers.

The film is most interesting perhaps for its lightness of touch (suggesting that Clouzot was actually rather adept at black comedy, despite his dour reputation). It would thus be a mistake to seek either psychological profundity or probing social comment in it, let alone formal innovation. Apart from Linz's ranting defence of the killer, little attempt is made to explain the trio's motivation; their fondness for drawing attention to themselves (for example, by calling the police after Mlle Cuq's murder) is hardly plausible. In fact, the point of *L'Assassin habite au 21*, like most detective stories, is to *avoid* issues such as psychological plausibility or social comment by posing an enigma and offering an amusing series of confrontations between the investigators and perpetrators as the solution is revealed. In contrast to later films like *Les Diaboliques*, its violent acts are highly stylised, presented for comic effect, and there is no real sense of anyone suffering. In his first feature film, Clouzot provided Continental with an innocuous, well-packaged entertainment, skilfully calculated to distract French audiences from the grimmer realities of life under German occupation.

Le Corbeau, on the other hand, is a far more ambitious and troubling work. The film is essentially a satirical and allegorical melodrama which sets out to expose hypocrisy and double standards in a provincial community seen as emblematic of French society in the mid-twentieth century. Its view of human behaviour is tragi-comic; its characters are memorably embodied by the actors, and their behaviour reveals considerable ambiguity and complexity, even if their motivation seems at times cursory. (One should note in passing that the exigencies or limitations of feature films which attempt to offer a social panorama within ninety minutes invariably demand a certain curtailing of characters, a need for rapid positioning to reveal behaviour and establish relationships which tend to seem elliptical and schematic if subjected to undue analysis.) The action takes place in Saint-Robin, 'A small town, here or elsewhere', apparently in the present. The ambulance which removes Laura at the end is from the Département de Seine-et-Oise (that is, the outskirts of Paris); the exterior scenes were in fact filmed in Montfort-l'Amaury (Yvelines). It is important to stress that, as is the case with all French feature films made under the restricted conditions imposed by occupation, there is no *overt* reference in the film to the war, the occupation or related political issues. The plot recounts the nefarious effects on the community created by a writer (or writers) of anonymous letters which denounce the misdemeanours committed by local worthies, and the atmosphere of suspicion, hysteria and persecution which is created as the culprit is sought out. 'Le corbeau' (meaning literally crow or raven) is the pen name adopted by the anonymous accuser (and has gone into the French language as a familiar expression for a writer of poison-pen letters). Despite their gravity, the truth of the writer's allegations is perceived as less important than establishing his or her identity and stopping his or her malevolent efforts (which lead to suicide, murder, and the arrest of at least one innocent person). These events last about two or three months.

It must also be stressed that delation (that is, denouncing one's neighbours to the authorities for mercenary or malevolent reasons) is a not uncommon practice in France, particularly at times of political and social crisis. The central theme of the film, in other words, is linked directly to a recognisable and controversial social reality, the tension between individual liberty, collective responsibility and authority. Anonymous denunciations reached a peak during World War Two, when as many as three million letters were sent to the occupation authorities and rewards were offered for denouncing Resistance activists (see Halimi 1983); at the liberation, supposed collaborators fell prey in turn to anonymous accusations which put them in prison or courtrooms. Since denunciation and the invasion of personal privacy are among the defining features of totalitarian and dictatorial regimes, *Le Corbeau* implicitly at least is questioning the authoritarian tendencies and double standards of the wartime authorities. As the film historian and critic Susan Hayward remarks (1993: 126), the encouragement of such nefarious activities exposes the lying paradoxes of Vichy moralising, 'a regime that decreed the constitutional legality of the logic of persecution, made a virtue out of spying and informing and yet, simultaneously, upheld the principles of moral regeneration and the triumvirate of the National Revolution' (the triumvirate being the values of work, family and patriotism). Films made a generation after *Le Corbeau*, which attempt a more dispassionate appraisal of the most discreditable aspects of occupation (such as Marcel Ophuls's documentary *Le Chagrin et la pitié* (1971) and Louis Malle's *Lacombe Lucien* (1974)), inevitably return to the disturbing subject of delation, which reveals not merely the uncharitable vindictiveness of ordinary French people but also a sort of civic and psychic derangement. Both these later films, with their relentless focus on such discreditable behaviour and their insistence on its banal normality, again aroused furious protests from establishment figures of all political persuasions. Such controversies, which arose a generation after the event in the liberal climate of the post-Gaullist years, are a further demonstration of the extraordinary paradox that Clouzot was able to produce and release his film during the occupation – when conformity and censorship were rigorously imposed by both German and French authorities.

There are three probable explanations why *Le Corbeau* was not stifled at birth. These are the fact that the subject pre-dated the Second World War (and indeed post-dates it too), the unusual status and independence of Continental as a film company, and Clouzot's own position of influence within the company. It has often been noted that Louis Chavance's original script (from which the film diverges significantly) had been written by 1937 and was inspired by Dr Locard's account in 1933 of a vendetta conducted in Tulle between 1917 and 1923 by an anonymous letter writer with the signature 'l'oeil du tigre' (the eye of the tiger). After more than a thousand letters were sent, the culprit was exposed, after an enforced dictation exercise and a failed suicide attempt, as one Angèle Laval, abetted by her mother and aunt; she was sentenced to five years in prison. Defending himself after the liberation, when the film belatedly became the target of self-appointed moral regenerators, Chavance (see Chavance and Clouzot, 1948) somewhat disingenuously noted the irony of a film about the evil of anonymous denunciations itself falling victim to anonymous denunciations (though the Resistance journalists who attacked *Le Corbeau* in 1944 perforce had to operate clandestinely). He also wondered how a plot dating from the 1920s and 1930s could allegedly serve German propaganda ends in the 1940s (with no great difficulty, one might retort, given that social conditions and attitudes were not so different). Finally, Chavance denied that the film had been released in Germany under the title *Une petite ville française*, as an object lesson in the decadence and corruption of French society. His denial was correct, although *Le Corbeau* was shown in Belgium, Switzerland, Czechoslovakia and Romania; and the *typicality* of Saint-Robin is deliberately established from the opening sequences. Indeed, the Laval affair has inspired a host of imitators, up to the present day. (See, for example, Lemoine 1995, for a report on a very similar court case about twelve years ago.)

This short-term independence soon exposed Clouzot and his associates to ferocious criticism from a variety of quarters, however: notably, the Church, the Resistance and jealous rivals. As a result, the director was banned from working between 1944 and 1946, and the film was withdrawn from public exhibition until 1947, and thereafter rarely shown again until 1969 (Lacourbe 1977).[4] At the same time, critical reactions to *Le Corbeau* in the 1940s (and ever since) nearly always acknowledge its effectiveness and impact as a piece of film-making (even if few commentators actually pay much detailed attention to the intriguing intricacies of its plot, characters and *mise en scène*). What principally divides critics is their moral (or moralising) position; as is

4 By contrast, in recent years nearly all of Clouzot's films have been aired on French television and have had selected re-releases in cinemas. *Le Corbeau* was even shown in selected arts cinemas in the UK in 2003–04.

usual with scandalous films, some take an authoritarian and others a libertarian stance. In this sense, François Vinneuil (the alias used by the notorious fascist journalist Rebatet) was unusual, and wrong, in observing in *Je suis partout* on 8 October 1943: 'ce film ne laissera pas dans notre mémoire un souvenir bien durable, et nous le regrettons' (quoted by Chavance and Clouzot 1948: 206).[5] The majority of film critics and the public have always treated the film with respect, as a technical success and an independent-minded social critique.

However, quite exceptionally, Clouzot and his team were accused both of economic collaboration and either of moral depravity (usually by right-wing critics) or of anti-patriotic betrayal (usually by left-wing critics). The first attack, entitled 'Le Corbeau est déplumé', appeared anonymously (the authors were Georges Adam and Pierre Blanchar) in number fourteen of the clandestine magazine *L'Ecran français*, the 'organe du Front National du cinéma' (a section of the CNE/communist *Lettres françaises*) in March 1944. They stated that the film was 'produit et encouragé par des boches camouflés' and 'alimente la propagande antifrançaise' (quoted by Barrot 1979: 15). A second article published in April 1944 by the communist Georges Sadoul reaffirmed the opinion that the film's merit 'n'excuse pas ceux qui se vendent à l'ennemi pour leur faire des films' (quoted by Chavance and Clouzot 1948: 219). In 1947, when the three-year ban on *Le Corbeau* was finally lifted, with the film being released in three Parisian cinemas in September, the Gaullist Joseph Kessel reiterated the complaint that it offered 'l'illustration la plus parfaite à la thèse allemande sur la pourriture de la France'. What was at issue was not the film's truthfulness but its appropriateness in the circumstances: 'En temps de combat, choisir de montrer, de son pays, le pire et avec la subvention de l'ennemi, c'est réjouir et servir les desseins de l'ennemi dans le domaine de la lutte psychologique' (quoted by Chateau 1995: 486).[6]

Unsurprisingly, the Centrale catholique du cinéma was equally keen to attack and suppress *Le Corbeau*, categorising the film as a

5 'This film will not make a very lasting impact on our memory, and this we regret.'
6 'Produced and encouraged by camouflaged Boches' and 'fed anti-French propaganda'. 'Does not excuse those who sell themselves to the enemy to make films for them.' 'The most perfect illustration of the German thesis that France was rotten.' 'In time of war, to choose to show the worst side of one's country, with the support of the enemy, is to aid and abet the intentions of the enemy in the domain of psychological conflict.'

'six', the most negative classification: 'A rejeter: film essentiellement pernicieux au point de vue social, moral ou religieux'. Valentin's *La Vie de plaisir* received the same grade, doubtless for its 'Notes anticléricales délibérément et fortement accentuées' (quoted by Siclier 1990: 447, 456).[7] Before we turn to closer analysis of the film, the validity of such criticisms merits brief investigation. As has already been suggested, their basis is moralising and authoritarian: the Communist Party, the Gaullists, the Catholic Church all represent conflicting forces of ideological and social order (just as did the Germans and Vichy regime). *Le Corbeau*, on the other hand, deliberately satirises the incoherence and double standards of authority (be it legal, political, medical or religious); its two most sympathetic characters (Dr Germain and Denise) are eccentric, if not deviant, individualists. The sluttish Denise first appears in *Le Corbeau* smoking in bed and painting her toenails, signs of depravity that are more likely to amuse than shock modern audiences. However, Ginette Leclerc was typecast in such roles and suffered the misfortune of being confused in real life with her acting persona (although in fact both Germain and Denise seem ready at the end of the film to adopt a more conventional family existence). As this example suggests, two separate issues need to be disentangled. One involves the actual behaviour of people in the entertainment industry, in other words the responsibility of film-makers, and the use made of their films in a particular historical context, namely wartime and the occupation of France by a foreign power abetted by a dictatorial government. As we have already seen, Clouzot's association with Continental and the world of cultural and economic collaboration made it virtually impossible for the Resistance to adopt *Le Corbeau* as a propaganda vehicle; tactically, it made more sense to denounce Clouzot and his associates as part of an oppressive nexus, even if the film's satirical programme by itself does not of course justify banning it and penalising those who made it. Kessel's objections do indeed carry considerable weight, in the circumstances of occupation: mercilessly exposing the divisions within French society is hardly likely to encourage resistance against the forces which have helped create them. The second issue is how, after the freedoms of liberal democracy were restored, the troubling complexities of the film have been or should be interpreted.

7 'To be rejected: a deeply pernicious film, from the social, moral and religious point of view.' 'Deliberate and strongly emphasised anti-clerical tone.'

Putting aside these wider historical factors, we can return to the film itself. A trenchant evaluation is given by the report of the Centrale catholique du cinéma in 1945, which is worth quoting at length:

Film pénible et dur, constamment morbide dans sa complexité. Amours libres provoquées cyniquement et avec une insistance crue par la femme. Médecin qui prête à l'équivoque par son attitude dans les accouchements. Atmosphère délétère pour laisser soupçonner les auteurs de lettres anonymes et qui s'étend jusqu'à une fillette de quatorze ans et demi d'une attitude équivoque et pénible. Profession de foi d'athéisme par le personnage sympathique. Suicide, meurtre, gros mots, jurons. (Quoted by Siclier 1990: 453)[8]

Beneath the ideologically motivated disapproval of a film which derides so many of the reactionary values dear to the Catholic church, one senses at the same time the curious fascination exerted by *Le Corbeau*. Its complexity is acknowledged, as are its equivocal and painful dissection of emotional and physical disturbance, its provocative exploration of taboo subjects (such as abortion, disease, religious faith, female sexuality).

Ostensibly, the plot of the film hinges on the initial appearance of the 'Corbeau', then on the revelations and turmoil caused by the anonymous and seemingly ubiquitous letters despatched by the writer, and finally on the identification and liquidation of the 'Corbeau', after suspicion has fallen on all the major characters apart from the actual perpetrator. I must apologise at this point to any readers unfamiliar with the dénouement for giving away the culprit's identity, since it is impossible to discuss the film meaningfully without doing so. In fact, *Le Corbeau* does not really depend on suspense or surprise for its effects: were it intended to be a standard psychological thriller, one would have to complain that Clouzot brazenly overturns convention and practises narrative duplicity by belatedly revealing the 'Corbeau' to be the chief investigator of the crimes, who is also an apparent source of sceptical wisdom. The Tulle affair (with its guilty female trio) and the

8 'A painful, hard film, constantly morbid in its complexity. Free love provoked cynically and with crude insistence by the woman. Doctor who behaves equivocally by his attitude to childbirth. Poisonous atmosphere to arouse suspicion against the authors of anonymous letters, which includes a young girl of fourteen and a half with an equivocal, painful attitude. Atheistic profession of faith from the most sympathetic character. Suicide, murder, bad language, oaths.'

characters' emotional and physical configurations lead us to suspect that the 'Corbeau' must be one (or more) of the women who surround Dr Germain, the chief object of the writer's vituperation. In fact, the 'Corbeau' is finally revealed to be his colleague and quasi-mentor, the psychiatrist Dr Vorzet (who has played the part of a world-weary Merlin). The film seemingly confirms the trite adage that psychiatrists are madder than their patients, except for the fact that Vorzet's mental state is barely explored; the sanity or malice of the 'Corbeau' are less important than his ability to expose unpleasant truths and his apparent omniscience about the community. Chavance's original script did not in fact identify Vorzet as the culprit. The 'archives scénaristiques' of *Le Corbeau* held in the Bibliothèque du film reveal that the characters' relationships went through various mutations: at an initial stage, Laura alone was guilty and was also Vorzet's daughter, while Dr Monatte (Germain) was married to Denise. Chavance's version was also more farcical than the bleaker film shot by Clouzot; for example, at one stage, the proliferating anonymous letters were delivered by a dog and by carrier pigeon (Sims 1999: 768).

This opacity is compounded by further complexities of plot, particularly in the relationships between major characters. One consequence is that critics who take the trouble to examine the film in detail sometimes conflate characters or misattribute their functions, in an unwitting urge to simplify or clarify. For instance, the original Tobis publicity erroneously says that Liliane Maigné plays Ginette Leclerc's sister, when in fact the character Rolande is Denise's niece (the daughter of her older brother) (see Chirat 1983: 101; Siclier 1990: 63; Burch and Sellier 1996: 195). Again, Ehrlich (1985) says that Laura Vorzet is Denise's sister, when Laura (played by Micheline Francey) is actually the sister of the nurse Marie Corbin (played by Héléna Manson); and Marie Corbin was the original fiancée of Laura's husband Dr Vorzet. Rather than mere carelessness (which it would be unnecessary to point out), such slips probably reveal an unconscious urge to normalise relationships which the film prefers to distort. Thus Rolande and Denise are near enough in age to be sisters, enjoy a considerable degree of emotional complicity, and are both treated in an authoritarian, paternal way by the school teacher Saillens (Denise gets a slap for feigning illness and for her sluttish comportment with the lodgers). It is never explained what has happened to Saillens's wife or why he is so much older than his sister (the actor Noël Roque-

vert who played Saillens was twenty years older than Ginette Leclerc).
Similarly, Laura and Denise are contrasting rivals for Germain's
affections (he clearly desires both of them), whereas Marie Corbin
is a more marginal figure. Since disrupted families, generational
mismatches and sexual frustration are central elements, it is helpful
to elucidate these group dynamics by enumerating the characters' and
actors' names and relationships:

Dr Vorzet [Pierre Larquey] husband of

Laura Vorzet [Micheline Francey] sister of
Marie Corbin [Héléna Manson] nurse of

Cancer patient [Roger Blin]
His mother [Sylvie]

Saillens [Noël Roquevert] father of
Rolande Saillens [Liliane Maigné] niece of
Denise Saillens [Ginette Leclerc] lover of

Dr Germain [Pierre Fresnay]

These nine central characters effectively form three conflicting and
disrupted family groups (at one point, Vorzet was engaged to his
sister-in-law Marie Corbin; Denise becomes pregnant with Germain's
child; the cancer patient's mother avenges her son's suicide when she
discovers Vorzet's culpability). A separate, less clearly defined group of
characters form the notables who in effect run the town (for example,
the doctor in charge of the hospital, his son the deputy prosecutor,
the mayor, the sub-prefect). While they are shown meeting together
to plot the letter-writer's downfall, in practice their rivalry, incompetence and corruption make their efforts worthless. Despite his father's
opposition, the prosecutor plans to discredit the outsider Germain,
but fails; when the letters reach epidemic proportions, the sub-prefect
is dismissed from his post. The fact that Vorzet is privy to their inves-
tigations evidently gives them little chance of success.

   To turn to the question of motivation, while the cancer patient
and Dr Germain are among the principal victims of the poison-
writer's missives, and the male characters Vorzet and Saillens are
given no obvious motive for sending anonymous letters, the four
women are all foregrounded as possible suspects. As a psychiatrist
and self-proclaimed expert in investigating handwriting and anonymous letters, Vorzet is granted a certain authority and removed from

suspicion (which allows him to initiate the dictation exercise and be exempted from it himself). His thesis that anonymous letter writers are 'toujours des refoulés, plus ou moins détraqués sexuellement' ('always repressed, more or less sexually disturbed') also directs suspicion towards the women, given their fixation on Dr Germain and 'hysterical' behaviour. The nurse Marie Corbin, apparently a frustrated spinster, is seen treating the cancer patient with callous brutality, stealing the morphine she is meant to give him, and reading a letter to her sister (the hospital social worker) which she has appropriated from Germain's coat. While she accuses Laura of being 'une petite grue' ('a little slut'), Laura's budding intimacy with Germain seems to be explained by her platonic marriage to a man old enough to be her father. The adolescent Rolande Saillens, who steals money from her till at the post office to buy clothes, spends her time spying on Germain. In a masked shot, Rolande is shown peering through a giant keyhole at Germain as he receives the first letter signed 'le Corbeau' to be shown on screen, accusing him of being Laura's lover. When Germain spends the night with Denise, Rolande is shown sobbing in the corridor outside their room. Denise herself, unlike the other three women, has no paid occupation. Her main activity appears to be seducing the lodgers and feigning illness (although she conceals the fact that she has a leg injury); when Germain finally succumbs to her advances, but refuses to commit himself to her, she is seen taking a stuffed raven out of a trunk and putting it outside his door. During the enforced dictation exercise, Denise collapses; later, she writes a letter signed 'le Corbeau' to Germain saying she is pregnant.

As a result of their misdemeanours, Marie, Denise and Laura each become the object of suspicion. Marie Corbin is sacked from the hospital and arrested; since the letters continue, she is vindicated but never returns to the screen. Similarly, after accepting Denise's explanation that she was merely imitating the 'Corbeau', Germain is finally persuaded of Laura's guilt by Vorzet and signs an internment order placing her in a mental hospital. Finally, these female suspects are exculpated as Vorzet is revealed as the real culprit, but it is never explained whether Laura will be freed or how far she shared her husband's guilt. In terms of the film's narrative economy, Vorzet's exposure seems somewhat arbitrary and perfunctory. Admittedly, one could argue that by making Vorzet the culprit Clouzot is perversely following (or deriding) the hackneyed convention of detective stories whereby the least probable character turns out to be the real villain. It is also true that Vorzet's reductive diagnosis of sexual malfunction can be seen retrospectively to apply equally well to his own case; as he says of his marriage, 'Une très jeune femme ... Un très vieux mari ... Voilà tout le drame!'[9] Vorzet does in fact teasingly hint at an early stage that he could be the culprit, when he says anonymous letter writers frequently accuse themselves. But given the film's creation of genuinely plausible and intriguing characters whose behaviour exceeds lazy stereotyping, one is left wondering why the conclusion is so cursory, leaving as many questions unanswered as resolved. For example, Vorzet is murdered in the act of writing a final letter accusing Laura, which (since she has been sectioned) actually would have suggested her innocence and confirmed his guilt as the main accomplice. We assume he has been killed by the cancer patient's mother, since she is seen disappearing into the background; but what has made her suspect Vorzet? And how has he persuaded Laura to abet him, in any case? In fact, Laura first accuses Denise, before being herself accused by Vorzet and counter-accusing him, as a consequence of which Germain is duped into having Laura interned. Laura also admits to penning the first letter, whereas it is left unclear whether subsequent letters were produced by one or both Vorzets acting in complicity and why, in an act of self-directed hostility, they feature in the accusations contained in their own letters (since hundreds of letters are eventually sent, it is indeed likely that they have several imitators).

Dr Vorzet's younger rival Dr Germain blunders his way towards the truth, wrongly suspecting everyone but Vorzet. While Vorzet's unexplored despair and mischievous penmanship lead to him having his throat cut, the jaundiced but honest Germain (whose brusqueness hides a cynical humanitarianism, it seems) is reconciled by these troubling events to accept human weakness and his union with the sluttish Denise. Although virtue thus seems finally to win against vice, both Vorzet and Germain are revealed to have a dual identity, and for much of the film Germain appears to be a rather unsympathetic, self-righteous figure, whereas Vorzet seems more worldly wise and tolerant. Thus Germain tells Vorzet, after Denise faints during the dictation exercise, 'si je la savais coupable, je n'hésiterais pas à la dénoncer'; to which Vorzet responds mockingly 'C'est cornélien!'.

9 'A very young wife ... A very old husband ... There's the whole drama!'

In other words, Germain rigidly sets civic duty before personal affection, casting himself as a tragic hero who can faultlessly take the right course of action. Vorzet, by contrast, adopts a less self-righteous, more relativistic moral position, asking: 'Où est la frontière du mal? Savez-vous si vous êtes du bon ou du mauvais côté?'[10] However, Vorzet is also clearly motivated by baser sentiments, such as envy of Germain's attractiveness to women and personal fortune; he inspects the furniture and handles the ornaments in Germain's apartment with inquisitive insolence, implying too that Germain has lied about his past career. In his manifestation as the all-seeing 'Corbeau', Vorzet reveals a much cruder obsession with sex and money, encapsulated in a rhyming letter to Germain which accuses him of being 'un farceur, un voleur, un menteur, un avorteur' ('a joker, thief, liar, abortionist').

To these configurations drawn by frustrated, destructive passions can be added the film's insistence on the physical or psychological mutilation of many characters. Denise is lame, following a car crash in which her brother Saillens lost an arm; Vorzet admits to being a drug addict, abetted by Marie; Germain has changed his identity after an incompetent surgeon killed his wife and unborn child, while his own deliveries suggest infanticide, since three infants have died in six weeks (hence the accusations of abortion made by the 'Corbeau'). Denise is accused of nymphomania by her brother, and attempts to induce a miscarriage by throwing herself downstairs. Outside the circle of principal figures, the atmosphere is equally deleterious: Dr Delorme regales his colleagues with an 'amusing' case of gangrene, while most of the accusations of corruption made against the town's leaders seem well founded.

Le Corbeau is celebrated for its expressive *mise en scène*, notably the use of highly contrasted light and shadow and distorted camera angles. Such stylistic devices in themselves are not particularly original, since they were much used from the mid-1930s 'whenever a macabre or gothic incident seemed to call for it' (Crisp 1997: 377), and in fact became defining features of film noir in the 1940s (see Chapter 1). A celebrated example would be Carol Reed's *The Third Man* (1949), shot on location in the ruins of post-war Vienna, whose shattered buildings, darkened doorways and labyrinthine streets and

10 'If I knew she was guilty, I wouldn't hesitate to denounce her.' 'That's like Corneille's tragedies!' 'Where is the boundary of evil? Do you know if you're on the right or the wrong side?'

sewers offer a forceful visual embodiment of the contorted personal and political drama enacted in the film. Clouzot's skill similarly is to invest his most striking images with a thematic significance which can outweigh the sometimes wordy or stagy dialogue. Thus lighting effects and spatial positioning which suggest the dominance of certain characters or the distortion of their perspective heighten this claustrophobic, oppressive atmosphere in *Le Corbeau*, while more subtly informing us about the characters' real situation. The hidden aspect of a character exposed in this way may in practice only become apparent on a second, more analytical viewing.

The most striking example is probably a shot of Vorzet descending the staircase in the gloomy hallway leading from Germain's apartment. As Vorzet goes out of sight, his gigantically enlarged shadow is projected on to the wall and bids Germain farewell by raising its enormous bowler hat. Briefly Vorzet is transformed into this dominant, shadowy presence, a second self whose mock civility does not conceal its intrusive menace and prefigures his eventual exposure as the arch-manipulator. If this brief scene silently shows us the real identity of the 'Corbeau', another sequence shows the falsely suspected Marie Corbin (whose surname is an archaic form of the word 'corbeau') fleeing from a mob down empty streets which are slanted at crazy angles. Her tiny shadow briefly appears on a wall as she turns a corner in long shot (suggesting vulnerability), and since we never see the mob, we may wonder if the threatening chants heard on the sound track are auditory hallucinations caused by her panic. Finally seeking refuge in her apartment, she discovers it has been vandalised and catches her reflexion deformed by a broken mirror, as stones are suddenly hurled through the window and two men appear in the doorway to arrest her. In reality, of course, her panic-stricken terror and distorted perspective reveal her as victim rather than perpetrator; whereas her sister Laura feigns a submissive but seductive posture by kneeling before Germain, seemingly a meek victim when she is actually another manipulator.

In conclusion, we need to return to broader, more ideological interpretations of *Le Corbeau*. The intricate details of characters' hidden motives and desires exposed by Clouzot's *mise en scène* may reinforce the impression that *Le Corbeau* is a dourly misanthropic and misogynous film which sets out to deride the hysterical indiscretions and disloyalties of the bourgeoisie. When Germain first refuses to continue his relationship with her, Denise's chosen insult is 'bourgeois'. The letter-writer does more than expose the alleged misdemeanours of his own social class, however. Significantly perhaps, his main victim in the film is the apparently working-class cancer patient hospitalised in bed number thirteen, who is identified only by the illness consuming him and offered little pity or proper medical treatment. He is first seen being brutalised by Marie and is finally driven to suicide by an anonymous letter revealing he is incurable. He is avenged by his mother (the school cleaning lady), who cuts Vorzet's throat with the razor which her son used to kill himself. 'Malade no 13' thus seems to be innocent of any crime or impropriety (unlike most of those accused by the 'Corbeau') and to be betrayed by all those who mission is supposedly to assist him. (In a parallel incident, which is less substantially developed, but again shows the letter writer's malevolent omniscience, a little girl tries to drown herself when an anonymous letter reveals she is illegitimate.)

Certain exchanges in the film seem to invite allegorical interpretation; for example, Vorzet's observation that 'Depuis qu'il souffle sur la ville un tourbillon de haine et de délation, toutes les valeurs morales sont plus ou moins corrompues', and Germain's conclusion that 'le mal est nécessaire'.[11] Although the letter dropped during the church service promises to continue the 'campagne d'assainissement',[12] the 'Corbeau' is really a force as corrupt as those he denounces. Just as the plague in Camus's famous post-war novel *La Peste* (1947) is conventionally read as an allegory of the Nazi invasion of France, so too the spectator of *Le Corbeau* is tempted to interpret such statements as barely disguised references to the compromises and betrayals wrought by occupation, particularly in a film which confronts social and personal divisions so caustically. Is it possible to derive a broader allegorical interpretation from the pattern of events and conflicts exposed by the film? For example, the sick patient might be taken as a symbol of France, betrayed and neglected by all those whose weaknesses and quarrels lead them to fail in their civic duty. That said, for all its bickering and unappealing *attentistes*, the film contains no very obvious equivalents to the main active participants (the invading Germans, the competing forces of collaboration and Resistance). Nonetheless, the contrasting

11 'Since a whirlwind of hatred and denunciation has been blowing over the town, all moral values have been more or less corrupted.' 'Evil is necessary.'
12 'Campaign of purification.'

characters of Vorzet and Germain could arguably be compared with the two competing political figures who each claimed that their leadership would lead France to salvation: Pétain and de Gaulle. Thus Vorzet masquerades as an upright member of the community, helping to seek out wrong-doers, when in fact he is the principal source of evil, just as Pétain's campaign of moral regeneration and policy of collaboration actually involved persecution of many French citizens and abasement to Nazism. Germain, on the other hand, is an outsider whose activities seem highly suspect, when in fact he is honourably serving a community which dislikes his non-conformism and abrasive personality. Compare General de Gaulle, who was the only important military and political leader to call for resistance and who was forced into exile in England after the armistice, where his refusal to compromise earned him a death sentence from the Vichy government and years of condescending treatment from his British and American allies, before he was finally recognised as the leader of the democratic government which replaced Pétain's discredited regime. The parallel cannot really be sustained, however, because the film eschews political issues; it may deride the authoritarian moralising favoured by the Vichy regime, but its relativism hardly amounts to support for Resistance.

In fact, the film does strive towards a more positive resolution, albeit of a somewhat sentimental and melodramatic variety, by placing the personal and private before the professional and social domains. Thus while professional males invariably fall down on the job in scenes sometimes played as farce (the deputy prosecutor or *substitut* fails to identify the 'Corbeau'; the sub-prefect is transferred to another town; and Germain is bamboozled by his patron Vorzet, who instigates a marathon dictation exercise to conceal his own culpability), women who are shown to be frustrated and hysterical nevertheless are able to discover the truth intuitively and act with far more humanity than male authorities. Thus Laura and Marie support Vorzet at great personal cost (though their motives for doing so are never explained); in the final scenes, Denise persuades Germain of Laura's relative innocence by personal entreaty, having earlier exculpated herself by a similar appeal to emotional authenticity: 'Tais-toi et regarde-moi. ... je ne suis pas intelligente comme toi, mais je sens les choses'.[13] In a scene like this, the film is clearly offering a positive

13 Be quiet and look at me. [...] I'm not intelligent like you, but I can feel things.

message. Ultimately, the misanthropic Germain (whose refusal of human contact was triggered by the surgeon who killed his family) is humanised by Laura and Denise. Whereas the opening scenes show him washing his hands like a vet in a farmyard vat, after failing to deliver a baby alive but saving the mother, and shutting out the noise of children playing outside Denise's bedroom ('Ces piaillements m'exaspèrent'), at the end he concedes that 'On ne peut pas sacrifier l'avenir au présent'[14] and re-opens Denise's window to let the noise of children back in. While the establishing shots which open the film take us through the churchyard's creaking gates into the town (suggesting the invasive presence of death), the final shot shows the black-veiled killer of Vorzet disappearing into the distance past a group of children, whose play suggests rebirth.

In a similar way, Germain's interaction with the 'Corbeau' (that is, the real culprit Vorzet, but also his imitators Laura and Denise) forces him to adopt a less rigorous and more humane posture. Most critics of *Le Corbeau* comment favourably on the chiaroscuro symbolism created in the scene where a swaying electric bulb alternately casts light and shadow over Vorzet and Germain, and over a globe in the room as well, burning Germain's fingers when he tries to steady it, although Chirat (1983: 117) remarks sarcastically: 'La conversation, d'une philosophie facile, sur le bien et le mal engagée entre Fresnay, Larquey et une ampoule électrique qui se balance devant le nez des protagonistes, enfonce une porte ouverte'.[15] Germain's conversion and acceptance of the necessity of evil may well seem facile, and in the context of occupation to imply an insidious moral relativism, implicitly dismissing all sides and choices as equally ambiguous. In fact, at this point Germain has still not realised that the real source of evil stems from Vorzet rather than the supposedly 'insane' Laura; indeed, Germain is duped by the 'Corbeau' throughout the film, even if in personal terms his reconciliation with Denise and future role as a paterfamilias restore him to humanity. This bird of ill omen remains highly mysterious and ambiguous. Retrospectively, at least, Vorzet has to be seen as a Mephistophelian, ironising figure, who

14 'These screeching brats get on my nerves.' 'You can't sacrifice the future to the present.'

15 'This conversation, with its facile philosophising about good and evil held between Fresnay, Larquey and a lightbulb swaying in front of the protagonists' noses, really labours the obvious.'

subverts his claims to knowledge, authority and truth by hinting at his true destructive role. Vorzet's lessons are intended not merely to curb Germain's rigidity (which could be seen as proposing a form of liberation from the hypocritical boundaries imposed by Vichy and by fascist attacks on supposed cultural and moral deviance) but also, more sinisterly, to propagate evil by making everyone seem more or less guilty or perverted. Hence his remark to Germain: 'Vous êtes atteint comme les autres. Vous tomberez comme eux!'[16] To the very end, we are left uncertain as to what motivated Vorzet and how many imitators the 'Corbeau' has spawned.

Such ambiguities may in part explain why some recent commentators have argued that the film actually supports Vichyist or collaborationist ideology. Burch and Sellier claim that *Le Corbeau* mirrors Vichy's anti-abortion and pro-natalist policies. The source of evil is shown to be the 'incestuous' marriage between Vorzet and Laura (that is, a sterile union between an old man and a woman young enough to be his daughter), whereas the promiscuous Denise is actually a 'fausse garce', a tart with a heart, and her final reconciliation with Germain and acceptance of childbirth are typical of many melodramatic films made during the period. Ultimately, the film's target is 'le pouvoir patriarcal, qu'il soit médical ou politique' (Burch and Sellier 1996: 192, 196).[17] This overlooks the fact that, for much of the film, Germain seems to practise infanticide (or at least to regard the survival of babies as much less important than their mothers'), or that Denise's brazen sexual conquests (presented as compensating for her injured leg, unlike her brother whose missing arm is matched by a defunct sex life) are hardly a model of the female submissiveness expected under Vichy's reactionary morality. Gregory Sims (1999: 759) points out the contradiction in claiming the film simultaneously promotes Vichy ideology and subverts patriarchy, although his own thesis that *Le Corbeau* deploys 'Nietzschean aesthetics' and is 'unambiguously fascistic' is hardly any more persuasive. While it is perfectly true that Denise's instinctiveness proves more effective than Germain's 'rigid rationality', it is hard to see what is gained by calling this 'Dionysian' (Sims 1999: 748, 744 n.4, 772). Fascism may well have an irrationalist component, but its defining nationalist, racist, imperialist, and gangsterish elements are manifestly missing from *Le Corbeau* (see

16 'You are infected like the others. You'll fall like them!'

17 'Patriarchal power, whether medical or political.'

Vincent 1992, for a concise but comprehensive account of fascism).

The current critical consensus about *Le Corbeau* is that a sometime 'film maudit' has now attained the status of a classic. In other words, 'la malédiction est levée'[18] for the contemporary spectator, who is doubtless able to set aside the issues of collaboration and anti-French propaganda which troubled earlier commentators, and to judge the film on its cinematic and aesthetic virtues, without direct reference to the socio-historical context of Occupation cinema. This approach implies that contemporaneous prejudices and preconceptions somehow temporarily block true understanding of artistic works, especially provocative and disturbing ones. An alternative reaction for later generations is occasionally one of disappointment or bemusement, when the object of critical adoration ceases to speak to a modern audience. In the case of films, this can simply be due to technical reasons which impair their quality irrevocably (damaged film stock, poor video copies, inaudible dialogue, unexplained cuts, etc.). A minor example in the case of *Le Corbeau* is that the scenarios of the film held by the Bibliothèque du film and the text published in 1948 refer to an opening shot of flocks of rooks which are invisible either in the transcript provided in *L'Avant-Scène Cinéma* (1977) or the versions shown in the cinema and on French television. My argument has been that we need both to undertake an archaeological reconstruction of occupation cinema and to interrogate the film as image and text in order to understand fully its value as a historical and artistic document. *Le Corbeau* succeeds as filmic drama and as a potent period piece full of satirical insights into the vices and virtues of Vichy France. In this sense, Claude Mauriac's equation of *Le Corbeau* with Renoir's celebrated *La Règle du jeu* as a satire of universal historical significance is entirely justified (cited in *L'Avant-Scène Cinéma* 1977: 80).

Bibliography

Assouline, Pierre (1990), *1944–1945: l'épuration des intellectuels*, Brussels, Editions Complexe

L'Avant-Scène Cinéma (1977), 186 (script and reviews of *Le Corbeau*)

Barrot, Olivier (1979), *L'Ecran français 1943–1953: histoire d'un journal et d'une époque*, Paris, Les Editeurs français réunis

---

18 'The curse is lifted.' The last words written by the 'Corbeau'.

Bertin-Maghit, Jean-Pierre (1984), '1945, l'épuration du cinéma français: mythe ou réalité?', in Marc Ferro, ed., *Film et histoire*, Paris, Editions de l'Ecole des Hautes Etudes en Sciences Sociales, 131–42

Bertin-Maghit, Jean-Pierre (1989), *Le Cinéma sous l'Occupation*, Paris, Olivier Orban

Bocquet, José-Louis and Marc Godin (1993), *Henri-Georges Clouzot cinéaste*, Paris, La Sirène

Bourdier, Jean (1996), *Histoire du roman policier*, Paris, Editions de Fallois

Burch, Noël and Geneviève Sellier (1996), *La Drôle de guerre des sexes du cinéma français*, Paris, Nathan

Chateau, René (1995), *Le Cinéma français sous l'Occupation 1940–1944*, Paris, Editions René Chateau et la Mémoire du cinéma français

Chavance, Louis and Henri-Georges Clouzot (1948), *Le Corbeau*, Paris, La Nouvelle Edition

Chirat, Raymond (1983), *Le Cinéma français des années de guerre*, Paris, Hatier

Clouzot, Henri-Georges, 'Le Corbeau', scripts, BIFI archives

Courtade, Francis (1991), 'La Continental', in Heike Hurst and Heiner Gassen, eds, *Tendres Ennemis: cent ans de cinéma entre la France et l'Allemagne*, Paris, L'Harmattan, 216–30

Crisp, Colin (1997), *The Classic French Cinema 1930–1960*, Bloomington, Indiana University Press/London, I.B. Tauris

Darmon, Pierre (1997), *Le Monde du cinéma sous l'Occupation*, Paris, Stock

Ehrlich, Evelyn (1985), *Cinema of Paradox: French Filmmaking under the German Occupation*, New York, Columbia University Press

Fresnay, Pierre and François Possot (1975), *Pierre Fresnay*, Paris, La Table ronde

Garçon, François (1984), *De Blum à Pétain: cinéma et société française (1936–1944)*, Paris, Les Editions du Cerf

Gauteur, Claude (1997), 'Le Mystère Clouzot', *L'Avant-Scène Cinéma*, 463, June, 100–8

Halimi, André (1983), *La Délation sous l'Occupation*, Paris, Editions Alain Moreau

Hayward, Susan (1993), *French National Cinema*, London, Routledge

Lacassin, Francis and Raymond Bellour (1964), *Le Procès Clouzot*, Paris, Le Terrain vague

Lacourbe, Roland (1977), 'Henri-Georges Clouzot', *L'Avant-Scène Cinéma*, 186, 94–124

Leclerc, Ginette (1963), *Ma vie privée*, Paris, La Table ronde

Lemoine, Françoise (1995), 'Deux corbeaux dans la nasse', *Le Figaro*, 25 May

Lindeperg, Sylvie (1997), *Les Ecrans de l'ombre: la Seconde Guerre Mondiale dans le cinéma français (1944–1969)*, Paris, CNRS Editions

Lloyd, Christopher (2003), *Collaboration and Resistance in Occupied France: Representing Treason and Sacrifice*, Basingstoke, Palgrave Macmillan

Mayne, Judith (2000), 'Henri-Georges Clouzot's *Le Corbeau* and the Crimes of Women', *Journal of Twentieth-Century French Studies*, 4, 2, 319–41

Médioni, Gilles (1995), 'Le Corbeau s'appelait Mlle Angèle', *L'Express*, 5 January, 42–4

Monjo, André (1947), 'L'Aigle hitlérien sous le plumage du corbeau', *L'Humanité*, 10 September

Pilard, Philippe (1969), *Henri-Georges Clouzot*, Paris, Seghers

Siclier, Jacques (1990), *La France de Pétain et son cinéma*, Paris, Ramsay Poche

Sims, Gregory (1999), 'Henri-Georges Clouzot's *Le Corbeau* (1943): the Work of Art as Will to Power', *MLN*, 114, 4, 743–79

Steeman, Stanislas-André (2000), *Œuvres choisies 1*, Tournai, La Renaissance du livre

Vincent, Andrew (1992), *Modern Political Ideologies*, Oxford, Blackwell

Williams, Alan (1992), *Republic of Images: A History of French Filmmaking*, Cambridge MA, Harvard University Press

1 False piety: Laura and Germain (Micheline Francey and Pierre Fresnay in *Le Corbeau*)

2 False slut: Denise (Ginette Leclerc in *Le Corbeau*)

3 False villain: Marie Corbin's shattered image (Héléna Manson in *Le Corbeau*)

4 False friend: Vorzet's shadow and Germain (Pierre Fresnay in *Le Corbeau*)

5 False protectress: Christina and Nicole (Vera Clouzot and Simone Signoret in *Les Diaboliques*)

6 Michel's resurrection (Paul Meurisse in *Les Diaboliques*)

7 False protector: Christina and Michel (Vera Clouzot and Paul Meurisse in *Les Diaboliques*)

8 Christina in peril (Vera Clouzot in *Les Diaboliques*)

9 José in bondage (Elisabeth Wiener in *La Prisonnière*)

10 Jo confronts Luigi (Charles Vanel and Folco Lulli in *Le Salaire de la peur*)

11 Linda's adoring posture (Vera Clouzot in *Le Salaire de la peur*)

12 Mario loses control (Yves Montand in *Le Salaire de la peur*)

13 Jo, Mario and woman in shower (Charles Vanel and Yves Montand in *Le Salaire de la peur*)

3

Reconstruction and retribution: Clouzot's post-war films

Despite the ultimate recognition of *Le Corbeau* as one of the most significant films made in France during the occupation, its caustic satire of authority and production by the German company Continental Films led to Clouzot and his associates being branded as collaborators and banned from working in the film industry after France was liberated in 1944. This chapter examines the four films with which Clouzot relaunched his career on his return to film-making in 1947 (having effectively been excluded from the profession for four years). Judith Mayne (2004: 41) has suggested that while Clouzot's first post-war film, *Quai des Orfèvres*, can be seen as a continuation of his previous work (its screenplay once again derives from a novel by S.-A. Steeman, and it offers a major role to the director's partner Suzy Delair), its preoccupation with sexual marginality also makes it a significant transitional film, which anticipates his work in the 1950s and 1960s. Clouzot's wartime record was soon forgotten or forgiven; in fact his next films, *Manon* and *Le Retour de Jean*, can be interpreted as a form of indirect self-justification, since both deal with issues of guilt and retribution for war crimes and collaboration. And though the fourth film in this cycle, *Miquette et sa mère*, is a rather plodding adaptation of a Belle Epoque boulevard comedy, it does at least show how within five years of the war's end Clouzot was firmly re-established as a mainstream director.

Two of Clouzot's post-war films have achieved popular and critical success: *Quai des Orfèvres* (1947) attracted over five million French spectators and was awarded a prize for best director at the Venice biennale, while a critics' poll conducted by the review *Positif* in 1995 ranked it as the second-best French thriller ever made (Gauteur 1997).

Manon (1949) likewise gained over three million French spectators and another Venice prize. It is an adaptation of the Abbé Prévost's classic story of tragic love (first published in 1731), skilfully updated to the liberation period; Clouzot and Jean Ferry published a novelised version of their script in 1949.[1] *Le Retour de Jean* (1949) is a short which was Clouzot's contribution to a compilation of five films collectively entitled *Retour à la vie*, about the problems of French prisoners of war returning to civilian life (the other directors were André Cayatte, Georges Lampin and Jean Dréville, the latter directing two episodes). *Miquette et sa mère* (1950) was a film which Clouzot made reluctantly to fulfil a contractual obligation; it was neither commercially nor critically successful. Clouzot co-scripted all four films with Jean Ferry.

Miquette is one of several filmed versions of a light-hearted comedy by Robert de Flers and G.-A. de Caillavet, first staged in 1906. As a period piece mainly played as farce, at first sight it seems rather remote from the sombre films which precede it, with their contemporary settings and acts of violent retribution. Like *Quai des Orfèvres* and *Le Retour de Jean*, however, *Miquette* does give a starring part to the celebrated stage actor Louis Jouvet. Like *Quai des Orfèvres* and *Manon*, *Miquette* also deals with sexual exploitation, rivalry and jealousy, although by conscripting the various protagonists and antagonists into his theatre troupe, the impresario-actor Monchablon (Jouvet) magically removes the social and emotional barriers which obstruct or destroy love and harmony. Like *Quai des Orfèvres*, again, *Miquette* is about the power of show business to transform lives or life, for better or worse; in both films, the lovers are reconciled and able to reconstruct their union (whereas in *Manon*, union is possible only in death). *Manon* and *Le Retour de Jean* deal with larger themes than *Quai des Orfèvres* and *Miquette*, in that the first two films attempt to transcend private conflicts and dramas by associating individuals with national destinies, most obviously the destructive effects of war (materially and morally) and the desperate (and probably doomed) struggle of the survivors to re-establish a stable existence.

Quai des Orfèvres has three alternative titles, all of which stress

1 Unlike Clouzot's other major films, *Manon* has not been available in video format in recent years and is therefore difficult to see, although it has occasionally been shown in arts cinemas. As a consequence of this limited distribution, it is now one of Clouzot's least well-known films. Copies are available for researchers to view in cinema archives in Paris and Brussels.

different aspects of the film and suggest its appealing diversity. The definitive title *Quai des Orfèvres* indicates to a French audience that the film is a police procedural, part thriller and part documentary, since this is the famous address of the headquarters of the Paris *police judici-aire*, where much of the second half of the action takes place. Since foreign audiences may be unaware of this association, versions of the film shown outside France are sometimes entitled *Jenny Lamour*; this is the stage name of the main female character (played by Suzy Delair), whose performances as a music-hall artiste and attempts to get a contract from a lecherous film producer drive the action in the first half of the film. Clouzot's provisional title, *Joyeux Noël*, was less specific and perhaps unduly sarcastic: the film is set in December 1946 and none of the central characters faces a very happy Christmas, since they are all involved in a murder investigation, either as suspects or investigators. Finally, as we saw in our opening chapter, Clouzot and Ferry adopted the film from S.-A. Steeman's novel *Légitime Défense* (1942), a title which expresses the supposed justification for murder of the two principal characters.

Quai des Orfèvres invites analysis as visual spectacle, narrative of suspense, and psychological or social drama. These are illustrated, respectively, by the music-hall scenes, the police investigation, and the intricate detail with which both places and people are presented and located. Clouzot and Ferry retained only the basic configuration of Steeman's novel (in other words, jealous husband, unfaithful wife, obnoxious lover, sympathetic female friend, intrusive detective), while changing the characters' identities, the resolution of the investigation, and the entire setting. *Légitime Défense* describes how the painter Noël Martin suspects his wife Belle of being the mistress of Judas Weyl, finally hitting the sleeping Judas on the head with a mallet in suppos-edly legitimate defence of his marital property. After Noël persuades his friend Renée d'Humain to give him an alibi, Belle informs him that she herself had already killed Weyl in self-defence; her jealous spouse had avenged himself on a corpse. The overweight *commissaire* Honoré Maria investigates the crime in a lethargic fashion. The setting of the novel is left curiously vague (while Maria says he is from the Quai des Orfèvres, in other words Paris, another reference to the 'procureur du roi' suggests we are actually in Belgium) and the characters' substance barely extends beyond their strangely symbolic names.

In *Quai des Orfèvres*, Jenny Lamour's morose husband, Maurice

Martineau (Bernard Blier), is a music-hall pianist who accompanies her singing performances (he has abandoned a career as a classical musician to marry her) and resents the attention she attracts from male admirers. When Maurice discovers that Jenny has a rendezvous with the libidinous film producer Brignon (Charles Dullin), whom he has already threatened to shoot, he takes out his pistol and drives to Brignon's house, only to find that Brignon has already been killed. Meanwhile, Jenny confesses to her friend, the photographer Dora, that she has killed Brignon with a champagne bottle while repelling his unwanted advances; Dora agrees to go to Brignon's house to retrieve the fox furs which Jenny left at the crime scene. Inspector Antoine has Maurice arrested as a prime suspect; Dora too is detained after a taxi driver admits to driving her from Brignon's house. While Maurice attempts suicide in his cell (he is saved by a blood transfusion), Antoine discovers that Maurice's pistol was not the weapon that killed Brignon (only at the end of the film do we discover that he had actually been shot). The gangster Paulo, who stole Maurice's car from outside Brignon's house and was arrested after using the car in a robbery during which he killed a policeman and rent collector, finally admits that he shot Brignon just as the latter was recovering consciousness after Jenny's attack, and just a few minutes before Maurice arrived to discover the corpse.

This denouement clearly marks a major change in the plot mechanism of Steeman's novel, and we may well share the disgruntled author's view (quoted in Lacassin and Bellour 1964) that Clouzot's addition of an outsider as the real murderer is somewhat contrived, not only because Paulo has no link with any of the other characters, but also because Jenny, Maurice and even Dora all have good reasons to kill Brignon. Paulo is very briefly shown stealing Maurice's car, and then preparing it for his robbery, but these inserted scenes make little sense on a first viewing, even if retrospectively they can be recognised as clues to Paulo's guilt. The police wrongly suspect Maurice and Dora, while spectators wrongly suspect Jenny after her confession, largely because the fact Brignon died of a gunshot is suppressed, although it seems highly implausible that the police do not start looking for the gun from the beginning of the investigation. Clouzot's films are of course notorious for their deceptive conclusions, which disrupt audience's expectations about the likely resolution of an enigma (thus there are three murderers in *L'Assassin habite au 21*, the chief investigator proves to be the culprit in *Le Corbeau*, and, most famously of all, a drowned corpse comes back to life in *Les Diaboliques*). What distinguishes these endings from *Quai des Orfèvres*, however, is that in the other films they are carefully, albeit surreptitiously, motivated and on a second viewing reveal a logical alternative plot development whose deviation from the apparent course of events strikes us as reasonably plausible. On the other hand, as Burch and Sellier (1996: 234) observe, Jenny is *morally* guilty of murder and betrayal, even if she is spared the disastrous consequences of her irresponsible behaviour by Antoine's persistence and Clouzot's convenient but somewhat gratuitous invention of a career criminal to take the blame.

Pierre Sorlin (1994: 99) argues that it is a mistake to see *Quai des Orfèvres* as a conventional thriller, when it is more a pseudo-documentary: 'We are offered no riddle and the police do not conduct a real inquiry'. While it is true that the film works better as a social and psychological drama than as a thriller, this is partly because Clouzot *conceals* the 'riddle' for much of the film; the audience assumes that Maurice will be unjustly punished for Jenny's crime and is left unaware of other possibilities (and thereby denied any real suspense). Antoine's belated discovery of another culprit at least allows a conventional happy ending to be grafted on to a grim account of marital infidelity and police incompetence. Jenny and Maurice are reconciled (though one wonders for how long, given her opportunism and his possessiveness), while Antoine is finally able to offer his neglected son a Christmas treat. Vice too is visibly punished: the sexual pervert Brignon has been disposed of, and the gangster who killed him has been imprisoned. Thus the survival of the 'virtuous' couples based on marriage and family and the elimination of the wealthy sexual predator and armed robber appear to offer a morally comforting conclusion.

Yet Clouzot rarely shows much faith or interest in conventional morality, banal normality and social respectability. Neither the childless Jenny and Maurice nor Antoine and his mixed-race son enjoy a stable family relationship (to gain professional advancement, Jenny conceals the fact she is married, while Antoine has no wife and usually leaves his son in a boarding school). Nor do the characters' occupations and activities (music-hall artiste, policeman, criminal) bear much resemblance to those of the average film spectator. In fact, what makes *Quai des Orfèvres* interesting as a social documentary and psychological drama are its exploration of unfamiliar and exotic milieux, its deviation from norms, (relative) refusal of sentimentality, and recognition of complexity and contradiction (even if a twenty-first-century viewer also perceives a considerable amount of sexual and racial stereotyping in some characters). Nearly all the central characters prove, on closer investigation, to be outsiders who are socially, sexually or professionally displaced.

This is most obviously the case with Maurice Martineau. We first see him reprimanding Jenny for her undue familiarity with a songwriter who beats time on her thighs (the camera following Maurice's jealous gaze in a close-up of the intrusive hand). Later, after her successful performance of the composer's song, she is embraced by three members of the music-hall team while Maurice sourly walks off. Jenny remarks: 'Il ne comprendra jamais!', to which the director Mareuil responds: 'Qu'est-ce que tu veux ... Il a été mal élevé ... C'est un fils de bourgeois, il voit le mal partout!'[2] In other words, Maurice's bourgeois upbringing prevents him from understanding the easy and unthreatening physical and emotional intimacy enjoyed by music-hall performers. In this instance, little more is involved than flirtatious camaraderie; the three elderly men who surround Jenny are shown as harmless admirers who are dominated by her presence (she is framed to appear literally larger than they are). On the other hand, as far as Maurice is concerned, the music hall is a place of sexual temptation and degradation: by marrying Jenny and becoming her accompanist, he has abandoned his career as a serious musician and broken with his parents. His suicide attempt follows his realisation that Jenny has deceived him (in other words, she seems certainly guilty of Brignon's murder since her alibi of visiting her grandmother has proved false) and that he has failed to protect her.

While Maurice appears hapless and over-wrought, and therefore unable to interpret others' behaviour correctly, let alone plan and execute a murder successfully, Jenny may seem to be more calculating and manipulative. Hence Antoine's accusation that she is 'une petite arriviste', that is unscrupulously willing to promote her career at the expense of truth or loyalty. Rather like the film's three titles, Jenny's three names reveal contrasting aspects of her identity. As Marguerite Chauffournier, her legal name, she is certainly a social climber,

2 'He'll never understand!' 'What do you expect? He was badly brought up. He's from a bourgeois family and sees evil everywhere!'

even if her ambitions are somewhat naïve and romanticised. While Maurice espouses a republican distrust of privilege, she claims she is a monarchist, on the rather comical grounds that the Ancien Régime would have allowed her to fulfil her true potential: 'Si j'avais vécu sous Louis XV j'aurais été la Pompadour, au moins'.[3] In practice, her attempt to manipulate Brignon in order to break into the movies fails lamentably, as she repels his undesirable advances with a champagne bottle like a valiant but affronted housewife. We learn too that Jenny emerged from an impoverished family; her ambitions in her view represent a justifiable urge for a better life. By marrying Maurice and launching her career as a singer, she has already succeeded both personally and professionally. As Mme Martineau, Jenny may appear to be a faithless if not unfaithful spouse; in fact, she insists on several occasions that their marital bond is sexually and affectively a strong one. Finally, as the singer Jenny Lamour, she has, on the smaller stage of the music hall, acquired her own mythic persona as an object of desire and femme fatale. Opening sequences of the film establish her as an alluring performer: thus we cut between Jenny in a revealing dress, singing her suggestive song, and various members of her audience, some of them enraptured (both male and female), others more distracted (a squalling baby, an irritated girlfriend, a canoodling couple). Then she is seen posing for publicity photographs in Dora's studio, encased in a brief costume that exposes her voluptuous body (but irritated by Dora's offers of physical and emotional intimacy).

Jenny has thus acquired some of the trappings of the star (fur coats and glamorous attire, a retinue of admirers, a recognisable, seductive image), however tawdry her surroundings still are in many respects. But her minor celebrity brings unwanted attention: not merely Brignon's advances, for example, but also the interest of the train conductor who destroys her alibi because he remembers the time he saw her. As a performer too, her situation is highly ambiguous: she clearly depends on the good will of producers, directors and songwriters, and her performance, however entrancing, is close to being a circus act. We see her rehearsing surrounded by performing animals and acrobats, and her act is followed by trick cyclists. While Maurice and Jenny inhabit the lower regions of show business, Inspector Antoine

3 'If I'd lived under Louis XV, I'd have been the King's mistress, or more.' Thanks to her erotic charms, Mme de Pompadour rose from being the plebeian Mlle Poisson to the rank of duchess and figure of legend.

is an equally marginal figure in the police hierarchy. He appears only after thirty-seven minutes, over a third of the way into the film, at which point however the focus of attention shifts from Jenny's performances to Antoine's investigation. Clouzot takes the trouble to sketch in Antoine's background in an expository scene (thereby giving his character a depth and poignancy generally lacking in the down-at-heel detectives whose stereotyped figures occur in innumerable films noirs).

While Martineau and his wife enjoy a certain opulence (such as a relatively spacious apartment, and most notably a motor car), as a mid-ranking official, Antoine lives in straitened circumstances which reveal incidentally but informatively, particularly to a twenty-first-century audience, the material hardship which most French people endured in the years of post-war reconstruction. He is first seen working on an elementary geometry problem, on behalf of his son who is asleep behind a screen; this child, together with a dose of malaria and an injured right arm, are all he brought back to France after fifteen years' service as an NCO in an African colony, as he tells his subordinate Picard. He has also failed to achieve promotion to *commissaire*, not through incompetence but because his face didn't fit.[4] After hearing Jenny's self-justifying account of her deprived upbringing, Antoine retorts sarcastically: 'Moi, mon père il vivait dans un beau château', then adding 'Il était larbin, on le payait pour nettoyer les saletés des autres ... J'ai pris la suite'.[5] When she complains about the police harassing the poor and defending the rich, he points out that the gangster Paulo, who has indiscriminately shot down a money collector and a policeman, is the real enemy of society. Whereas Jenny's complaints about the police merely disguise her own dishonesty and fear of being found out, Antoine is thus established as an affectionate father and honourable albeit poorly rewarded servant of the state. In a telling contrast, while the egotistical Jenny forgets her fox furs at the murder scene, Antoine deliberately leaves his overcoat over his sleeping son.

The presence of this child (who sleeps through Maurice's protracted interrogation at police headquarters) no doubt adds a sympathetic

---

4 Antoine is an *inspecteur principal adjoint*, roughly the equivalent of a detective sergeant, a rank mid-way between the basic *inspecteur* and the more senior *inspecteur principal*. I have followed the usual convention of translating his rank as 'inspector'.

5 'My father lived in a fine château. He was a flunkey and was paid to clean up other people's messes. I've followed in his footsteps.'

element of human interest to Antoine, although the boy himself is barely individualised. Indeed he is never given a name in the film (and the actor who played him is not identified in the credits). The published version of the script of *Quai des Orfèvres* (*L'Avant-Scène Cinéma* 1963) refers to this child generically or racially as 'le marmot', 'le petit noir' and even 'le négrillon' (the kid, the little black, the piccaninny). Dictionaries inform us that this last term is nowadays deemed offensive, although any offence was clearly unintended by the scriptwriters, since the boy's relationship with his father and Antoine's colleagues is portrayed positively. Although there is no explicit reference to the boy's ethnic origin, the fact that Antoine has taken responsibility for educating his mixed-race and possibly illegitimate son is meant to show he lacks the racial prejudices of many Europeans from the colonies. (Whether he will achieve his ambitions is another matter: the boy fails the maths exam to enter the *lycée* which is probably his passport to academic success.) We should recall that the French Empire (which had played a key role in the resistance to Vichy and liberation of mainland France from the Germans) was still seen as an integral and important part of the French community in 1946; most of the negative associations of Empire which we retain in our post-colonial age derive from bitter conflicts which still lay in the future sixty years ago.

Nonetheless, modern audiences may well see Antoine's son as revealing an unconscious racial stereotyping which corresponds to the conventional stereotyping of most secondary characters in genre films. In *Quai des Orfèvres*, the engaging piccaninny matches other schematic types such as the tart with a heart (the garrulous prostitute Manon (Claudine Dupuis), who saves Maurice from bleeding to death when she sees his blood dripping under the partition between their cells), or the 'vieux dégoûtant' (dirty old man; the voyeuristic businessman Brignon, played with caricatural relish by Charles Dullin as a slavering hunchback). Although Clouzot would offer a more sensitive exploration of voyeurism twenty years later in *La Prisonnière*, Brignon is cast rather crudely as an obnoxious pervert, even if his main indulgence seems to be the relatively harmless one of picking up prostitutes and paying them to pose nude and Dora to photograph them while he watches. As he remarks, this is a 'chaste' spectacle, more aesthetically appealing in his opinion than a Manet or Picasso. Brignon is thus burdened with a large number of repellent characteristics: he is physically unattractive, uses his wealth to buy women, seems however to be sexually impotent, and prefers pornography to high art. It is rather surprising that this diminutive voyeur should frighten Jenny so much that she defends herself with a champagne bottle; she never explains what, if anything, he did to her, referring only to the fact he was old enough to be her father.

If Brignon thus attracts further obloquy as an incestuous lecher (abusing his position as Jenny's patron), neither Jenny nor Dora attracts much criticism for their venal complicity in his sexual fantasies. Admittedly, both women pay the price of their association by becoming suspects in his murder, but there is no suggestion that there is anything wrong with Jenny displaying herself half-naked or Dora taking pornographic photographs; this is all part of the legitimate erotic glamour of show business. It is worth noting that Dora emerges as a stronger and more sympathetic character than either Maurice or Jenny, both of whom abuse her fidelity and good will. Nor does she conform to the crude stereotyping of lesbians often found in popular films and literature (man-hater, marriage-destroyer, masculine woman, and so on). Whereas Brignon seems irredeemably vicious, Dora is endowed with many positive qualities, which appeal to both male and female viewers. The fact that the actress Simone Renant was a strikingly beautiful woman inevitably adds to Dora's charm; Suzy Delair may have had magnificent legs, but her chubby face looks very ordinary compared to Renant's sculpted cheekbones.

Neither Maurice nor Jenny is aware of Dora's proclivities (though they are obvious to Antoine and the audience). The married couple's self-centredness (Maurice's petulant jealousy, Jenny's inept careerism) is contrasted with Dora's loyalty and restraint. A succession of scenes discreetly reveals Dora's attraction towards Jenny, and simultaneously her willingness to sacrifice her own desires and well-being for the married couple (she sustains their convenient but implausible fiction that she is a heterosexual spinster more interested in Maurice than Jenny). For example, her handling of Jenny during the photography session is ostensibly meant to improve her pose, though Jenny rebuffs this physical contact and dislikes Dora's unwarranted interest in the couple's sex life. Dora's willingness to retrieve evidence incriminating Jenny from Brignon's house is supposedly an act of friendship on behalf of Maurice, although the risk involved clearly demands a much stronger attachment. In a scene cut from the film, Dora embraces

Jenny, but is again rejected because she is not a man; another deleted scene at the end showed Dora brusquely leaving and Maurice and Jenny concluding she must have been in love with him. Ironically, while Dora asserts that men rarely understand women, Inspector Antoine tells her that she is 'un type dans mon genre ... Avec les femmes vous n'aurez jamais de chance.'[6]

Antoine recognises Dora's sexual marginality, since he too fails to conform to the usual norms of professional and marital behaviour. (He is also an amateur photographer, a hobby picked up from a previous 'client'.) Nevertheless, for all their emotional conflicts and material frustrations, the main characters' deviancy in reality barely exceeds the limits of bourgeois respectability, compared with the violent law-breaking of a professional gangster like Paulo; however, he is presented too summarily to be more than a sneering tough guy who eventually confesses. When Antoine encounters a well-dressed gangster in the corridor at police headquarters, the latter derides the inspector's shabby appearance; but we learn nothing about his ill-gotten riches other than that his is another world. Despite Clouzot's celebrated preliminary research at the Quai des Orfèvres, we actually learn very little about the criminal underworld and its denizens; as already suggested, they function mainly as a convenient means of closing the plot and absolving Jenny of murder.

The enigma is essentially resolved by Antoine's patient (at times brutal) interrogation of Maurice, Jenny and Dora, during which he breaks down their defensive and (as it proves) unnecessary lies, as he does too with ancillary figures. Thus he gets the truth from an elderly taxi driver (Pierre Larquey), who is reluctant to identify Dora as the passenger he picked up outside Brignon's house, until Antoine threatens to confiscate his licence. Much of the action in the second half of the film is driven by lengthy verbal confrontations between characters. Hence the conclusion drawn by Pierre Jouvet (1978: 18) that 'Le dialogue a une fonction structurale très forte et commande les images' and that

> C'est une film essentiellement parlant, où ce que font les personnages est rarement aussi important que ce qu'ils disent. Le rôle des acteurs est presque entièrement défini par leur parole, elle leur désigne toute la *mise en scène*. Tous ont de la verve, du répondant, des formules colorées.[7]

6 'A type like me. With women you'll never have any luck.'
7 'Dialogue has a very powerful structural function and drives the images. The

At the same time, however, and at the risk of a certain contradiction, Jouvet (1978: 19) notes that music is 'le fil conducteur de certaines images', so that *Quai des Orfèvres* 'est un film musical, ou peu s'en faut'.[8]

There is less contradiction here if we note that the film effectively shifts from music to words as it moves from the expository scenes based around the music hall (lasting about forty minutes) to the police procedural set largely at the Quai des Orfèvres (occupying much of the final sixty minutes). What might be called the open world of cabaret artistes, with its accompanying interiors set in private apartments and exterior Parisian street scenes, is followed by the enclosed world of police headquarters, which consists of crowded, shabby offices, corridors and cells; the film becomes more theatrical and less cinematic as it moves into these enclosed spaces. As a result, the most memorable and striking effects of editing and *mise en scène* are largely found in the opening scenes. Four successive scenes, linked by the soundtrack which plays the verses of Jenny's song, cut with swift efficiency from the initial to the final stages of her performance: first from the songwriter's office to Jenny's apartment (we see her examining her multiple image reflected in a three-sided mirror as she rehearses her movements, watched in turn by Maurice and Dora), then to a full-scale rehearsal on the music-hall stage (accompanied by orchestra, stage crew and other artistes), then to the first live performance before an admiring audience. (The sequence may well be borrowed from a very similar one in Welles's *Citizen Kane*.) Nevertheless, apart from the appeal of hearing Jenny's song evolve, a great deal of introductory information about characters and setting is delivered purely visually by this montage, with hardly any dialogue at all, and music is skilfully integrated into the action (whereas in musicals, musical numbers typically function as interludes that stop the narrative).

As the film shifts from social documentary to thriller, it tends to become less formally innovative. For example, jarringly melodramatic extra-diegetic music is used much more conventionally to underscore the lengthy exterior sequence which presents Maurice's silent,

film is essentially spoken; what the characters do is seldom as important as what they say. The actors' roles are almost entirely defined by their words, which determine the whole *mise-en-scène* for them. All of them are endowed with eloquence, repartee and colourful idioms.'

8 'The thread linking certain images.' 'Is a musical, or very nearly.'

protracted odyssey across Paris when he returns to the music hall after finding Brignon's corpse. It is, however, misleading to imply that *Quai des Orfèvres* degenerates into filmed drama, with little visual impact. For example, throughout the film there are noteworthy shots or edited sequences inserted for comic and/or metaphorical purposes. An amusing case occurs in the expository scenes when Jenny opens her coat and reveals her scanty costume to Maurice; as they embrace, we cut to a close-up of a pan of milk on the stove boiling over, a parodic symbol of steaming passion wittily linked with a more banal illustration of distraction from domestic duty. While Jenny is narcissistically and flatteringly reflected in mirrors as she rehearses, the brooding Maurice sees his reflection chopped off at the neck as he is about to set off to shoot Brignon, a premonition of the punishment that awaits murderers. The sombre and protracted interrogation scenes in the second half of the film are also alleviated with some comic touches: such as a rapid montage cutting from Dora to Maurice to Manon, all repeating 'je n'y étais pas' to their separate interrogators, followed by a fourth scene when a detective ironically completes the same phrase for Paulo: 'Puisqu'il vous dit qu'il n'y était pas'.[9] All of them, as this suggests, are predictably lying. More farcical effects are obtained from the antics of the press pack, eagerly awaiting the identification of the killer; when Antoine emerges, they fall downstairs over one other in their eagerness to quiz him.

Finally, it is worth noting how the repetition of some devices and scenes throughout the film reinforces its incidental impact as a social documentary. Certain exterior shots serve almost entirely to add local colour, establishing the atmosphere of Paris night life and film noir (porters unloading fruit and vegetables at the central market, crowds pouring out of the metro, the sheen of street lights on rain-soaked roadways). The physical discomfort and material deprivation of the immediate post-war years are frequently suggested by such incidental details (for example, wearing coats indoors against the cold).[10] In fact,

9 'I wasn't there.' 'Since he's telling you he wasn't there.'
10 Chronicling post-liberation Paris, the historians Beevor and Cooper (1995: 219) note that 'The inconveniences and discomforts of daily life seemed endless. ... For many, the winter cold was a more terrible memory than the shortages of food.' Scarcity of most basic commodities meant that rationing continued until 1949 (along with the black market that allowed the wealthier to bypass official restrictions). Apart from human fatalities, enormous damage to property and infrastructure was caused in mainland France during the last year of the

motifs such as smoking and resisting the cold have a more direct thematic value, serving both to highlight the film's documentary impact and to convey characters' vulnerability. For example, a group of men are shown standing in the music-hall gallery, all wearing heavy coats and smoking vigorously throughout the performance (smoking presumably providing some illusion of added warmth). Maurice, on the other hand, whose paranoiac jealousy drives him to mental and physical collapse, surrenders his coat to the cloakroom attendant, in an inept attempt to acquire an alibi while he crosses Paris to seek out Brignon; under interrogation by the police, he is deprived of his jacket, so that exposure to cold is again added to his torment. In other scenes, he is seen listlessly examining the unappealing ingredients of a meagre meal, or anxiously observing Antoine as the detective unwittingly lights his pipe with a piece of paper containing evidence incriminating Jenny. Such examples of material details that skilfully link the austerity of the times to the narrative and characters' dilemma could be endlessly multiplied; they give *Quai des Orfèvres* a visual appeal and richness of texture that distinguish it from more workmanlike thrillers.

At the end of the war, less than half the French rail network and its rolling stock was serviceable; in these conditions, the journey from Paris to Strasbourg took over fifteen hours (Rioux 1980: 33–4). This example is highly relevant to Clouzot's next film, *Manon* (1949), because the director claimed that this film was originally inspired by his idea of a scene on a packed train in which two separated lovers are desperately trying to find each other (see Clouzot 1965). Unlike *Quai des Orfèvres* (where war and politics are glimpsed only very obliquely, insofar as they are the distant causes of the material hardship which intrudes into the film), *Manon* addresses historical and ethical issues related to the defeat and reconstruction of France much more directly. The subject of the film is the punishment and survival of former collaborators in post-war France (or elsewhere). There is little need to spell out the biographical parallels with Clouzot's own predicament, other than to observe that commentators have seemed curiously blind to them; this is perhaps due to the classic status of Prévost's original

---

war; some towns in Normandy were almost totally destroyed. The Ministry of Reconstruction estimated in 1946 that investment of up to three years' national income was needed to restore economic activity comparable to the pre-war period (Rioux 1980: 33).

novel, which (along with its multiple operatic, theatrical and film adaptations) is remembered principally as a romantic story of tragically thwarted love. Apart from its portrayal of a beguiling femme fatale, the novel does however contain important reflections on historical circumstance and personal responsibility; these merit brief revaluation, since they are also central to Clouzot and Ferry's version.

The *Histoire du Chevalier des Grieux et de Manon Lescaut* is the seventh volume of a lengthy picaresque novel entitled *Mémoires et aventures d'un homme de qualité* (1728–31). The principal narrator encounters des Grieux twice: first, when the Chevalier is accompanying a convoy of prostitutes, including Manon, who are being deported to North America; then two years later, on des Grieux's return to France, at which point the Man of Quality learns the full story of the lovers' fate and transcribes des Grieux's account in the first person. Unlike des Grieux, Manon, who is of common birth, has not survived their ordeal in the New World. Des Grieux met Manon when he was seventeen and she was somewhat younger; helping her escape detention in a convent, he flees with her to Paris, abandoning his studies and indulging in a life of pleasure. Des Grieux is kidnapped by his father's lackeys (with Manon's connivance); but she robs her wealthy lover and returns to him. When they lose this money, Manon's cynical elder brother suggests that she should be able to keep all three of them by selling her favours. However, their plans to cheat another elderly admirer lead to the lovers' arrest. Des Grieux escapes by shooting dead a guard; Lescaut is shot after they assist Manon to escape. From this point on, dishonesty and duplicity become their way of life, until their bungled attempts to cheat another wealthy man lead to Manon's deportation as a common prostitute. Misfortune continues to follow them in America. They flee into the wilderness after des Grieux wounds the governor's nephew in a duel over Manon. After a night spent in the open air, des Grieux discovers that Manon has died of exposure; he is rescued while awaiting death on her grave.

Montesquieu famously said of *Manon Lescaut* 'Le héros est un fripon et l'héroïne une catin'[11] (quoted in Prévost 1963: lxi). Yet this is not how most readers perceive them, for des Grieux's skilfully sentimentalised account blinds us to the gravity of their misdemeanours. Both he and Manon are constantly tempted by the venality of an inequitable, hypocritical society; des Grieux likes to blame everyone but himself

11 'The hero is a rogue and the heroine a whore.'

for their misfortune (his father, society, fate), while seeing the passion that ensnares him as a vitalising rather than a destructive force. His defence is that their acts do not match their true nature; rather than wickedness or weakness, 'It is merely the unfortunate accidents of existence in the shape of law, morality and convention that make them act as they do' (King, quoted in Prévost 1963: lxi). Clouzot and Ferry's adaptation of the novel respects this central premise of youth and love corrupted by circumstance; if anything they reinforce it, by insisting more explicitly on the violence, immorality and rapacity of post-liberation France. Thus their Robert Desgrieux blames 'l'époque abominable' for the couple's misdeeds (he was introduced to the black market as a schoolboy during the occupation and then to a life of violent adventure when he joined the maquis), and we are told that 'La France libérée avait une reine qui s'appelait la combine'.[12] Like their fictional counterparts, the film's central characters are innocents ruined (and finally destroyed) by an abominable age (a point empha-sised by the youthful ingenuousness of the actors: Cécile Aubry, who played Manon, was twenty and Michel Auclair and Serge Reggiani who played Desgrieux and Léon Lescaut were twenty-seven).[13]

Such deterministic fatalism, which conveniently acquits the protag-onists of any real personal responsibility for immoral and criminal acts, doubtless struck a chord with contemporary audiences eager to forget or to excuse the humiliations and uneasy compromises brought by life under German occupation. However, at a more straightforward level, Clouzot's *Manon* derives its popular appeal from being an exemplary adventure story and visual spectacle, which benefited from a more generous budget than his previous films. This permitted the full-scale reconstruction of a ship in the Joinville studios, as well as extensive location shooting in Normandy and Morocco. The film also moves out of mainland France, when Desgrieux and Manon take refuge on

12 'Liberated France had a queen whose name was dealing.' Note that the spelling Desgrieux is the form adopted in Clouzot's novelised version of the film (Clouzot 1949)

13 Clouzot thought Cécile Aubry projected an appealing image of provocative innocence. Her unsuccessful rival for the part, Danielle Godet, later commented sourly that his selection process 'faisait penser au calibrage des petits pois dans une usine de conserves' and that 'Clouzot me reprochait ma réserve et mon côté jeune fille de bonne famille' (Godet 1981: 51, 53). ('Made you think of grading peas in a canning factory. Clouzot objected to my shyness and my bourgeois, lady-like manner.')

a ship carrying illegal immigrants to Palestine. The enclosed urban spaces of *Le Corbeau* and *Quai des Orfèvres* are replaced by the wider expanses of the natural world, though the sea and desert prove even more hostile to the protagonists. The audience's sympathy is almost entirely engaged with them, mainly because (as generic conventions dictate) they are physically appealing and beset by adversaries (whether human or natural) who are much more obviously malevolent. Though Montesquieu's caustic judgement could in theory apply equally to the film, spectators are given little opportunity to achieve the critical distance necessary to observe the characters with such hostility. Clouzot has followed the novel's oblique mode of narration, shifting the sequence of events so as to favour the protagonists' retrospective self-justification. There is also added appeal for readers of the original novel in discovering how skilfully Clouzot and Ferry have relocated it in wartime France and Palestine.

Most of the film consists of an extended flashback, presented from Desgrieux's perspective, preceded by a prologue set on the ship where he and Manon are stowaways, and followed by an epilogue set in Palestine. The Man of Quality is replaced by the ship's captain, a more functionally important narratee, since the couple's fate depends on the success of Desgrieux's narrative (and Manon's emotional entreaties as she weeps on his shoulder) in persuading him not to turn them over to the police. Desgrieux is wanted for murder and is separated from Manon, who bribes a crew member to let them meet. The sailor thereby acquires more and more of her property; this exchange of valuables, money and eventually sex effectively encapsulates Manon's precarious survival tactics and Desgrieux's somewhat abject dependence on her. The captain, however, puts a stop to these transactions and restores Manon's belongings to her; he is a rare example of a figure in authority who behaves honourably and impartially.

While this prologue strikes a rather sentimental, melodramatic tone (to which the chanting of the Jewish refugees hidden in the hold adds a certain pathos), Desgrieux's account of his encounter with Manon takes the form of a more cynical documentary on the liberation and its aftermath. Virtually every person we see is motivated either by venal self-interest or vengeance. Desgrieux's *maquis* unit, which is fighting with the Americans in Normandy, rescues Manon from a mob of women in a devastated town; the women are intent on shearing her hair as a punishment for frequenting German soldiers.

Desgrieux is told to guard Manon in a ruined church; while she tries to persuade him to let her go, on the grounds that enjoying herself was no crime, we see the bodies of hostages shot by the Germans brought out on stretchers to a solemn drum beat, and the mob passing with two shorn women. Desgrieux finally relents, and they flee to Paris in a stolen jeep, where they take refuge with Manon's brother Léon and his associate Monsieur Paul.[14] It takes the ingenuous Desgrieux some time to realise that these two are black-market dealers and that Manon's work as a model is a euphemism for upmarket prostitution; he is sent on business trips to Oran to keep him out of the way.

Shedding his naivety, Desgrieux tracks down Manon in a high-class brothel, by posing as a client, in a sequence where social comedy is followed by a melodramatic confrontation when he spits in her face. They are rapidly reconciled. Realising that Manon's whorish behaviour is in her nature (or that honesty and fidelity are for dupes), Desgrieux becomes more tolerant of her clientele and an unabashed trafficker himself (dealing in penicillin stolen from the US army, like Harry Lime in *The Third Man*). But Léon is unwilling to tolerate Desgrieux's interference and has him locked up in a cinema basement to stop him pestering Manon; in a showdown beneath the projection room, with the soundtrack of a western playing in the background, Desgrieux strangles Léon with an electric cable and then flees to Marseille. There follows Clouzot's long-planned sequence on the train, further combining sardonic comedy and documentary, as Manon seeks him out in the crowded station and packed corridors and carriages. This train is literally overflowing with travellers (so that one woman has sought refuge in the luggage rack), though allied forces, in a telling contrast, have a quiet carriage, unlike the French civilians whom they have liberated. The lovers find each other and we return to the ship.

Persuaded by this account of their tribulations that the couple deserve the chance to start a new life (the Promised Land replacing the New World of the novel), the captain lets them leave with the Jewish refugees, reporting them drowned to the authorities. They disembark

14 The episodes showing the shorn women and the couple's flight to Paris have been cut from the copy of *Manon* conserved at the Cinémathèque archives at the Fort Saint-Cyr (viewed in July 2004), whether by accident or design. Clouzot's film is possibly the first feature to refer to this punishment, which was extensively inflicted on alleged horizontal collaborators in the months following the liberation; the victims were usually young unmarried women and the perpetrators men (see Virgili 2002 for details).

joyously from three sailboats on a beach in Palestine, accompanied by lyrical music. However, the lorry transporting them to a settlement breaks down and they have to cross the desert. They reach an oasis and enjoy a brief idyll (we see their silhouettes romantically framed by the sunset). But this glimpse of paradise proves illusory: the carcasses of dead camels indicate the hellish conditions they will endure on their forced march and the likely outcome. One man foolishly throws away his ill-fitting boots and walks barefoot; none of them are adequately equipped for a desert journey. They are spotted by an Arab on a camel, who summons the rest of his patrol to attack the refugees. Manon is shot, along with most of the other refugees and their lightly armed guards, though Desgrieux is unhurt.[15] Manon's death is extended operatically, as Desgrieux carries her body across the sand dunes, suffering auditory hallucinations which recall their life together. Finally, we see him lying next to a dead camel with her corpse; then with her body buried in a shallow grave, kissing her face with necrophiliac passion; she is fully his at last in death. The film ends with him prostrated on the grave, awaiting his own end.

Noting the scathing portrayal of liberated France given by *Manon*, where dealing in flesh, drugs and other commodities replaces the nobler Resistance ideals of freedom, equity and justice, Marcel Oms argues that the film's epilogue universalises this pessimistic vision. Manon perishes in the Promised Land, 'sur les lieux mêmes du commencement d'une culture, au terme d'un nouvel Exode qui marque l'épilogue de l'Histoire récente' (Oms 1987: 56).[16] Other critics have been less sympathetic to Clouzot's interpretation of recent history, drawing attention to its tendentious aspects. For example,

15 Despite the melodramatic pathos of its ending, the film does continue to respect historical reality in these closing scenes. As the British mandate in post-war Palestine drew to a close, and a vicious three-way conflict between Jews, Arabs and British forces developed, the UK Labour government placed draconian restrictions on the departure of Jewish immigrants from Europe, forcing would-be settlers to attempt illegal landings on the coastline. About 40,000 Jewish immigrants entered Palestine clandestinely between 1945 and 1948, while a further 52,000 were caught and detained in Cyprus. Attacks on Jewish settlements by neighbouring Arab communities had occurred since the late nineteenth century. By 1947, fighting between Arab and Jewish units was a daily occurrence; the unilateral declaration of an independent Jewish state on 14 May 1948 brought full-scale war (see Gilbert 1998).

16 'On the very site where a culture began, at the end of a new Exodus, which forms an epilogue to recent history.'

the novelist Roger Vailland (a Resistance activist and member of the Communist Party, and thus an implacable ideological adversary of an ex-collaborator like Clouzot) observed in a review published in March 1949:

> Il y a chez Clouzot une volonté délibérée de montrer qu'en 1944 tous les Français sans exception étaient des veules. D'où à conclure que ceux qui passent maintenant pour des héros ne le furent que par hasard, par erreur, il n'y a qu'un pas. (Quoted in Vailland and Ballet 1973: 115)[17]

Vailland's complaint that Resistance fighters like Desgrieux are carica-tured as self-interested thugs little better than outright collaborators has some justification (we might also note that important figures in Prévost's novel who represent honesty or moral righteousness, like des Grieux's father and his friend Tiberge, are omitted from the film). On the other hand, Burch and Sellier's more recent attempt to convict Clouzot of both sexism and xenophobia in the conclusion of *Manon* is less persuasive. The dying Desgrieux, they assert, is a 'nouveau Christ sacrifié pour racheter les péchés de la Femme', ignoring the fact that there is no religious dimension in the film and that his passion is purely carnal and morbidly obsessive. As for showing Arabs massa-cring Jews, this is racism and a cynical ploy 'pour faire oublier les complicités françaises dans le génocide des juifs' (Burch and Sellier, 1996: 235–6).[18] This overlooks the historical reality of such attacks in post-war Palestine, as partition of the two communities and British departure approached, or the fact that French complicity in genocide seems rather remote from the story Clouzot has filmed.

One might indeed praise Clouzot for revealing some awareness of the suffering of the Jews and linking their epic attempts to found a new homeland with the tragic odyssey of his lovers, who escape one war only to perish in another. Few film-makers in the 1940s were able or ready to confront the monstrous immensity of genocide. Racially motivated deportation of French or foreign Jews was not immedi-ately distinguished from deportation of Resistance activists or of conscripted civilian workers and prisoners of war, partly because only

17 'In Clouzot's film there is a deliberate intention to show that in 1944 all French people without exception were spineless rogues. To draw the conclusion that those who are considered heroes nowadays achieved this merely by chance or by mistake takes only one more step.'

18 'A new Christ sacrificed to redeem the sins of Woman.' 'To make us forget French complicity in the genocide of the Jews.'

a few thousand of the 75,721 Jews deported to death camps survived to bear witness to their experiences, whereas 50 per cent of Resistance activists returned, as did most civilian conscripts and military prisoners. The return and reinsertion in French society of deportees and prisoners represented not only a psychological and social process of readjustment for the individuals concerned and their families, but also a significant political and logistical problem (demanding the creation of a ministry specifically dedicated to solving it), given the vast numbers involved. Apart from 700,000 conscripted civilians and 1.2 million soldiers returning from Germany and its satellite territories, several million people had been displaced within occupied France in the course of the war (see Rioux 1980: 26).

The film *Retour à la vie* (1949) represents a worthy and relatively uncommon attempt to deal with these issues in fictionalised form. Following a newsreel-style introduction reminding the audience of the basic historical facts, the film presents five separate short episodes. Clouzot's, *Le Retour de Jean*, is the third and runs for twenty-eight minutes. Unsurprisingly, given its brevity and budgetary constraints, this episode has none of the dramatic complexity of *Quai des Orfèvres* or the epic breadth of *Manon*. In fact, it is less about the problems of readjustment of French prisoners than German war crimes, and who has the authority to pass judgement on them. Jean Girard (Louis Jouvet) has spent five years as a prisoner of war, having been wounded in the leg, and on returning to France has taken refuge in a boarding house, without resuming his former occupation. In other words, he remains socially and psychologically displaced, lacking a job, family or other form of commitment; he neither escaped from imprisonment nor became a resister or collaborator (options which are not even mentioned), and is sunk in despondency. When a wounded German prisoner (Jo Dest) takes refuge in his room, Jean discovers (having first viewed him with sympathy as a fellow POW) that the man was a Gestapo killer and torturer. The core of this episode is thus a confrontation between the passive but humanitarian Frenchman and the mendacious Nazi, whose fate now depends on the erstwhile prisoner. Jean seeks to discover the man's motivation, but is told only that he had done his duty. After denouncing Nazi atrocities, Jean kills the prisoner with an overdose of morphine before turning his body over to the authorities, whose self-important representatives have been leading a bungled search in the vicinity. Does Jean act from vengeance or mercy? As with *Le Corbeau*, a disempowered individual is shown to act more decisively and ruthlessly than the representatives of the state, whose self-seeking incompetence has helped create the initial crisis. But the central confrontation is melodramatic and schematic, since the German proves to be an indefensible villain and Jean wearily virtuous (the man is likely to die from his wound anyway, without Jean's intervention). French individualism is more humane than German totalitarianism: the message seems banally consoling, is crudely emphasised via long-winded speeches, and once again elides French complicity in German war crimes (a taboo subject which is considerably more relevant in this instance).

While an austere normality is restored in *Quai des Orfèvres*, *Manon* and *Le Retour de Jean* show places and people ruined by the aftermath of war, and how little relevance conventionally good behaviour and morality have to those seeking to reconstruct their existence. In comparison to such sombre and stirring films, *Miquette et sa mère*, with its ponderous humour, overdone performances and happy ending where differences of class and gender are conveniently but implausibly resolved, is an extraordinarily frivolous work. Jean-Pierre Jeancolas (1992: 93) dismisses *Miquette* by saying that it is the only film of Clouzot's which could have been made by any director in the late 1940s, in other words that it lacks any interesting, distinctive features. *Miquette* (which was preceded by several other adaptations of the original play) belongs to a tradition of filmed theatre, mainly drawn from boulevard comedies. Colin Crisp observes that on average 15 per cent of films made between 1936 and 1954 derived from plays; while their undemanding comedy was popular with audiences, they are usually hated for their staginess by the 'cinematic fraternity'. In fact, *Miquette* was commercially unsuccessful. Crisp remarks that its only notable formal feature is direct address to camera by characters (whereas conventionally, the camera is treated as an invisible eye, usually matching the perspective of the audience or a character: Crisp 1997: 291, 399).

However, such addresses only mimic the asides to the audience which are a common feature in stage plays and indeed occur in the original text (for example the Marquis to camera: 'Je l'adore cette petite').[19] They show how Clouzot's adaptation deliberately exaggerates the play's theatricality and artifice, though he also added facetious

---

19 'I adore this dear little girl' (i.e. Miquette).

intertitles which recall silent film comedies. The theatre is shown to have the power to transform lives and remove social barriers. The point is made in the original play, when the stage-struck Miquette says of Monchablon's performance as Corneille's Rodrigue that theatre transforms 'un affreux petit ratatiné en un héros magnifique' (Flers and Caillavet 1907: 11),[20] but considerably extended in Clouzot's film. Significantly, he replaced the third act, set in Miquette's salon, with the performance onstage of a rumbustious romantic drama, and, not content with this play within a play, in a further *mise en abyme* introduced the authors of the play as characters who appear at the end to announce they will write a play about Miquette. One could also note self-reflexive elements in themes and devices reintroduced from earlier films, although here they are recycled as sentimental comedy. Thus Jenny's casting-couch flirtation with Brignon is reworked when the amorous Marquis establishes Miquette as an actress in Paris; Miquette and Urbain's silhouettes are projected on the canvas of a tent, just as Jenny and Maurice's were in *Quai des Orfèvres*. All this makes for harmless entertainment, an innocuous interlude in a career which spawned more controversial and powerful films, of which the most celebrated are *Le Salaire de la peur* and *Les Diaboliques*, to which we now turn.

Bibliography

L'Avant-Scène Cinéma (1963), 29, script and reviews of *Quai des Orfèvres* (reprinted in no. 487, 1999)

Beevor, Antony and Artemis Cooper (1995), *Paris after the Liberation: 1944–49*, London, Penguin

Burch, Noël and Geneviève Sellier (1996), *La Drôle de guerre des sexes du cinéma français 1930–1956*, Paris, Nathan

Clouzot, Claire (1965), 'Voix off: Henri-Georges Clouzot', *Cinéma 65*, 96, 58–64

Clouzot, Henri-Georges (1949), *Manon 49*, Paris, Bibliothèque France Soir

Clouzot, Henri-Georges (n.d.), *Manon*, script, BIFI archives

Crisp, Colin (1997), *The Classic French Cinema 1930–1960*, Bloomington, Indiana University Press/London, I.B. Tauris

Flers, Robert de and G.-A. de Caillavet (1907), *Miquette et sa mère*, Paris, Librairie théâtrale

Gauteur, Claude (1997), 'Variations critiques autour de Henri-Georges Clouzot', *L'Avant-Scène Cinéma*, 463, 1–13

---

20 'A hideous shrivelled midget into a magnificent hero.'

Gilbert, Martin (1998), *Israel: A History*, London, Doubleday

Godet, Danielle (1981), *Si tu n'es pas gentille, tu ne feras pas de cinéma*, Paris, Editions France-Empire

Jeancolas, Jean-Pierre (1992), 'Clouzot en 1991', *Positif*, 374, 92–5

Jouvet, Pierre (1978), 'Sur *Quai des Orfèvres*', *Cinématographe*, 37, 16–20

Lacassin, Francis and Raymond Bellour (1964), *Le Procès Clouzot*, Paris, Le Terrain Vague

Mayne, Judith (2004), 'Dora the Image-Maker, and Henri-Georges Clouzot's *Quai des Orfèvres*', *Studies in French Cinema*, 4, 1, 41–52

Oms, Marcel (1987), 'Manon 49, l'irrécusable témoin', *Les Cahiers de la Cinémathèque*, 46–7, 55–8

Prévost, Abbé (1963), *Histoire du Chevalier des Grieux et de Manon Lescaut*, ed. Clifford King, London, Harrap

Rioux, Jean-Pierre (1980), *La France de la Quatrième République*, vol. 1, Paris, Seuil

Sorlin, Pierre (1994), *European Cinemas, European Societies 1939–1990*, London, Routledge

Spaak, Charles, Henri-Georges Clouzot and Jean Ferry (1949), *Retour à la vie*, Paris, La Nouvelle Edition

Steeman, Stanislas-André (1985), *Quai des Orfèvres*, Paris, Librairie des Champs-Elysées (first published as *Légitime Défense*, 1942)

Vailland, Elisabeth and René Ballet (1973), *Roger Vailland*, Paris, Seghers

Virgili, Fabrice (2002), *Shorn Women: Gender and Punishment in Liberation France*, trans. John Flower, Oxford and New York, Berg

4

Beyond genre: *Le Salaire de la peur*

Following Rick Altman's argument (1999: 20) that genre is not merely 'a hollow commercial formula' but 'a culturally functional category', the main purpose of this discussion is to study Henri-Georges Clouzot's *Le Salaire de la peur* and 'the particular ratio it exhibits between convention and invention, between the requirements of genre and the ingenuity and world view of an auteur working with that genre' (Andrew 1984: 116). Although there may be some initial hesitation about what genre *Le Salaire* belongs to (for example, Hayward (1993: 170) calls it 'a newly styled buddy-and-road movie'), in practice the film shares many of the defining features of the action-adventure movie (a categorising term first used in 1927, even if we tend to associate it with Hollywood blockbusters of the last thirty years: Neale 2000: 55). At first sight, Clouzot seems to adopt many of the conventions of the expensive and expansive adventure film with considerable relish; my argument is essentially that he invests them with added value, formally, psychologically and morally.

Le Salaire de la peur was released in April 1953, to immediate critical acclaim and commercial success, winning prizes at the Cannes festival for best film and best actor (for Charles Vanel) and proving the second most popular film of the year in France, with some seven million spectators. Along with *Le Corbeau* and *Les Diaboliques*, it is Clouzot's most memorable and enduring film, thanks to the brilliant ensemble playing of actors who create roles that far exceed the stereo-typed figures found in most thrillers and adventure films, and to the masterly handling of narrative and *mise en scène* by Clouzot and his cinematographer Armand Thirard and art director René Renoux. While *Le Corbeau* and *Les Diaboliques* are confined to the claustrophobic and gloomy spaces of urban and suburban France, largely following the stylistic and psychological conventions of film noir, *Le Salaire de la peur* moves to a more exotic and less familiar locale. The film is set in an unnamed Central American country and describes the perilous odyssey undertaken by four unemployed and impoverished European truck drivers, who agree to drive two lorries containing nitro-glycerine across 500 kilometres of mountainous terrain for an American oil company, which needs the explosive to extinguish a conflagration raging in a remote oil-field. Only one of the four survives the outward journey to collect his large fee, but on the return trip to the township where his girlfriend and friends are celebrating his survival, he loses control of the lorry and plunges to his death in a ravine.

The resolution of an enigma and identification of a criminal which drive the plots of most thrillers, including Clouzot's, have little relevance to *Le Salaire de la peur*.[1] The film is essentially about the accomplishment of a mission and the obstacles which progressively eliminate the protagonists as they move towards their goal. These obstacles include human frailty and malice, but primarily they are elemental (gravity pulls the truck into the abyss, fire and explosives blow men into the air without trace, the mountain rains boulders on them, they nearly drown in a viscous flood of oil). In other words, the protagonists are threatened and destroyed by super-human forces, in their quest for lucre, a quest which represents for these individuals an attempt to buy their way back to civilisation (that is, the Europe from which they are exiled), and in a wider sense the greedy and destructive urge of Western capitalism to exploit the natural resources of under-developed countries, whatever the cost to the workers involved or the local economy and environment. One man fulfils the mission, but is cheated of his reward when his premature and reckless celebration of his success causes his death. Destiny grimly disposes of the last overweening survivor. Before returning to these broader philosophical and ideological aspects, we will examine the film's structure, characterisation and *mise en scène*; first of all, some contextual information about Clouzot's intentions, sources and production methods is needed.

The fact that *Le Salaire de la peur* shares certain generic charac-

1 It is therefore odd that Robin Buss (1994) includes *Le Salaire de la peur* in a filmography of 101 French films noirs, since this is neither formally nor thematically justified.

teristics of adventure stories and films is undoubtedly one of the main reasons for its lasting appeal. One important characteristic is that the ideological and mythic elements just outlined are skilfully contained within and expressed by plot, character and *mise en scène* (there is none of the portentous philosophising which mars *Les Espions*). Clouzot aimed to create 'essentiellement un film plastique', 'une épopée dont l'accent majeur porterait sur le courage. Et sur son antithèse, car le contraste est pour moi la base de ma conception cinématographique' (quoted in Bocquet and Godin 1993: 83–4).[2] The speechifying, or subordination of image and action to dialogue, used somewhat theatrically in order to delineate character and sustain confrontations, which drives many scenes in *Le Corbeau* and *Quai des Orfèvres*, is thus replaced by a visually dominant *mise en scène* which essentially shows men at odds with a hostile landscape, a landscape captured both in vast panoramas dwarfing the human scale and in the minute details which human resourcefulness can conquer. There is no extra-diegetic music to underscore lyrical or dramatic moments after the opening credits; some of the most dramatic scenes play almost entirely without dialogue. Fear and suspense are sustained by a silent struggle to overcome apparently insuperable hazards and by the expectation of catastrophe, teasingly deferred so that it strikes at times when characters seem nearer to safety. Thus when joyful music is heard within the action of the film, it dupes characters and spectators into a false sense of security, since it is frequently interrupted by violence and disaster (the discovery of Bernardo's body, the bar brawl, the destruction of both lorries). To appreciate and enjoy the film, the spectator needs to accept an emotional engagement with the characters' plight and situation, although this need not be uncritical; the two main characters are in some ways extremely unsympathetic.

Courage, fear, myth, ideological conflict, a laconic hero battling through threatening terrain in search of a goal that brings destruction

2 'Essentially a plastic [formally beautiful] film.' 'An epic whose main emphasis would be on courage; and on its antithesis, for contrast is the basis of my conception of cinema.' Clouzot's aspiration could be seen as generic as much as aesthetic, for as Yvonne Tasker argues (1993: 6): 'the cinema as sensuous experience is too often neglected. Features such as the breathtaking nature of visual spectacle, or the feelings of exhilaration at the expansive landscapes in which the hero operates, are fundamental to the action cinema. ... popular cinema is as much concerned with visual pleasure as it is with narrative development and in the action cinema visual display is elevated to a defining feature of the genre.'

when attained, with an audience vicariously participating in his deeds: such features are also much on display in well-known adventure films like the Indiana Jones series. It is worth recalling, for instance, that the plot of *Raiders of the Lost Ark* (Steven Spielberg, 1980) hangs on the struggle between Nazi and American archaeologists to discover the Ark of the Covenant; when the Nazis attempt to use the magical powers of the Ark for their impious ends, it annihilates them. What most obviously distinguishes *Le Salaire de la peur* from the Indiana Jones cycle and other Hollywood adventure films, however, is the virtual indestructibility of their heroes, in this case the character tirelessly replayed by Harrison Ford: however large or numerous his adversaries, whether human, natural or supernatural, he survives an interminable series of extremely violent escapades unscathed, packs up his adventurer's kit and returns to his more placid, civilised existence as a university professor until the next adventure. While the simple morality and commercial imperatives of such films demand that the hero (and heroine) are normally handsome, heterosexual, American and survivors, their adversaries are generally disposable and therefore marked out as losers (by being ugly or non-Americans: European, African or Asian). In any case, none of these characters seems to suffer physically or emotionally, or to exhibit convincingly human emotions.[3] A typical adventure film, in other words, is a formulaic, juvenile, chauvinistic fantasy, often made with lavish resources and immense technical skill, but aspiring only to offer the dubious thrills of wanton spectacles of destruction and showing little interest in representing the complexity of human behaviour and society plausibly. In Clouzot's film, on the other hand, although five central characters meet violent deaths, very little violent action is actually represented on screen (a kick, a punch, a few slaps, a leg crushed by a lorry wheel, the final crash); what interests him is not the glamorised, balletic scenes of combat, mayhem and pursuit which rhythmically punctuate most action films, but characters' reactions to extreme circumstances, their discomfort and suffering, shown in elaborate but low-key detail.

A better point of comparison with Clouzot's film is John Huston's

3 Yvonne Tasker (1993: 39) observes that the action hero's physical prowess tends 'to lead him into narrative situations in which he is subjected to torture and suffering'. But such ordeals are almost invariably temporary and rapidly surmounted (however implausibly); the James Bond novels and films repeatedly recycle such instances.

The Treasure of the Sierra Madre (produced by Warner Bros in 1948), which it resembles in plot, setting and tone. Three American adventurers, reduced to beggary in a Mexican town, are able to fulfil their dream of becoming prospectors when one wins the lottery. After an exhausting journey to remote mountains, they finally strike gold. But an intruder who joins the group is killed by bandits, while the leading character Dobbs, driven insane by greed and fear of the others, shoots one of his partners and steals the gold, before being killed and robbed by the surviving bandits. Ultimately the two survivors lose everything when the bandits let their sacks of gold dust blow away into the desert, not realising its value. Apart from their location shooting, memorable characterisation and compelling narration, both films can be interpreted as sardonic philosophical fables about human ingenuity and degradation, the fragility of civilised norms, and the lure and futility of desperate aspirations. While the strutting gangster Jo (Charles Vanel) in *Le Salaire de la peur* is reduced to abject terror when confronted with the perils of the road, Dobbs, the character played by Humphrey Bogart in Huston's film, is possessed by paranoid delusions when faced with losing his riches.

Although *The Treasure of the Sierra Madre* (with its unprepossessing heroes, lack of love interest, and cynical view of human nature) was considered daringly downbeat by the sentimental and escapist standards of 1940s Hollywood, Huston does however offer a more morally uplifting conclusion than Clouzot, by showing that the two survivors are those who retain their loyalty and decency. Howard (the old man inspiringly played by his father Walter Huston) abandons the quest for impossible gains in favour of a comfortable existence as a medicine man in a village, where he has resuscitated a drowned child, while Curtin (Tim Holt) recovers from his wounds and returns to the USA. Unsurprisingly, no doubt, the homoerotic and anti-capitalist elements easily discernible in *Le Salaire de la peur* have no equivalent in Huston's film, which is also structurally more conventional, with setpiece scenes and other characteristics recognisable in any western (for example, gunfights with bandits, a bar-room brawl where a villain is punished, the insistent use of extra-diegetic music to underscore the mood). Whereas Dobbs's descent into insane delusions is emphasised verbally (with Humphrey Bogart delivering ranting monologues more appropriate to the theatre than an action movie), Clouzot shows Jo's decline far more through his actions than his words. We will come back to Clouzot's use (or avoidance) of such generic conventions in discussing specific episodes from *Le Salaire de la peur*.

As we saw in the introductory chapter, Clouzot was forced to abandon his plans to make a documentary film during his extended visit to Brazil with his new wife Vera in 1950, publishing instead a quasi-ethnographic study, *Le Cheval des dieux* (1951), about the religious rites and animal sacrifices practised by fetishist sects, whose members enter trance-like states when they are apparently ridden by the gods (hence the book's title). One can note an obvious parallel with *Le Salaire de la peur*, in that the film is also a quasi-ethnographic study of a Central American country: in particular of the shanty town Las Piedras (presented in a prologue which lasts thirty-five minutes, nearly a quarter of the whole film) and its community of dispossessed natives, impoverished European exiles, and ruthless American oil-men. But the unnamed country is actually an imaginary place: despite the plethora of exotic social details, characters and landscapes, the film was shot entirely on location in the south of France. It was Clouzot's most ambitious project to date, proving extremely costly in time and money. The film was a French–Italian co-production (as were many larger-budget films in the 1950s); hence the presence of an Italian assistant director (Roberto Savarese) and an Italian actor (Falco Lulli) playing the sympathetic and industrious Luigi. We should recall too that Yves Montand, who plays the lead role as the Corsican Mario, was himself of Italian origin. Clouzot is also credited as an executive producer, having set up his own production company, Vera Films, to part-finance this and subsequent films. (The film offered Vera Clouzot her first part as the bar servant Linda, exploiting her fluent command of Spanish.)

Le Salaire de la peur was a best-selling novel published by Georges Arnaud in 1950. Clouzot and his brother Jean (credited as Jérôme Geronimi) spent ten months producing a screenplay, with a further three months devoted to creating a storyboard with the art director René Renoux. Clouzot was determined to shoot on location to create a sense of authentic, expansive landscapes, despite the cost and logistical problems (whereas the great majority of films at the time continued to be made almost entirely inside studios on stage sets). The town of Las Piedras and other exterior sets were therefore built from scratch in the Camargue in 1951, while the lorry scenes were shot near Anduze in the Cévennes. Needless to say, Clouzot insisted on using real oil in the burst pipeline sequences, with Charles Vanel, Yves Montand and the camera crew consequently spending days soaked in oil. Vanel also played the horseman briefly seen galloping across the flames roaring from the burning well, ostensibly because no extra was willing to go near enough to the flames to provide the director with this effect of perspective. Shooting began in August 1951, but was delayed by unseasonable, torrential rain and cost overruns. After refinancing, filming recommenced in June 1952 and lasted till November.

Georges Arnaud and his novel merit further attention, not merely as the source of the film, but because both author and book were unusually colourful. In 1941, at the age of twenty-four, Arnaud, whose real name was Henri Girard, was accused of murdering his father, aunt and a female servant in the family's chateau in the Dordogne. After spending nineteenth months on remand, he was tried and acquitted. In 1945, this former student at Sciences Po moved to Venezuela, where he became a gold prospector, smuggler and truck driver; his novel thus derives in part from testing personal experience. As with his other adaptations, Clouzot retained the skeletal structure of the novel, while redefining the central characters and their relationships, eliminating some episodes and adding others. It has to be said that the book (which is dedicated to Arnaud's deceased father) is far more brutal and cynical than Clouzot's film; this probably reflects the considerably greater freedom of expression enjoyed by literary authors compared with the censorship imposed on film-makers until the 1970s, as well as Arnaud's own adventurous existence.

Arnaud devotes the first 17 pages of his novel to describing the gas explosion and the oil company men whom it affects, before spending 50 pages on Las Piedras and the European 'tramps' who are stranded there; his final 107 pages describe the mission and its aftermath. Clouzot and Geronimi largely dispense with the preamble, saving their scenes showing the conflagration until the film's conclusion, apart from a few rapid intercalations when news of the disaster reaches Las Piedras. Unlike the film, Arnaud locates his story in Guatemala and offers a great deal of technical information about oil-drilling and its dangers. American oil-men are generally shown as contemptuous of the safety and welfare of their native employees; most of the casualties in the well explosion are Indians. Most of (if not all) the principal characters are extraordinarily callous and unpleasant; the production of oil, it seems, involves the sacrifice both of human lives and of moral scruples. (We are remote from the clean-cut heroics of a contemporary British novel like Hammond Innes's *Campbell's Kingdom* (published in 1952, filmed in 1957), whose virtuous protagonist finds love and salvation prospecting for oil in the Canadian Rockies.)

The town of Las Piedras is described as shrouded in fog from the surrounding coastal swamps (Clouzot and his team preferred to shoot the daylight scenes in harsh sunlight, suggesting unbearable tropical heat, although the puddles which fill the innumerable potholes in the streets suggest frequent downpours). The town is economically moribund, because the oil revenue is paid directly to the central government and brings nothing to the local community. The central meeting place is the Corsario Negro, a café-cum-brothel, owned by a European, Hernandez; one of its inmates, Linda, is a mixed-race prostitute and notionally belongs to the Parisian Gérard Sturmer, a former smuggler who arrived from Honduras a year before (getting Hernandez to pay for his taxi, like Jo in the film). Although Linda appears to have a sexual relationship with both Hernandez and Mario in the film, the brothel has disappeared and Linda has been ethnically cleansed (Mario's rejection of her would in fact make more sense if she had remained a fallen native woman, rather than become a stunning beauty like Vera Clouzot). We also learn that Linda has been paid by Gérard to have sex with the desperate young Italian Bernardo, whose suicide precedes the deaths of the drivers (Bernardo is the only character transferred unchanged to the film, apart from this venal sexual episode, which is omitted).

Apart from Gérard, the three other men selected by O'Brien to drive the trucks are the Romanian Johnny Mihalescu (a murderer on the run), the Italian Luigi Stornatori (about whom little is said), and the Spaniard Juan Bimba, a Republican exile in Mexico after the civil war who has fallen out with his Stalinist compatriots. The reserve driver, Hans Smerloff, takes his revenge for not being picked by sabotaging one truck's shock absorbers (in the film, Jo eliminates Smerloff in order to take his place as the fourth driver). During the journey, despite his violent past, Johnny is overcome by fear and proves incapable of assisting Gérard in passing the obstacles which block their progress, although despite his agonising leg injury, he does suggest how to set up the haulage mechanism which allows them to cross the oil flooding the road. In other words, Clouzot retained major incidents in the novel, some of the characters' names and characteristics, and some of the dynamics of the group. Jo and Mario, however, as their different names indicate, are really new creations, while Bimba changes his nationality and biography to match the acting persona of the German Peter Van Eyck. It is worth noting too that nearly all the journey in the novel takes place at night, whereas the most dramatic events in the film occur in daylight (they would otherwise be inconceivable, either in terms of plausibility or the practicalities of filming in darkness).

The omission of a major episode from the novel is also significant, since it reveals how Clouzot shied away from Arnaud's virulent anti-clericalism, anti-Americanism, and lurid cult of violent retribution. When the trucks reach the village of Los Totumos, they encounter the local mayor and priest. While the mayor launches into an anti-gringo tirade (claiming that Americans drain the blood of local inhabitants when they go to their hospitals), the priest asks them to take a 'safe' detour to reduce the risk to the village from their explosive cargo. In fact, they discover that the detour is highly dangerous and that the priest's main concern is for his own house and church. While the pious Luigi accedes to the priest's request (and receives a blessing), the priest-hating Bimba gives the duplicitous cleric a severe beating and desecrates the sacred objects in the church. Their lorry is destroyed shortly afterwards. Clouzot probably omitted this incident for political, personal and plot reasons, knowing that neither censors nor distributors would find it tolerable. He was a man of religious interests, if not convictions (as his book on Brazil and exploration of Christian mysticism in later life show). His widow remarked to me that a sense of sin hangs heavily over his films and he avoids blasphemy (thus in *Le Corbeau* the Church is spared the satirical jibes directed at most other civic institutions). While the destruction of Luigi and Bimba in the novel suggests a vengeful providence at work (the blasphemer is chastised, alongside his pious companion), Clouzot avoids such a crude underscoring of some invisible power directing events. The encounter in the village also disrupts the coherence of the narrative, by pitting the drivers against outsiders, the local representatives of society and civilisation; in Clouzot's film, their journey takes them beyond civilisation and their contest is against nature and the flaws of human nature, observed by natives who are silent witnesses to the folly of Westerners.

The film, then, streamlines the plot of Arnaud's novel, in order to make Mario the constant centre of interest. Unlike Gérard Sturmer, he is not a professional criminal; this perhaps explains why Mario is fascinated by the gangsterish Jo and prefers the company of this ageing hard man to the ravishing Linda (Linda, Jo and Luigi all compete for Mario's attention and friendship in the expository scenes set in Las Piedras). Like Johnny, Jo is ostensibly a man of violence (we assume he is responsible for Smerloff's disappearance)[4] who nonetheless proves unequal to the nerve-wracking challenges of the journey. Unlike their counterparts in the novel, Luigi and Bimba are neither gullible nor sadistic, but form an admirably loyal and efficient team. Consequently, their truck rapidly overtakes the faltering Jo and Mario and leads the way through the first three major obstacles, although their role as secondary characters in the narrative economy effectively guarantees their demise before the final destination. While Mario is in a sense corrupted and duped by Jo in Las Piedras (gratuitously humiliating Linda and Luigi in order to please him), Jo's subsequent failings turn Mario into a harder and more ruthless character, as the *rapport de force* between them is reversed and he has to do the work of two men. Eventually, Mario drives the truck over Jo's leg when he fails to get out of the way, thereby causing his death. No doubt this incident could be read as a symbolic castration and punishment for Jo's posturing and betrayal; we will return to the film's (homo)sexual politics later on.

Clouzot dispenses with Arnaud's prologue at the oil well, since the sequences set in Las Piedras serve this introductory purpose better, both spatially and temporally. Their relative lengthiness (about two-fifths of the film) reflects their threefold function: to establish the setting in considerable ethnographic detail; to present the main characters and their evolving relationships (the four drivers, Linda, Hernandez and the oil company manager O'Brien); to establish a highly dynamic *mise en scène*, where everything we see is skilfully motivated, often visually arresting, sometimes unpleasant or shocking. The film has run for thirty-five minutes before the fire is reported; the

4 The spectator probably assumes that Jo has shot Smerloff in the back (as Mario implies he has done). In fact, a careful viewing of the closing sequence in the bar reveals that Smerloff is still with the rest of the 'tramps' awaiting Mario's return and joins in the celebratory dance. How Jo took his place as the fourth driver is left unexplained.

selection of the drivers and other preparations take another twenty-three minutes. The journey itself thus commences an hour into the story and occupies nearly all the rest of the film (in other words about eighty minutes; the epilogue showing Mario's return trip and death lasts about three minutes).[5]

The voyage breaks down into four episodes, of roughly equal duration, each consisting of a hazard barring the route which the drivers have to circumvent. These obstacles become progressively more arduous: while the first two test the drivers' skills in manoeuvring the lorries, the last two also require considerable mechanical ingenuity in overcoming physical barriers obstructing the road. The first involves negotiating a lengthy stretch of bumpy road, where, in order to avoid jolts that would detonate the volatile nitro-glycerine, the drivers have the choice of driving either extremely fast (to skate over the bumps) or extremely slowly. Mario boldly takes the more dangerous first option and therefore nearly collides with the preceding lorry, forced to go slowly after a breakdown. The second obstacle involves a hairpin bend which can only be rounded by reversing the lorries on to an overhanging wooden pontoon, which is both rotten and slippery with mud. The third is a massive boulder blocking the road, which they finally succeed in blowing up with some of the nitro-glycerine. (The sequences showing the second and third obstacles are not in the novel; they were invented by Clouzot and Geronimi, and last thirty-five minutes, about a quarter of the film.) Both lorries survive all these tests, although Jo is incapacitated by fear. Then Bimba and Luigi's lorry explodes inexplicably ahead of Mario and Jo, causing oil from a ruptured pipeline to flood the road. The crossing of this final obstacle leads to Jo's death.

The shooting style of *Le Salaire de la peur* matches Clouzot's expressed desire for images built on striking contrasts and showing dynamic plasticity. Although considerable use is made of close-ups and medium shots (typically in order to show key intricate details as

5 Most filmographies give the running time of *Le Salaire de la peur* as 156 minutes, whereas the DVD released by René Chateau and used for this analysis actually runs for 142 minutes. There is no obvious explanation for this discrepancy, since the DVD version matches the screenplay published in *L'Avant-Scène Cinéma* (no 17, July 1962), apart from some minor variations most probably due to transcription errors. It is possible that distributors cut fourteen minutes from the original version of the film.

well as dialogue and confrontations between people), the camera is also extremely mobile, with considerable use of elaborate long shots and tracking shots that reveal the expansive landscapes surrounding characters and, in the initial sequences, the three-dimensional and exotically filled community of Las Piedras. In one sense, this makes us aware that we are seeing a big-budget adventure film, whose production values allow elaborate camera set-ups and extensive and authentic décor filled with large numbers of extras. But while the prologue of a more conventional adventure film typically starts in an exotic locale with an elaborately choreographed piece of derring-do (for example, Indiana Jones in pursuit of lost treasure being thrillingly albeit absurdly pursued by a gigantic boulder), *Le Salaire de la peur* seems at first to be about inaction, torpor and frustration, as well as local colour presented for its own sake, in a fashion more appropriate to an ethnographic documentary.

Thus the first image we see on screen is a close-up of insects apparently caught on sticky string being idly poked with a stick; their tormentor is revealed to be a small black boy, clad only in a ragged vest and straw hat, his buttocks and penis unashamedly displayed to the camera. The image, with its gratuitous cruelty and nudity, is both unsettling and informative: on a symbolic level, we can no doubt relate the struggling insects to the truckers tormented by a malevolent fate; more literally, we are being shown a primitive, impoverished society, where oppressive tropical heat and meagre resources lower inhibitions and encourage cruder pleasures than those enjoyed by most spectators of the film.[6] Other establishing shots of Las Piedras show women washing clothes in a mucky pool, while they exchange ribald insults in Spanish, a beggar and a man riding a donkey. *Le Salaire de la peur* is indeed a multi-lingual film, with much of the dialogue being spoken in Spanish, English, Italian and German, as well as French. These opening exchanges are not sub-titled, no doubt because their meaning is readily guessed, but also to emphasise the foreignness of this setting, where Westerners are displaced persons and intruders. While these samples of native behaviour suggest a timeless, under-developed culture, the American oil company motor bike and jeep which busily roar through the street crowded with people and animals

6 Sam Peckinpah's western *The Wild Bunch* (1969) opens with a similar scene of children tormenting a scorpion, before proceeding to eliminate most of its grown-up protagonists in a series of famously violent episodes.

show the aggressive purposefulness of Western, capitalist technology, which brings no apparent benefits to the local community.

The camera finally brings us to the principal building on the main street, the Corsario bar, where the group of unemployed European exiles idle away their time (the only reason the Americans hire four of them to drive their trucks is because they are non-unionised and expendable). One throws a stone at a dog tied to an ice-cream cart, uttering the first words in French: 'J'aime pas les clebs' (although this is the German Smerloff, played by Jo Dest). To which Mario replies: 'On te demande pas l'histoire de ta vie.'[7] As this sample suggests, the dialogue is laconic, colourful and conforms to the stylised norms of the tough-guy genre, whereby characters who would probably be inarticulate in real life display a gift for quick-fire slangy repartee even in languages of which they are not native speakers. Smerloff's unmotivated dislike of dogs and the fact we never do learn his life story mark him out as an unsympathetic secondary character. Mario, on the other hand, is quickly established as the central figure by his frequent presence on screen, his youthful good looks, and the emotional and physical attraction he exerts on others. At the same time, his indifference to Smerloff typifies a more general indifference to others, whose affection he exploits quite cynically. Linda first appears on all fours, washing the floor, her breasts well in evidence beneath a low-cut blouse, caressing Mario's hand like an affectionate dog. Neither Linda nor Mario seems unduly perturbed when the bar-owner Hernandez interrupts their canoodling to assert his sexual rights over her; when she re-appears from Hernandez's upstairs room, we first see her legs and then her hands rebuttoning her blouse. Since Linda carries the (heterosexual) love interest of the film, some twenty-first-century viewers may find her submissive posture unappealing. One needs to remember, however, that all the central characters are required to give highly physical performances, involving feats of endurance that test them to the limits in sometimes humiliating situations. Vera Clouzot's winsome displays of her alluring body are surely far less degrading (either for the actor or the character) than the ageing Charles Vanel's displays of cowardice. While Linda is obviously restricted by her supporting role, her character actually ranges beyond meek compliance to express seductive joie de vivre, piety and terror in her various scenes.

7 'I don't like dogs.' 'We don't need your life story.'

The aeroplane overflying the village marks the first major event of the film, since its passengers, as well as a man with a goat, include the second major character Jo. His confident pose, pristine white suit and fly-whisk mark him out as an apparently more dominant figure than the denizens of Las Piedras, although his lack of luggage and need to bribe the immigration official also suggest this is a mere façade. His first encounter with Mario clearly has sexual undertones; his appraisal is so insistent that Mario asks menacingly (in Spanish) 'Tu veux ma photo?'. Their moment of recognition is however musical and cultural, when Jo picks up Mario's whistling of 'Valentine' (a mildly bawdy song about male sexual conquests made famous by Maurice Chevalier in the 1920s) and they realise they are compatriots. Whereas the hard-nosed oil-company manager O'Brien has known Jo for twenty years and refuses to do him any favours (he ignores his threats and entreaties, failing to select him as one of the drivers), Mario is seduced by Jo's posturing and betrays both Linda's and Luigi's friendship in order to curry favour with him. An oddly jerky zoom on to Mario and Jo sitting at a bar table is, we realise, a subjective shot from Linda's point of view, as she suddenly spots this unexpected rival. Jo tells Mario that 'Les gars comme nous, on n'est pas fait pour les filles' ('Guys like us aren't made for girls'), deliberately disrupting his planned outing with Linda. Mario brutally rejects her possessive displays of affection with a slap, and later by throwing her off the lorry door.

A skilful montage of brief scenes linked by dissolves shows Mario explaining to Jo how escape from Las Piedras is virtually impossible; while the dialogue is continuous across the scenes, they are spatially and temporally discontinuous, compressing a guided tour probably lasting several days into a minute or so of filmic time. Thus a shot of an unfinished building (abandoned with the economic downturn) is followed by a funeral procession, since death from disease or starvation is the only obvious way out. The Americans have their own cemetery and live in an enclosed camp, excluding everyone else. Jo's immaculate white suit is besmirched by mud splashed by an oil-company jeep, symbolically anticipating his subsequent ordeal and degradation, which culminates with him mutilated and nearly drowning in the oil pool, covered in a shining black suit of oil from head to toe. More immediately, this incident triggers Mario's break with Luigi, since he casually lends Jo Luigi's trousers, answering Luigi's protests with the retort 'On n'est pas mariés!' In fact, the unemployed Mario does appear to live off the more industrious and prudent Luigi; we see Jo and Mario strolling along arm in arm while Luigi works as a bricklayer (although the cement dust is seriously damaging his lungs). A striking scene shows Jo reclining on a lounger while Mario sits attentively on the ground at his feet.[8] Neither pays any attention to the nude young black woman who is shown from the rear taking a shower in the background behind them, until her screams alert Mario to the fact that a large spider is sitting on her towel; he leaps up and promptly crushes it. The scene is evidently meant to reveal both Mario's decisive agility in a minor crisis and his sexual indifference to a nubile native woman, who falls below his erotic aspirations and outside his patriotic nostalgia (he keeps a used metro ticket as a fetish to retain his link to Paris and France). We have already seen that he has a 'museum' of photographs of nude models from Pigalle above his bed, 'Pour penser à autre chose quand tu pelotes une négresse'.[9] Shifts in taboos over the last fifty years are likely to make us see this scene as revealing a certain implausibility, as well as unconscious racism and sexism on the film-maker's part; while a 'primitive' native woman is so uninhibited she can be shown nude virtually in view of the street, she is still too fearful to fend off a spider.

The prologue in Las Piedras concludes with the first major setpiece action scene: the bar-room confrontation between Luigi and Jo. This is introduced by an elaborate, lengthy tracking shot, taking full advantage of the three-dimensional set to reveal both the community and the central characters in depth. We start with the crowded night-time street at the front of the bar; the camera then withdraws down the side of the building, showing Smerloff and Bimba watching Luigi's arrival, before turning the corner and entering the inside of the bar from the rear. While Jo and Mario sit apart at a separate table, Luigi invites Linda to dance and buys champagne for the others. Their noisy celebrations are interrupted when Jo cuts off the music by ripping out the radio lead and then seizes the champagne bottle and sprays its contents over Luigi and his friends. Luigi advances on Jo brandishing

8 This shot therefore illustrates rather effectively Yvonne Tasker's observation (1993: 154) that 'homoeroticism is central to the male action movie, and while gay desire may be unspoken within dialogue, it is very much present within the frame.'

9 'So you can think of something else when you're groping a negress.'

the champagne bottle, but is deterred by Jo's revolver; when Jo contemptuously hands him the revolver, inviting him to shoot and slapping his face, Luigi is unable to pull the trigger, and backs down, finally retreating in humiliation.

Bar brawls are entirely conventional occurrences in action films, demonstrating the toughness of the characters in a lawless environment, displaying their directors' skill in staging fight scenes, and gratifying spectators' delight in vicariously experiencing violent confrontation. In *The Treasure of the Sierra Madre*, Dobbs and Curtin take on an employer who has cheated them of their wages (and who with further duplicity starts the unprovoked fight by smashing Curtin over the head with a bottle). After a protracted and vicious exchange of kicks and blows (mostly shot using stuntmen to protect Huston's stars from injury, though the editing skilfully conceals this), they extract their money from the battered employer's wallet. The next scene shows them barely damaged by this encounter. The heroes reveal their courage, assert their rights, and re-affirm their camaraderie, in other words, and a rogue is punished. What is most striking about the comparable scene in *Le Salaire de la peur* is how far Clouzot deviates from these conventions and the moral code which underlies them. While close-ups in Huston's film are mainly used to create the illusion his stars are participating in a fight whose rapid choreography was actually too dangerous for them to attempt, close-ups in Clouzot's scene are mainly reaction shots of characters observing the stand-off. In fact we have not brutal action so much as hesitant inaction. The most dramatic close-up is of Luigi's finger on the revolver trigger, but he refuses to fire (just as Jo refuses to engage in fisticuffs). Tension and expectation thus replace violence, for there is no fight, merely the threat of violence (which is deferred), and certainly no simple moral justification behind either the confrontation or its outcome. A gangsterish bully humiliates a decent worker, as both vie for the attention of another man. Hence John Weightman's observation (1974: 18), that this is 'a subtly sadistic scene, in which goodness and generosity are made to appear almost as effeminate attributes'.

Luigi's attempt to win back Mario fails, although retrospectively at least we can see that Jo's victory is largely due to bluff. The voyage exposes Jo's real cowardice and re-establishes Luigi's courage and good sense. In other words, Mario has chosen the wrong partner. Weightman (1974: 18) has also noted that Jo and Mario's relationship has at least three configurations: as master and disciple, father and son, male and semi-female. To experience, age and sex we should add the ties of shared nationality. Jo reassures Mario as they start with the words 'T'en fais pas, ma gosse!' ('Don't you worry, girlie!'), thereby patronisingly asserting his supposedly greater wisdom and masculinity. Soon, however, Mario emerges as the dominant partner, as Jo's pretences are stripped away. His lack of nerve and malaise are at first disguised as prudence or even the effects of malaria. In fact he is sick with fear (which drives him first to vomit literally, then to flee in panic from the lorry on two occasions, as he proves incapable of controlling his emotions). Although Mario is enraged by his betrayal and contemptuously dismisses him as a 'gonzesse' and a 'lavette' (in other words, an effeminate, cowardly weakling), Jo's collapse actually makes him a more sympathetic character. As Jo himself says, with a certain wit, his weakness is due to his greater imagination and cautiousness, as opposed to Mario's reckless bravado: 'C'est ça la division du travail: toi, tu conduis et moi je crève de peur! Crois-moi, t'as la meilleure place!'[10]

Charles Vanel embodies Jo's transition from swaggering, white-suited adventurer to cringing and finally crippled old man with engaging gusto and pathos. The part had originally been offered to Jean Gabin, who declined this 'rôle de lavette' (Bocquet and Godin, 1993: 79), since the part of a homosexual poltroon hardly conformed to the mythic star persona which all his films had to perpetuate.[11] It is hard to conceive of Gabin either being capable of acting a part which demanded such sensually realised abjection or being willing to play second fiddle to Yves Montand's Mario, let alone to Clouzot's uncompromising vision. That Vanel and Montand fit their parts so well is a consequence not merely of their acting skill, but also of a certain correspondence between their careers and their characters in the film. Like Jo, Vanel had known better days, having appeared in starring roles in many films since 1912; by his late fifties, however, he had been reduced to taking parts in mediocre post-synchronised

10 'That's the division of work: you drive while I die of fear! Believe me, you've got the better job!'
11 Ginette Vincendeau (2000: 76) points out that Gabin did in fact play the part of a lorry driver and accept a role with 'clear homoerotic components' in *Gas-Oil* and *L'Air de Paris* in the early 1950s. His screen persona however is nearly always heroic, dominant and basically virtuous (some might say monolithic and predictable).

Italian co-productions. Montand's cinema career had also failed to take off; after a series of unsuccessful films in the late 1940s, he was still far better known as a cabaret singer and reluctant at first to risk taking on an unfamiliar and demanding part. Some contemporary critics of *Le Salaire de la peur* referred mockingly to the contradiction, despite Clouzot's coaching, between Montand the seductive crooner and the hard man Mario (forgetting that before he broke into show business, Montand had actually been a manual worker, including a spell as a docker). In any case, Mario's position as a neophyte and his initial hesitancy are skilfully motivated within the film; during the voyage, he has to acquire the ruthless efficiency which Jo only pretends to master. Stripped down to a tight singlet which becomes progressively filthier with each obstacle (thirty-five years before Bruce Willis relaunched the fashion for action heroes in dirty vests in the *Die Hard* films), Montand converts himself into a lean and muscular man of action.

A second fight scene shows Mario dropping the constraints of civilised conduct, unlike Luigi's earlier confrontation with Jo. A brief stand-off between Mario and Jo, caused by Jo's flight on hearing the other lorry explode, is rapidly concluded by Mario lobbing a rock at Jo before kicking and punching him (we see the rock hit Jo's head in close-up, and Mario delivering the blows in medium shot towards the camera, with Jo's body concealing their impact). As Mario drily observes, the ritualised conventions of combat are no longer relevant: 'C'est peut-être pas régulier, mais de toutes façons, j'étais le plus fort. Alors, ça gagne du temps.'[12] When Mario subsequently drives the lorry wheel over Jo's leg, we have clearly gone even farther beyond the usual bounds of the rivalry between partners which is a conventional feature of adventure films. Whereas Dobbs's gunning down of the loyal Curtin in *The Treasure of the Sierra Madre* demonstrates that Bogart's character has become a psychotic maniac, Mario acts only through deliberate albeit desperate expediency. In their final scenes together, Mario displays an almost maternal tenderness towards the dying Jo, cradling him on his shoulder and reminiscing about home. In an ironic epilogue, after Jo's death, Mario reasserts their patriotic camaraderie and intimacy by praising Jo's supposed toughness to the waiting Americans; the myth of friendship is restored, if not the reality.

12 'Maybe it's not on the level, but anyway I was stronger. So it saves time.'

The summary treatment of this second fight contrasts with the meticulous detail used to film the obstacles that impede the journey: overcoming objects and the forces of nature has become the real source of drama. The first are, typically, represented by rapid close-ups (for example, the lorry wheel spinning on muddy planks), the second shown in their insuperable vastness by extreme long shots (for example, the lorry approaching the hairpin bend, a tiny shape in the landscape). The sequence on the bend lasts fourteen minutes; in fact it is protracted sufficiently long so as to take place almost in real time. This particular sequence employs a wide variety of camera positions in order to reveal the hostile terrain, the difficulties of the manoeuvre, and the characters' varying behaviour. Thus the lorry is shot from both right and left, while low-angle shots show the lorry's inner front wheel teetering over the abyss on the crumbling pontoon bridge and Bimba and Luigi looking down as the second truck approaches, along a road marked with memorial crosses and a skull and crossbones. The rotten planking gives way under the rear wheel as Bimba reverses, but Luigi levers the wheel out and uses a loose plank to provide traction. When Mario's heavier truck attempts the same manoeuvre, Jo is nearly crushed between the lorry and a trolley which plummets over the edge. Mario leaps dramatically from the cab down on to the hillside to look for Jo, in an elegant low-angle shot, which cuts in mid-leap from a long shot showing his take-off to a close-up of his feet landing right by the camera. Then Jo is discovered climbing up the hill in panic; a high-angle shot shows Jo's perspective on the lorry; while Jo cowers behind a wall, we cut back to the lorry's wheels spinning on the muddy planks and Mario wedging them with branches. Finally, after clearing the bend, Mario forces Jo to run after the lorry, laconically lighting a cigarette while he catches up, the gesture contemptuously encapsulating the contrast between Mario's efficient calmness and Jo's lack of self-control.

There is the same meticulous, protracted attention to detail in the sequence where Bimba siphons off a flask of nitro-glycerine to blow up a huge boulder blocking the road. The drama and suspense are in the preparation of the task, rather than the final explosion. The others wait as Bimba pours the explosive into a hole drilled in the rock and ingeniously improvises a detonator and fuse. Extreme close-ups of their hands and Luigi's mouth and moustache moving anxiously are intercut with Bimba's intricate preparations, the only sound being his breathing, their tapping and noisy crickets chirruping (although these are more appropriate to the South of France than Central America). Bimba's patient work is successful: the road is cleared, the debris blasted out by the explosion misses the lorries, and Luigi, though flattened by the blast, escapes uninjured. Luigi and Mario embrace and congratulate Bimba, all three jokingly celebrating their triumph by urinating together (off screen). Jo, who has contributed nothing to their endeavours, is pointedly excluded from this act of homoerotic bonding. This may seem ironic since he is the only one of the four who is (unavowedly) homosexual. The exclusion (and subsequent mutilation and death) of Jo, one might argue, restores the norm of heterosexual camaraderie and sexuality (Mario is reconciled with Luigi and drives back to Linda); indeed, by revealing himself to be an obnoxious bully and a coward, Jo also illustrates the stereotyped dictum that a sexual deviant is not a true man ('a pansy has no iron in his bones', as Philip Marlowe puts it in *The Big Sleep*: Chandler 1948: 99).

This interpretation, whereby homoeroticism effectively excludes homosexuality, certainly matches Yvonne Tasker's observation about more recent American action films, in which 'homoeroticism is a constant presence, acknowledged and played with by films which ... simultaneously deploy an anxious disavowal of gay desire' (Tasker 1993: 29).[13] On the other hand, Clouzot's film avoids both the knowing self-consciousness of post-permissive cinema and the pitfall of homophobic caricature. The character Bimba is a good example of Clouzot's discretion in this respect. While possibly sharing Jo's sexual orientation, unlike Jo he emerges as a physically heroic and resourceful figure, effectively leading the team for most of the journey; he is also the most impressive physical specimen of the quartet, the only one to display his lithe torso stripped to the waist. Bimba's cigarette-holder

13 The earliest example which she cites of an American film which includes 'the covert exploration of the homoerotic possibilities of male bonding' (Tasker 1993: 45) is *Butch Cassidy and the Sundance Kid* (1969) (a film whose triangular configuration of desire incidentally includes a playful homage to Truffaut's *Jules et Jim*). *Le Salaire de la peur* is unusual for a film of the early 1950s in emphasising homoeroticism (a feature which, as we saw in the introductory chapter, Truffaut in his guise as acerbic critic found offensive). Sexuality, whether overt or sublimated, is virtually eliminated from the central action in *The Treasure of the Sierra Madre*; the quest for gold demands single-minded chastity and the characters find heterosexual release either before or after undertaking their search for mineral riches.

(all that remains of him when his truck finally explodes) and concern about his appearance (he shaves in the cab) could be seen as rather equivocal characteristics, as is his refusal to discuss his background with Luigi. He reveals only that he dislikes women and that he is a hundred years old. The spectator is likely to assume at first from these enigmatic hints that Bimba is a misogynous Nazi on the run (the sort of character which Peter Van Eyck was typecast to play in several of his films). Only shortly before their death does Bimba admit to Luigi that his father was hanged and that he has survived three years as a slave labourer in a Nazi salt mine; his stoical refusal of emotional display and affective ties is the result not of past crimes but of past suffering for unexplained acts of resistance.

Reviewing *Le Salaire de la peur* in the communist newspaper *Les Lettres françaises*, Georges Sadoul (cited by Gauteur 1997) found Luigi to be the most sympathetic central character, no doubt because he conforms most obviously to the stereotype of the cheerful, heroic worker whose labour is exploited by the evil oil company. Luigi's ambition is to use his earnings to return to Italy and found a family. Yet he and Mario initially form an odd couple, in which Luigi mixes convention-ally male and female characteristics (for example supporting Mario by working, but also undertaking household duties like cooking). Clouzot, in other words, avoids simplistically categorising either Bimba or Luigi, showing toughness and sensitivity as qualities that are unexpectedly compatible. Although both men emerge as more loyal and self-sacrificing than the pusillanimous Jo and the ruthless Mario, in practice such positive features help seal their fate. In a more conventional adventure film, the sacrifice of secondary characters usually at least guarantees the survival of the principal hero, who is evidently the main focus of spectators' interest (not to mention that of producers and distributors intent on making profits from sequels and merchandising). While Huston reverses customary expectations in *The Treasure of the Sierra Madre* by disposing of his leading player, Humphrey Bogart, this does allow for a morally uplifting conclusion, since the character Dobbs seems irredeemably wicked and his more virtuous comrades survive. Once again, Clouzot goes much further by killing Mario in the final sequence of *Le Salaire de la peur*, thereby cancelling out the success of his mission, the loss of his three comrades, and the possibility of reintegration for the character (through return to Paris or reconciliation with Linda). The only winner is the brutally exploitative oil company, which will be able to resume production.

Yet this mercilessly bleak conclusion plays a key part in the film's impact, aesthetically, psychologically and morally. In other words, it allows Clouzot to escape the comforting commonplaces of the adventure genre and to drive home the full implications of his character's behaviour and the world he inhabits. To the very end, the audience is left anxious and uncertain about Mario's survival. Collecting a cheque for $4,000 (which includes Jo's fee), Mario refuses to be driven back to Las Piedras. He heads back alone in the surviving truck, ploughing through the oil pool where Jo's leg was crushed (peasants are glimpsed collecting the oil). His survival and impending return are announced at the Casario, where a celebration begins. The final sequence cross-cuts between Linda, Doc, Hernandez and the others waltzing in the bar to the 'Blue Danube' and Mario rhythmically spinning the steering wheel of the truck as he listens to the same tune on the cab radio (on which his good luck metro ticket is stuck). At first the increasing tempo of cross-cutting between spinning dancers and lorry suggests exhilaration and euphoria; but as the truck reaches the dangerous bends winding down the cliffs, the camera angles become increasingly distorted. Unusually low and high angle shots show the dancers whirling dizzyingly, while tilted shots of the truck from outside and the landscape from Mario's point of view are followed by Linda's collapse (which we take as a premonition of disaster) and Mario's loss of control of the lorry. An extreme long shot of the lorry going off the road is followed by a medium shot of Mario trapped in the cab; after the truck plummets down the ravine, we are shown a close-up of Mario's wounded head and the metro ticket clutched in his left hand (no longer a passport to a new life). The sound of the klaxon wailing fades down and the film ends.

This conclusion is formally satisfying partly because of the intricate montage used to stage the crash (the temporal overlapping with the dancers giving it an added emotional and spatial resonance), and partly because Clouzot has saved the most violently detailed incident for this final crescendo (thereby completing the series of disasters and respecting Arnaud's novel); what may seem unexpected in terms of a conventionally happy ending in fact entirely matches the economy of his narrative. While Mario's comrades are killed by despair (Bernardo), weakness and incompetence (Jo), or bad luck (Bimba and Luigi), Mario is the agent of his own destruction, killed by reckless driving and tempting fate (the very qualities which have allowed him to complete the mission successfully). As John Weightman remarks, 'He commits suicide, we might say, through high spirits, a form of *hybris* no less dangerous in the godless, than in the god-ridden, world'. Yet this final surge of excitement is likely to leave the spectator with a 'sense of elation, because of the intelligence and vitality with which [such sequences] are conducted' (1974: 18–19).

It is no doubt more tempting to read an ideological (rather than metaphysical) message into *Le Salaire de la peur*, as a denunciation of American capitalism as much as an absurd, malevolent universe. A review published in *Time* in 1955 objected to the film's alleged anti-Americanism, while more recently in 1991 a critique in *Village Voice* condemned it as 'aggressively racist' (cited by Buss 1994: 20). Both charges are somewhat overstated, disingenuously confusing Clouzot's brutal presentation of corporate ruthlessness or cultural difference with xenophobic prejudice. A few scenes certainly show that the American oilmen place expediency and efficiency ahead of humanitarian concerns, although their main representative O'Brien makes no attempt to deceive the European drivers about the dangers they face, and ensures they get a fair deal financially. Thus, following the report of the explosion at the oil rig, we are shown trucks arriving at Las Piedras with the casualties; while this provokes rather half-hearted protests from the locals, O'Brien tries to cover up the disaster. A very brief scene shows three near-naked Indians (one man and a male and female couple) silently watching the blazing inferno, as a fire fighter tries to usher them away. The contrast between primitive culture and technological civilisation is strikingly captured; but far from appearing in a demeaning light, the Indians are placed there as impassive witnesses to the destructive folly and greed of Westerners. Despite their impoverishment, the Indians express 'attitudes of wise resignation', as Buss observes (1994: 110), unlike the desperate and ultimately futile striving of the equally marginalised heroes. Apart from their documentary interest, in drawing attention to ethnographic and social differences between conflicting groups, such sequences are incidental to the main action and do not really preach any political message or imply a hierarchy of cultural and ethnic superiority.

Clouzot's great achievement in *Le Salaire de la peur* is to revitalise the adventure film, so that it no longer seems a juvenile and formu-laic genre whose main purpose is to offer the spectator the vicarious pleasure of ritualised violent confrontation in a fantasised universe. Reviewing the film in 1953, André Bazin praised its 'synthèse originale et positive du neo-réalisme italien et des conventions de la *mise en scène* américaine' (quoted by Gauteur 1997: 7), thereby drawing attention to its combination of pseudo-documentary realism and the dynamic shooting style of American action movies. What distinguishes Clouzot is the seriousness with which he takes his characters and the suffering they endure; as a consequence, violence ceases to be the recurrent and predictably stylised phenomenon which it is in most action films. Clouzot holds the viewer's attention less through the impact of violence (devastating though it is) than through its expectation and the postponement of catastrophe. It is thus no surprise that his next major film was a brilliant variation in suspense: *Les Diaboliques*.

Bibliography

Altman, Rick (1999), Film/Genre, London, BFI Publishing

Andrew, Dudley (1984), *Concepts in Film Theory*, New York, Oxford University Press

Arnaud, Georges (1955), *Le Salaire de la peur*, Paris, Le Livre de poche

L'Avant-Scène Cinéma (1962), 17, July, script and reviews of *Le Salaire de la peur*

Bocquet, José Louis and Marc Godin (1993), *Henri-Georges Clouzot cinéaste*, Paris, La Sirène

Buss, Robin (1994), *French Film Noir*, London/New York, Marion Boyars

Cartier, Jacqueline (1989), *Monsieur Vanel*, Paris, Robert Laffont

Chandler, Raymond (1948), *The Big Sleep*, Harmondsworth, Penguin

Clouzot, Henri-Georges (1951), *Le Cheval des dieux*, Paris, Julliard

Crisp, Colin (1997), *The Classic French Cinema 1930–1960*, Bloomington, Indiana University Press/London, I.B. Tauris

Ford, Charles (1986), *Charles Vanel, un comédien exemplaire*, Paris, Editions France-Empire

Gauteur, Claude (1997), 'Variation critiques autour de Henri-Georges Clouzot', *L'Avant-Scène Cinéma*, 463, June, 1–13

Hayward, Susan (1993), *French National Cinema*, London, Routledge

Neale, Steve (2000), *Genre and Hollywood*, London, Routledge

Tasker, Yvonne (1993), *Spectacular Bodies: Gender, Genre and the Action Cinema*, London, Routledge

Vincendeau, Ginette (2000), *Stars and Stardom in French Cinema*, London/New York, Continuum

Weightman, John (1974), Introduction to *Masterworks of the French Cinema*, London, Lorrimer Publishing

5

Suspence and surveillance:
Les Diaboliques and *Les Espions*

Les Diaboliques was released in January 1955 and proved to be Clouzot's most commercially successful film. Although it was awarded the prestigious Prix Delluc and the New York critics' prize, the film's critical reception was mixed. While its combination of ingenious plot twists, moments of horror and black humour captivated cinema audiences, for many reviewers such features were taken as evidence that Clouzot's aspirations were cynically limited to meretricious manipulation of spectators' emotions in the cause of low-brow entertainment, as were his requests that latecomers be barred from entering the cinema and that viewers did not betray the conclusion to friends who had yet to see the film. Such hostile responses were encapsulated by J.-L. Tallenay's grudging judgement in *Cahiers du cinéma* that 'Il est dommage de dépenser tant de talent pour une devinette' (quoted by Lacourbe 1977: 106).[1] British reviewers struck an overtly moralising tone, complaining about the film's 'queasy moments' and 'relentless sordidness' (Moskowitz 1955: 172). As Robin Buss suggests (1994: 23), by exhibiting evil for pleasure, the film was deemed to have offended public morality and ignored social responsibility.

Changes in critical and aesthetic conventions over the last fifty years may make such complaints now seem either quaint or mealy-mouthed. There is some irony in the fact that the journal *Sight and Sound*, having damned *Les Diaboliques* with faint praise on its initial release, in 1996 treated Clouzot's film as a sacred classic which Jeremiah Chechik's American remake *Diabolique* had wantonly defiled (Newman 1996). It is true that, in comparison with Chechik's coarsely

---

1 'It's a pity to waste so much talent on a riddle.'

violent adaptation and the visceral excesses of contemporary horror films, Clouzot's film now seems a model of decorous restraint and subtle understatement; the existence of this and at least three other forgotten remakes (one French, two American) of *Les Diaboliques* is a perverse tribute to his inimitable mastery of the suspense thriller, which inevitably invites comparison with Hitchcock. Yet Clouzot himself was inclined later in his career to dismiss *Les Diaboliques* as a shallow and trivial exercise in manipulating the formulaic conventions of a genre unworthy of a serious film-maker.

Such reservations may explain why *Les Espions*, released in October 1957, makes far less effort to engage or beguile the spectator. Although this film, like *Les Diaboliques*, is set in a run-down institution on the outskirts of Paris, and peopled by enigmatic and duplicitous characters who plot each other's downfall, its narrative and characterisation are deliberately disrupted and elliptical. Clouzot's intention was not to construct another pleasing puzzle but to convey an atmosphere of alienation and absurdist uncertainty. The film's theme, he claimed, was metaphysical: 'L'angoisse, l'inquiétude, l'homme et ses fantômes dans le monde actuel, c'est ça le sens du film' (quoted by Bocquet and Godin 1993: 113).[2] In fact this description applies rather better to *Les Diaboliques*, which evokes a mood of haunting anxiety with none of the ponderousness of *Les Espions*. Audiences and critics were deterred by the apparent incoherence of *Les Espions* and it was a commercial failure, despite its cast of international stars. Perhaps recalling the director's abortive attempt to adapt *The Trial* and eventual recourse to the less well-known Czech novelist Egon Hostovsky for his source text, the critic Henri Jeanson remarked with acerbic wit that 'Clouzot a fait Kafka dans sa culotte' (quoted by Bocquet and Godin 1993: 113).[3]

A critical rehabilitation of *Les Diaboliques* needs to revisit some of these reservations, summed up by one reviewer's caustic judgement that Clouzot was 'un fumiste abusant scandaleusement de ses dons',[4] but also to encompass the film's wider generic resonances (most notably the mastery of suspense and the creation of the fantastic).

2 'Anguish, anxiety, man and his ghosts in the modern world, that's what the film is about.'

3 'Clouzot has Kakfaed/crapped his pants.' In other words, he had made a noxious mess of his metaphysical fable.

4 'A charlatan scandalously abusing his talents.' François Vinneuil (i.e. Lucien Rebatet), in *Dimanche-Matin*, quoted by Gauteur 1997: 3.

Comparison with Clouzot's source text and imitators offers another way of understanding the particular secrets of his success; in the case of *Les Espions*, his generally acknowledged failure to repeat this success suggests that Clouzot himself underestimated or misunderstood what he had achieved with *Les Diaboliques*. Jean-Pierre Bertin-Maghit (1996: 278) notes that critics have seen terror as the key emotion aroused by *Les Diaboliques*, terror triggered by 'l'intrusion de l'irrationnel dans le monde de l'autoritarisme – le danger est inconnu et tout devient possible'.[5] For spectators who identify with the situation of the victim Christina (rather than her character), such strong emotions have a cathartic power. While it is true that the film contains one or two highly memorable, horrific scenes (notably, the drowning of Christina's drugged husband in a bathtub, and his subsequent emergence from another bath like a vengeful vampire), to my mind a much clearer distinction needs to be made between the reactions of audiences watching the film and characters within the film. Christina (apparently) expires of fright when her drowned husband returns from the dead; spectators, on the other hand, may be variously shocked, amused or disgusted, but are fully aware their reaction is primarily aesthetic (in other words, their response to violent or supernatural events in a filmed narrative is patently quite different to what it would be if such events occurred in real life).

It thus seems highly unlikely that anyone watching *Les Diaboliques* is terrified by the experience, since watching a film, vicariously enjoying a mediated representation, is hardly a life-threatening activity; if one is engaged by the film's narration and characters' plight, one more probably feels a pleasurable sense of curiosity, anxiety and surprise about the outcome of events. Creating the conditions which sustain such emotions, more specifically maintaining narrative tension and suspense, even after repeated viewings, requires a skill and ingenuity that demand detailed attention (rather than summary dismissal). For that matter, the implicit assumption that entertainment is incompatible with more serious aspirations also needs challenging. Like all Clouzot's films, *Les Diaboliques* offers a sharply observed satirical portrait of a social world captured in considerable detail; what distinguishes this film is not simply its intricate manipulations of plot and characters' relationships, but also its evocation of the irrational and

5 'The intrusion of the irrational into the world of authoritarianism. The danger is unknown and everything becomes possible.'

supernatural. The spectral presences of murder victims returning to haunt their tormentors form the central enigma, which is never entirely resolved; we are thus remote from the violent but basically rational world of detective thrillers, and much closer to the fantastic, whose defining features include the uncanny, the return of the repressed, ontological uncertainty and 'different regimes of verisimilitude' (Neale 2000: 35; cf. Freud 1990 and Todorov 1976).

This is no doubt why Charles Derry excludes *Les Diaboliques* from his taxonomic study of *The Suspense Thriller* (1988), classing it as a horror film, although horror and suspense tend to go together. As Steve Neale (2000: 2) observes, 'most films are multiply generic'. Moreover, Clouzot's film patently belongs in the first category of the six which Derry elaborates in his typology, that is the thriller of murderous passions, typically involving the triangle of husband, wife and lover. In *Les Diaboliques*, the wife and mistress of an abusive man plot and carry out his murder, only to find he has apparently come back to haunt them. While the detective figure represents order and rationality, he may fail to understand an enigma that defies resolution. The retired policeman arrests the real plotters in *Les Diaboliques*, but apparently at the cost of allowing their plan to kill the wife to succeed (or does she too return from the dead?). Nor is Clouzot alone in subverting rationality: in Hitchcock's *Psycho* (1960), the interfering detective is himself killed by a mysterious figure who appears to have returned from the dead; the glib explanation offered by a psychiatrist when the killer is finally captured again fails to address the possibility that he is genuinely possessed by the malevolent spirit of his dead mother.

These reservations aside, Derry skilfully delineates some important generic aspects of suspense thrillers, thereby providing a useful guide for contextualising and understanding *Les Diaboliques*. These include manipulating the expectations of the spectator regarding the fate of a character; suspense clearly involves the anticipation and relief of anxiety and our emotional response may well reflect unconscious desires and fears which the vicarious experience provided by a film helps resolve. In terms of *mise en scène*, he observes that objects frequently have a dual nature, implying something else beyond themselves and acting as 'visual correlatives' or metonyms. Thus the dead man's clothes which mysteriously re-appear in Clouzot's film act as a baleful reminder of their owner and his inexplicable disappearance. More generally, 'Physical environments seem constantly to either threaten the protagonist or comment obliquely on the action in which he or she is involved'. Above all, he argues, what is primarily suspended in narrative terms is time (Derry 1988: 36, 50, 21, 32). Truffaut (2000: 120) makes a similar point in discussing Hitchcock, arguing that suspense involves not violent subject matter, but 'la dilatation de la durée, l'amplification d'une attente'.[6] We might add that suspense can also be spatial as well as temporal: witness the innumerable films like *Vertigo* or *Cliffhanger* where characters are protractedly suspended over a void, literally enacting the nightmare of falling endured by most spectators. And shifting viewpoints, restricting and expanding the field of vision, are further ways of revealing or concealing information and thereby controlling the spectator's response, as Gordon Gow observes (1968: 14).

The deadly passions fictionalised in *Les Diaboliques* were replicated to a lesser degree by the tensions provoked during the film's production, with Clouzot deliberately seeking to boost the intensity of his actors' performances by maintaining a confrontational and hostile mood on set. Although his wife Vera had no professional acting experience beyond her minor role in *Le Salaire de la peur*, Clouzot was determined to give her the leading part as the persecuted wife Christina (radically altering Boileau-Narcejac's original novel *Celle qui n'était plus* in the process). Christina's death from heart failure at the sight of her drowned husband climbing out of the bath grimly anticipated Vera's premature demise from chronic cardiac disease a few years later (although there is no evidence that Clouzot precipitated her decline, as malicious biographers sometimes allege).[7] Shooting began at the Saint-Maurice studios in August 1954 and lasted four months, although Paul Meurisse's scenes took only two weeks to film, and Simone Signoret (1978) complained she was only paid for two months' work. The cast of schoolboys included Jean-Philippe Smet

6 'The dilation of duration, the amplification of expectation.' Hitchcock himself remarked in his discussions with Truffaut: 'The ability to shorten or lengthen time ia a primary requirement in film-making. As you know, there's no relation whatever between real time and filmic time.' Thus 'a fast action has to be geared down and stretched out; otherwise, it is almost imperceptible to the viewer' (Truffaut 1985: 72).

7 The legend of Clouzot as a merciless tyrant is perpetuated in Eddy Vicken's recent documentary film, *Henri-Georges Clouzot le diabolique?* (2004). See Wiel (2005) for a brief review.

(better known as Johnny Hallyday), Patrick Dewaere, and his brother Yves-Marie Maurin (playing the important part of Moinet).

Paul Meurisse recounts his confrontations with Clouzot with a certain relish. Filming the bath scenes took two days, but contrary to legend the water in the bath was tepid. Having failed to roll back his eyeballs sufficiently to convince Clouzot that he resembled a drowned man, Meurisse had recourse to white contact lenses. (In fact, this bit of trickery intensifies the scene when he removes them, since it marks the shift from supernatural horror to a potentially rational elucidation.) Meurisse's main complaint was that he and Signoret were obliged to subordinate themselves to the amateurish Vera:

> Que d'éclairages savants, élaborés pendant des heures, pour donner à ce visage un soupçon d'expression! Que de grincements de dents et de révoltes rentrées de la part de Simone Signoret, qui voyait son talent servir de support au vide absolu de sa partenaire. Supreme astuce, on «tramait» la lumière pour que sa beauté ne vienne écraser l'insignifiance du visage de Vera. (Meurisse 1979: 239)[8]

What probably annoyed Meurisse most was that such devices were entirely successful: Vera's passivity and helplessness are adroitly embodied in her character and cleverly complement her more domineering partner Nicole.[9]

The thriller writers Pierre Boileau and Thomas Narcejac shared Meurisse's ambivalent attitude towards Clouzot, admiring his creative talent while resenting his shameless appropriation of their own work. Both had been moderately successful novelists and essayists before they joined forces to produce the first of innumerable collaborative works, *Celle qui n'était plus*. Despite their subsequent notoriety and prolific output, they had difficulty publishing their initial joint efforts. When *Celle qui n'était plus* was finally accepted by Denoël in 1952,

8 'How skilfully the lighting had to be set up, taking hours, in order to put a glimmer of expression on her face! How often Simone Signoret had to grind her teeth and restrain herself from protesting when she saw her own talent being used to support her partner's absolute emptiness. The worst trick was when they diffused the light to stop her beauty completely overwhelming the insignificance of Vera's face.'
9 Susan Hayward (2005: 71) observes, however, that Vera Clouzot was unable 'to make her face provide a nuanced performance', in contrast to Signoret's subtle versatility. Nonetheless, Signoret's subordination is shown by the fact that she appears in barely half as many solo shots as Vera, while Vera appears three times more often in close-up or medium close-up.

however, both Hitchcock and Clouzot expressed interest in acquiring the film rights. The writers' contract with Clouzot left them 'séduits et vaguement floués', for they were given no role in the adaptation:

> Disons-le tout net: il a conçu, écrit et réalisé une histoire qui n'a plus qu'un air de parenté avec la nôtre. ... Bref, il régnait et nous étions bien chétifs près de lui. ... Ce roman, il s'en voulait presque de ne pas l'avoir conçu le premier. ... Au fond, son film est le récit d'une longue crise cardiaque. ... C'était peut-être génial, mais la subtile mécanique du roman était remplacée par un nouveau mouvement d'horlogerie. [...] si l'on va au fond des choses, le contenu psychologique du film est plutôt banal. (Boileau-Narcejac 1986: 77–91)[10]

Although their encounter with Clouzot launched them into minor celebrity, it also reduced their role as writers to that of industrial producers of storylines and scripts.

The plots of Boileau-Narcejac novels typically depend on characters making and breaking oppositional and collaborative configurations. The central figure is not the detective of the classic crime novel intervening to resolve a mystery, but rather the victim of events that seemingly defy rational explanation (a victim who may erroneously think he or she is controlling events). The reader is gripped more by the situation and the curiosity which it provokes than by any real engagement with the characters, probably because their motivation (and therefore their plausibility or interest as literary creations) has to remain opaque in order to prolong the mystery until the catastrophic dénouement. In *Celle qui n'était plus*, a travelling salesman called Fernand Ravinel lures his wife Mireille to Nantes, where he and his mistress Dr Lucienne Mogard drug her and drown her in a bath, before smuggling the body back to the Ravinels' house in the Paris suburbs. Their plan is to make Mireille's death look like an accident, to give themselves an alibi, and to claim on Mireille's life-insurance policy. The fact that an autopsy would probably destroy this alibi, or that a healthy young woman is highly unlikely to drown accidentally in

10 'Beguiled but somehow cheated.' 'Let's be frank: he conceived, wrote and directed a story that only vaguely resembles ours. ... In short, he was the boss and next to him we cut a fairly sorry figure. ... He almost resented not having been the first to conceive our novel. ... Basically, the film is about a protracted heart attack. ... It was no doubt ingenious, but the subtle mechanism of the novel was replaced by a new sort of clockwork. [...] when all's said and done, the psychological content of the film is pretty banal.'

the wash-house is barely considered. In any event, Ravinel is bemused to discover that Mireille's body has vanished on his return home. The rest of the novel recounts her apparent spectral resuscitation. In the penultimate chapter, the despairing Ravinel hears the footsteps of what he supposes to be the vengeful ghost of Mireille outside his door and shoots himself rather than confront her. An epilogue then reveals that Lucienne and Mireille had faked the murder plot in order to terrorise Fernand; however, the final page implies that Lucienne is likely to turn her homicidal impulses back on to Mireille, whose health has been ruined by their conspiracy.

In *Celle qui n'était plus*, the perpetrator, investigator and ultimate victim of a crime are thus intriguingly revealed to be the same person, as Ravinel's quest draws him towards self-destruction. Although Boileau-Narcejac objected to the supposed 'banality' of the characters' psychology in Clouzot's film, a more obvious objection to both novel and film is that their behaviour is both extraordinary and implausible. For instance, what could possibly attract Dr Lucienne to the down-at-heel Ravinels (a question posed by Ravinel himself)? Why should Mireille risk drowning, or at least pneumonia, for no very tangible reward (she has not claimed on the life-insurance policy)? How could the conspirators be sure that Ravinel would obligingly commit suicide? *Les Diaboliques* retains the central features of the faked murder plot and dual conspiracy, while changing the characters' social positions and temperaments, and most of the background and setting. Now the wife and husband (Christina and Michel Delassalle) own a run-down boarding school, while the mistress (Nicole Horner) is one of the teachers. But why should Christina murder Michel, when divorce on the grounds of adultery and abuse seems a less dangerous solution? Why should she trust Nicole, whom she has suspected of wanting to kill her? Both questions are raised within the film, though never answered convincingly. And what has Nicole to gain from her association with Michel's plot to terrorise Christina, except a lengthy prison sentence? If the retired policeman played by Charles Vanel has seen through the plot, why does he not intervene and save Christina's life? Is the schoolboy Moinet lying when he claims to have seen Christina alive at the end of the film?

Another obvious point to make here is that we do not necessarily expect plausible behaviour or logical motivation from characters in thrillers. That such questions remain largely unanswered may only demonstrate their irrelevance to the real objectives of either novel or film, which are to engage and bemuse us with a universe whose stylised, fantastical mystery evidently deviates from mundane reality. Truffaut observes that Hitchcock's films tend to dispense with the utilitarian, retaining only dramatic scenes, and that their screenplays rarely bear logical analysis. Thus the lack of plausibility of the celebrated plane-in-the-cornfield sequence in *North by Northwest* is deliberate, part of a 'fantasy of the absurd'. Hence Hitchcock's assertion that 'Our primary function is to create an emotion and our second job is to sustain that emotion' (Truffaut 1985: 99, 256, 111). What Clouzot achieved in *Les Diaboliques* was a memorable 'perfidie de l'image', as Boileau-Narcejac grudgingly acknowledged (1988: 1219); the film's psychology is more a matter of visual enticement and duplicity than of profound character studies. The problem with *Celle qui n'était plus*, on the other hand, is that the novel does aspire towards a much fuller and more conventional analysis of character (mainly taking the form of Ravinel's interior monologue, through which most of the action is narrated), even though this rather contradicts the constant evocation of the intangible nature of the self and others, of 'un monde où les lois de l'existence commune ne s'appliquent plus de la même façon' (Boileau-Narcejac 1988: 203).[11]

While the characters in *Celle qui n'était plus* are shadowy figures, who literally dissolve in the fog which surrounds them, Clouzot's film has a violent immediacy and intensity in its protracted suspense and scenes of horror which have no equivalent in the novel; his characters are also far more sharply delineated and more effectively integrated into the enclosed community of the boarding school. Before studying the film's structure and *mise en scène* in more detail, it is worth noting one or two possible losses in the adaptation. Boileau-Narcejac (1986: 92) remarked that 'si les convenances obligeaient Clouzot à terminer son film par l'arrestation des coupables, en revanche nous étions libres d'assurer l'impunité à nos deux complices'.[12] The social morality of the 1950s allowed novelists considerably more freedom than film-

11 'A world in which the laws of everyday existence no longer apply in the same way.' For a fuller discussion of Boileau-Narcejac's literary aspirations, see Lloyd (2000) and Young (2000).
12 'If convention obliged Clouzot to end his film with the arrest of the guilty couple, on the other hand we were free to let our two accomplices remain unpunished.'

makers to deviate from norms of acceptable behaviour, whether in dealing with politics, crime or sexual behaviour. While Clouzot delivers Nicole and Michel over to justice, the novelists leave us to infer that their plotters will bring destruction on themselves. In this respect, the American remake of *Les Diaboliques*, directed by Jeremiah Chechik and produced by Morgan Creek in 1996, is closer to the novel than Clouzot's film: after the plot to terrify the wife to death fails, the two women join sides to kill the brutish husband, this time abetted by the female detective. Justice is thereby redefined in a supposedly more radical way: law-breakers are no longer mechanically punished, but justified on the grounds of a dubious feminist morality which allows the elimination of an odious male. Boileau-Narcejac (1986: 88) also note the summary nature of Clouzot's conclusion, arguing that 'il ne supportait pas l'appendice des explications. Si mystère il y avait, la solution devait survenir d'un bloc, dans une image-choc'.[13] A succession of startling images successively reveal that Michel is alive, that Christina is overwhelmed by his re-appearance, that Michel and Nicole are accomplices, that Fichet is waiting in the shadows to arrest them. What the novelists overlook, however, is that whereas they restore a sort of rationality in their epilogue, the film does not resolve the mystery of Christina's possible return from the dead, irising out on the pupil Moinet's insistence that he has indeed seen her alive. Clouzot's conclusion thus becomes considerably less conventional, at least in Boileau-Narcejac's sense of restoring bourgeois order and asserting legality (although generically speaking, refusing to resolve a supernatural enigma is a common narrative convention in the fantastic).

Sexuality is another area where one can argue more convincingly that the film loses some of the novel's transgressive force. Boileau-Narcejac observed that '*Les Diaboliques*, en filigrane, c'est un problème d'homosexualité' (1986: 170).[14] They were presumably implying that there is an understated sexual attraction between the two women. The problem, at least for some critics, is that Clouzot largely keeps sex off screen. Hence Susan Hayward's bold assertion that 'the queerness seeps out despite a heterosexualizing of the original lesbian text', in for example the complicity between Nicole and Christina that makes

13 'He couldn't bear adding protracted explanations. If there was a mystery, the explanation had to come in one go, in a shock image.'
14 'Reading between the lines, *Les Diaboliques* is about homosexuality.'

them 'a simulacrum of the heterosexual couple' (2003: 5, 12). Judith Mayne finds the ultimate 'revelation of Nicole's heterosexuality', her transformation into 'a simpering, fussing woman in love' (with Michel) as shocking as Michel's resuscitation (2000: 56). The twist in the plot certainly produces a strange shift in Nicole's behaviour, from active partner with Christina to subservient accomplice of Michel. Whereas Clouzot respects conventional (hetero)sexual morality (if adultery, violence and betrayal can be deemed either conventional or moral), 'The secret of the novel is lesbianism' (Mayne, 2000: 43). Despite Boileau-Narcejac's reticence, a careful reading of *Celle qui n'était plus* supports this interpretation, which indeed makes the conspiracy between the women considerably more plausible. For example, apart from Lucienne's mannish physique and behaviour, complementing Mireille's delicate femininity, Ravinel's sexual relationship with both mistress and wife is forced and passionless (Boileau-Narcejac 1988: 141, 143, 144).

It is far harder to find convincing evidence of lesbianism in *Les Diaboliques*. Heterosexual relations may well be shown to involve violence and exploitation (at the beginning of the film, we learn Michel has given Nicole a black eye during a quarrel, while he subsequently appears to rape Nicole off screen), but while Michel's odious brutality explains the women's plan to dispose of him (and gains them the audience's sympathy), an overtly sexual relationship between Christina and Nicole would surely make Nicole's final betrayal even more implausible than it already is. In the fairly prudish climate of 1950s France, neither Simone Signoret's nor Vera Clouzot's image would have benefited from any hint of lesbianism (whereas in 1990s America, Sharon Stone extended her audience appeal by playing bisexual characters in films like Paul Verhoeven's *Basic Instinct* (1991) and Chechik's *Diabolique*). Christina's religious piety and fragile health also limit her to the role of a passive, albeit alluring victim, who behaves like a distressed child rather than a mature or sexually autonomous adult.

Apart from the reconfiguration of the central trio's relationship and social background, Clouzot also significantly altered the structure of the original novel. In *Celle qui n'était plus*, the opening chapter immediately reveals the plot between Ravinel and Lucienne. The drowning of Mireille is carried out in the second chapter, while chapters two and three describe the transportation of her body from

Nantes to Enghien. The remaining two-thirds of the novel describe Ravinel's tormented quest to track down the missing body. By significantly delaying the revelation of the plot and accomplishment of the murder to the middle of the film, Clouzot and his fellow scriptwriters (Jérôme Geronimi, René Masson and Frédéric Grendel) allowed themselves more time to establish the setting and the characters' relations in considerably greater detail, and to arouse the audience's curiosity about the outcome of the conspiracy. Having provisionally entitled their adaptation *Les Veuves*, they ultimately opted for the more ambiguous *Les Diaboliques*, borrowing the title of a collection of stories published in 1874 by the Catholic novelist Jules Barbey d'Aurevilly. This literary reference (which otherwise would probably remain obscure to most spectators) is affirmed by the epigraph from Barbey's preface (1967: 41) which concludes the credit sequence: 'Une peinture est toujours assez morale quand elle est tragique et qu'elle donne l'horreur des choses qu'elle retrace'.[15] It is tempting to dismiss this quotation as a spurious attempt to claim some cultural capital for the film by referencing a literary classic (despite, or rather because of, the equivocal mixture of sexual depravity and decadent Catholicism in his book, Barbey claimed he was a Christian moralist in order to forestall a threatened prosecution for obscenity). The intertitle which concludes the film suggests a less lofty or more commercially orientated ambition: after the word 'fin', we read the following injunction: 'Ne soyez pas diaboliques! Ne détruisez pas l'intérêt que pourraient prendre vos amis à ce film. Ne leur racontez pas ce que vous avez vu'.[16] Arousing tragic pity and moral revulsion do not really seem compatible with inviting audiences to conceal from others what they have seen in the film, or with the underlying urge to preserve the key elements of surprise and suspense from somehow being contaminated by discussion outside the movie theatre.

I have of course disobeyed Clouzot's instruction in the course of this discussion, on the assumption that most people reading it will be already familiar with the film. In any case, knowing the outcome or unexpected plot twists does not automatically destroy one's interest; such is the skill with which the film is constructed and with which

15 'A painting is always sufficiently moral when it is tragic and arouses horror at the things which it portrays.'

16 'Don't be diabolical! Don't destroy the interest your friends might have in this film. Don't tell them what you've seen.'

it engages us that second or repeated viewings acquire an added, analytical dimension, as we look for the hidden traces (many of them essentially cinematographic) of the dual conspiracy, clues which remain invisible to the uninitiated spectator. A striking example is the opening shot of a pool of stagnant, filthy water, on to which the credits are superimposed, to the sound of Georges Van Parys's strident music (an orchestra accompanying a boys' choir). Only retrospectively do we realise that this is the swimming pool from which Michel's drowned corpse mysteriously vanishes. The image is a powerful metonymy, representing not only the literal scene of crime, but the central enigma of the film; the polluted water also evokes the sordid world of the malfunctioning boarding school and its duplicitous denizens. Whereas Boileau-Narcejac's prose is often verbose and opaque, attenuating the violence of their story and turning their characters into shadowy phantoms, Clouzot's images and *mise en scène* have a far greater dynamic impact, while retaining less readily apparent meanings or symbolic possibilities.

Paul Guth remarked in *Le Figaro littéraire* that 'Les deux principaux personnages des *Diaboliques* sont une piscine et une baignoire' and that 'l'eau y est l'élément du drame' (quoted in Boileau-Narcejac 1988: 1222).[17] Objects and spaces are as important as characters, since they cease to be neutral appurtenances filling the décor but become functional presences; characters are defined less by any sense of psychological interiority than by gesture, appearance and positioning. The school and swimming pool apparently took Clouzot and his collaborators a long time to invent. The Institution Delassalle derives from childhood memories and provides much of the incidental social humour of the film (largely absent in Boileau-Narcejac). Thus Pierre Larquey as the bibulous, downtrodden teacher M. Drain adds a further comic, liquid element. As in *Le Corbeau* and *Les Espions*, the opening sequence of the film takes us through the gates which enclose a small community whose customs and rites are both recognisable and murderously deviant. On its way up the drive, the small Citroen van driven by Michel splashes through a muddy puddle, crushing a paper boat under its wheels; this image suggests both the gratuitous destruction and material austerity that will characterise the film.

Although the school belongs to Christina Delassalle, a wealthy

17 'The two main characters in *Les Diaboliques* are a swimming pool and a bath. Water is the key element in the plot.'

Venezuelan who bought it in the mistaken belief it was a viable business, the institution is ruled tyrannically by her husband Michel. He dominates the schoolboys (who seem to number only a few dozen), the male teachers Drain and Raymond, and his wife and mistress Nicole Horner. Apart from his abuse of power and the anxious watchfulness it arouses in others, the introductory scenes also establish the conspiracy mounted against Michel; the surprising but overt complicity between Christina and Nicole is contrasted with more covert signs of the underlying plot against her. Thus Drain is amazed by the intimacy between the meek Christina and the bossy Nicole (sarcastically noting the latter's black eye and recalling her dismissal from a post in a reputable state school). Retrospectively, we can of course interpret his suspicions as a warning that the women's friendship is not genuine. While Michel imposes himself through physical violence on the women, he treats Drain and Raymond like flunkeys. In a grimly comic scene set in the school refectory, he forces Christina to eat a meal of rotten fish, while the subservient Raymond (played by a youthful Michel Serrault) assures him it is 'extrêmement nutritif' (despite visibly finding it nauseating) and Drain humbly asks for a glass of wine. The boys are so disgusted by the food that they stage a mini-riot, demanding their money back, until Michel orders Drain and Raymond to evict them from the room.

Moinet (the only pupil who acquires an identifiable name and personality) is shown spying through the glass door of a classroom as Christina and Nicole study a little bottle. While he reports to his schoolmates that they are secret drinkers (a more innocent interpretation of their plan to spike Michel's whisky with the contents of the bottle), we may again think it strange that Michel makes no effort to discover what they are plotting when he too interrupts their discussion. If his lack of inquisitiveness implies prior knowledge of the women's secret, the domineering attitude of Nicole and Michel tacitly suggests theirs is the real partnership, as do their body language and positioning in certain scenes. Just as Michel's dandyish confidence, his stylish Prince of Wales suit and cigarette-holder contrast with Drain's cringing resentfulness and old-fashioned wing collar, so too Nicole physically and emotionally dominates the diminutive Christina, whose schoolgirlish plaits, frailty and desperate piety all convey pathetic vulnerability. The spatial relationship between the trio in some shots discreetly betrays their real *rapport de force*: Christina is shown with her back to the camera while Michel and Nicole face her together and discuss her malady and flimsy high-heeled shoes. At the end of the dining-hall scene, we see Christina weeping at a separate table, as Michel and Nicole sit together and watch her; he says explicitly that he wishes Christina dead.

Although Christina maintains a shrine in her bedroom and her superstitious piety makes divorce inconceivable, nevertheless she embarks with Nicole on the journey from Saint-Cloud to Niort: the first stage in their plan to murder Michel. Their conversation during this journey (whose ostensible purpose is to give them an alibi) pointedly underlines the improbability of their murder plot and thus effectively reveals that the real victim is to be Christina. Christina tells Nicole she does not believe her capable of killing Michel; indeed Christina admits she has assumed Nicole desired her own death as a rival. Claiming she changed her attitude towards the spouses, Nicole responds that Michel is counting on Christina dying of heart failure. (Though Clouzot shifted the murder scene from Nantes in the original novel to his birthplace Niort, in practice most of the sequences set there were eventually shot on studio sets, apart from a few exterior shots marking the journey.)

A high-angle view of the van parking in the street is revealed as the perspective of the nosy lodgers who live on the top floor of Nicole's house, as a crane shot takes the camera from outside the window into their room. Apart from their functional role as potential witnesses, M. and Mme Herboux generate some incidental satirical comedy about provincial small-mindedness. Supported by Thérèse Dorny, Noël Roquevert does his standard number as the 'éternel rouspéteur',[18] the beret-wearing petty bourgeois who regards taking an evening bath or eating in a café as unheard-of luxuries and whose only entertainment is listening to a radio game show. The straitened circumstances in which these characters live remind us that post-war provincial France remained economically backward and hierarchically divided; this may surprise modern audiences who take less deferential behaviour and the conspicuous consumption of consumer goods for granted. Although Mme Herboux is introduced as an 'agrégée de grammaire' (that is, a highly qualified schoolteacher), she cannot afford to pay the rent, and she and her husband resent Nicole's more privileged

18 'The eternal grumbler.' The title of Floc'hlay's biography (1987); see chapter one for more details.

status as the owner of a house (which, quite unusually for the 1950s, includes a bathroom and a telephone). In fact, Nicole's background seems equally modest; thus she claims she has never drunk whisky, a luxury item costing 2,500 francs for a bottle (more than twice the price of a tank of petrol). We never learn how she acquired a house, or what drove her from Niort and from her job in a more reputable school, but could deduce from such minimal details that her association with Michel is driven by mercenary ends.

Michel is more obviously a hedonist. He complains that the school is a pointless drain of money and that they live like paupers (he alleges he had to sell his encyclopaedia to pay the train fare to Niort), while making eyes at a woman on the train and drinking the drugged whisky like lemonade. He also asks salaciously whether Christina and Nicole share the bed on which he then collapses. In practice, we see little evidence of any physical intimacy between the women, other than when Nicole holds Christina's arms to calm her (a gesture which Michel repeats in a further example of subtle mirroring). Such apparently consoling movements actually suggest restraint rather than desire or affection. In Michel's case, violence rapidly follows: after Christina nervously spills whisky on his suit, he retaliates with a couple of slaps (effectively removing her scruples about killing him).

The murder scene is a bravura piece of film-making, which still remains shocking, macabre and comic. Reviewing *Les Diaboliques* in *Franc-Tireur*, Georges Altman observed enthusiastically that in scenes like this or Michel's subsequent return from the dead, 'le réalisme atteint au fantastique qui l'apparente à certaines pages d'Edgar Poe' (quoted in *L'Avant-Scène Cinéma* 1997: 95).[19] Observed dispassionately, of course, nothing could be less realistic than a plan to scare one's wife to death by persuading her to participate in a faked murder. Clouzot's success, in other words, is to make events and behaviour that could be risible seem not merely believable but supernaturally horrific. He does this essentially by duping us, by playing with our expectations about cinematic characters, narration and realism, that is the fact that we (mistakenly) think we understand his characters' motivation, line of action, and the limits of what can be represented. Most crucially, the omissions which we interpret as standard editing conventions (such as eliding extreme violence, curtailing protracted actions, cross-cutting) prove to have an added level of significance.

19 'Realism achieves a fantastic impact comparable to some of Poe's best pages.'

Dudley Andrew (1984: 114) argues that the fantastic as a genre (which involves a sort of dialectic of belief and doubt) particularly suits the technology of film, 'for the cinema is at once exact in its reproduction of the minutiae of everyday life (belief) yet eager to startle its audience with tricks in optics, chemistry, and *mise en scène* (doubt)'. Audiences know that murders in feature films are simulations, performed by actors, but also that these fictitious acts will be filmed so as to appear realistic and believable within the imaginary world represented by the film. Clouzot's joke on his audience is to appear to follow these conventions when in fact he is breaking them: the murder, despite its excruciating details, really is a fake. He appears to transgress taboos about representing violence when he is mainly twisting the rules of narration. Thus *Les Diaboliques* violates the sanctity of the bathroom, normally a place which evokes purification, domestic intimacy, privacy and comfort, not merely once but twice: the initial murder scene *chez* Nicole is replicated when Christina seeks sanctuary in her own bathroom, only to discover Michel's corpse awaiting her. That these sequences have been much imitated by subsequent film-makers suggests how disturbing this disruption of domestic space is but also, if we compare Clouzot with his successors, how restrained *Les Diaboliques* is. The most obvious comparison is with the notorious stabbing in the shower in *Psycho* (1960), if only because one of Hitchcock's ambitions was to outdo Clouzot in macabre horror (this included adding a shot of a toilet flushing away evidence, apparently the first time this everyday object had been shown onscreen). Hitchcock's scene is memorably shocking because of its location, its combination of extreme violence and vulnerability, its unexpectedness, the anonymity of the killer, the fact the film's heroine is eliminated and the narrative thus radically disrupted, and, above all, because of its brilliant editing, involving a montage of some seventy-eight pieces of film lasting forty-five seconds. The rapidity of the editing creates the illusion of the knife puncturing both the woman's bare flesh and the screen itself in the blows aimed directly at the camera, their thrusts rhythmically underscored by Bernard Herrmann's strident music (McGilligan 2003: 583–5, 594).

In contrast, Clouzot's murder scene is understated, slowly paced, and grimly business-like. As in *Le Salaire de la peur*, he foregoes the facile emotional and auditory emphasis offered by extra-diegetic music; apart from the credit sequence, only diegetic sounds are heard in *Les Diaboliques*, even if they are highlighted in some key scenes to intensify a desired effect (water running, footsteps moving, doors creaking, voices off). The murder is intercalated with comic scenes, as the noise of the bath filling and pipes clanking drowns out Herboux's quiz programme and the indignant tenant notes that Nicole takes twelve hours before emptying the bath. The drowning lasts about two minutes: the women carry the unconscious Michel to the bath, where Nicole holds his head under water until the camera cuts to Christina fetching the bronze statue to weigh him down. As they manoeuvre the heavy statue, his head floats back to the surface, at which point Christina leaves the bathroom and collapses. We then see Nicole covering the bath with a plastic tablecloth and locking the door (ostensibly, one assumes, from a sense of decorum; in reality, we infer retrospectively, to prevent Christina discovering Michel is still alive). He later tells Nicole that he spent an hour in the bathwater before getting out; we see his body in the empty bath the following morning, before M. Herboux unwittingly helps its removal in the wicker trunk. (What is not explained is how Michel and Nicole manage to fill the bath in Nicole's apartment at the end of the film without Christina hearing the water running.)

Whereas Hitchcock concludes the shower sequence in *Psycho* with a macabre and showmanlike superimposition of bloody water spiralling down the plughole on to a close-up of Marion's staring dead eye, Clouzot ends the murder scene in *Les Diaboliques* with a much simpler and less gratuitous close-up of the bathroom tap dripping on to the plastic sheet. The effect is one of chilling banality, matching the cold-blooded efficiency of Nicole's actions (even if there is another reason for her calmness). Retrospectively, we can see too that the tap announces that death and water will continue to dominate the film. The second half of *Les Diaboliques* recounts a series of uncanny events that ineluctably destroy Christina's fragile security (Michel has called her a 'ruin' waiting to collapse); she is effectively haunted by increasingly menacing, inexplicable signs of her guilt and his presence. After returning to the Institution Delassalle, the women hide Michel's body in the filthy swimming pool. They are shown wearing pyjamas the following morning, as they look from a window at the pool; yet far from having an erotic charge, their intimacy becomes increasingly antagonistic. Christina is seen giving an English lesson, while the concierge Plantiveau pokes half-heartedly at the scummy surface of the pool, his action matching the boys' recital of the verb 'to find'. We see Christina and Nicole marking scripts at the same desk and patrolling round the pool, Nicole telling Christina she is like an anxious child and rebuking her for biting her nails. A boy dives into the pool when Nicole drops her keys in the water, but discovers only Michel's cigarette lighter. When the pool is finally drained, the body has disappeared and Christina faints.

A succession of deliberately ambiguous shots and incidents suggests that Michel has come back to life; like the audience on a first viewing, Christina apparently interprets them as quasi-supernatural evidence of her guilt rather than as a rational conspiracy against her. In each case, a rational explanation is hinted at, however. The checked suit Michel was wearing when he drowned is brought back from the cleaner's by a man whose face is hidden behind it (but he is then revealed to be the concierge). Christina visits a hotel room which Michel has rented; the bathroom door suddenly swings open, catching her startled expression in a mirror, but behind it there is only a cleaner who has never encountered Michel. She visits the morgue to identify a drowned man's body; we see only the nose of this unknown corpse. Here too she meets the retired *commissaire divisionnaire* Alfred Fichet, who interrogates her and launches his investigation. As he remarks, 'Quand même, les clefs dans la piscine, le mari à la morgue; j'ai l'impression que vous rêvez beaucoup d'eau dans la maison'.[20] Christina's nightmarish misinterpretation of these clues is countered by Fichet's scepticism. When she eventually confesses to killing Michel, he evidently disbelieves her, but seems content to let the conspiracy run its course. The pupil Moinet claims he has been punished by Michel for breaking a window with his catapult; he is disbelieved and further punished, but a school photograph session captures Michel's spectral image in the background gazing from a window.

Fearing the worst, Nicole abandons Christina; a jump cut makes Nicole literally vanish like another phantom in the middle of the corridor, as a voice-over from a pupil is heard reciting lines from Racine's *Athalie* that proclaim God will chastise wrongdoers. As Christina awakes from a troubled sleep, a mysterious prowler is revealed as Fichet, who listens to her confession before disappearing again.

20 'All the same, with keys in the pool and the husband in the morgue, I get the feeling you dream a lot about water in this place.'

After this teasingly false dénouement, Christina's final ordeal is protracted over seven minutes, in a skilful montage of shots showing her increasing fear and vulnerability, the presence of further prowlers, intrusive noises, and sinister objects. Christina's sleeping figure is cross-cut with a long shot of a door opening and a shadow moving; a close-up shows a gloved hand in a checked sleeve gripping the banister rail. Christina is awoken by light cast over her from a window across the courtyard, where another shadow is moving. Our unfamiliarity with the exact spatial location of the rooms which appear to contain these threatening presences means that we effectively share some of her anxiety as she investigates the source of the disturbances. The long, dark, twisting passage between her bedroom and Michel's study is a particularly sinister space, although the real danger will be in the illusory safety of the bathroom. As Christina cautiously advances down the corridor, backlighting reveals the curve of her breasts and hips in her translucent nightdress (making her an eroticised victim). The camera moves from her to look along the corridor at the light under the door; we see male legs walking and hear a door squeaking, a voice speaking, and a typewriter clattering in the room ahead of her. Entering the study, she sees a man's hat and gloves on the table and the name 'Michel Delassalle' repeated several times on the paper in the typewriter. When the light is extinguished, she screams and flees back to her bedroom, bolting the door and retreating to the bathroom, where nemesis awaits her.

After the climactic revelation of Michel's resuscitation and Christina's death from terror, the film's epilogue seems curiously perfunctory: in only two minutes, Michel and Nicole's plot is explained, Fichet interrupts their rejoicing, and a dissolve shows Moinet's catapult shattering another window. How should we interpret the boy's claim that Christina is not in fact dead, since she returned his confiscated weapon? Is he a liar or the victim of an hallucination (despite the fact his previous sight of Michel proved not to be imaginary)? Has Christina faked her own death, or become a ghost? By leaving such questions unresolved, Clouzot conforms to Todorov's well-known assertion (1976: 29) that sustained ambiguity is the defining feature of the fantastic. The success of *Les Diaboliques* is to entice the spectator into pursuing an enigma that is only partially resolved (thereby encouraging further viewings of the film). Observed dispassionately, the characters and their situation may seem shallow and implausible, but Clouzot draws us so skilfully and persuasively into his imagined world that such objections seem irrelevant; we certainly adopt an anxious identification with Christina's plight, even if our vicarious experience of what terrifies her is pleasurable.

A brief discussion of Jeremiah Chechik's remake, *Diabolique* (1996), by way of conclusion and comparison, offers further evidence of Clouzot's subtle mastery of suspense and the uncanny. Chechik's film might be taken as a tribute to his European sources, were it not for the fact that Clouzot and Boileau-Narcejac are acknowledged only at the very end of the closing credits and that Morgan Creek failed to acquire the rights to *Les Diaboliques* from Clouzot's estate. (Clouzot's widow eventually won significant compensation from the producers: Dacbert and Lamassoure 1996.) Neither of his two female stars offered Chechik much support. Sharon Stone insisted on wearing her designer wardrobe in the film (despite her role as a low-income schoolmistress), but refused to go to Cannes to promote *Diabolique*. Chechik claimed he aspired to create 'a much more complex version' of Boileau-Narcejac's novel than Clouzot's original screenplay (Pizzello 1996: 37), though in practice his version copies Clouzot's until the conclusion. Isabelle Adjani (who plays Mia, the equivalent of Christina) observed with rather damning tact to a French interviewer that '*Diabolique* est un film de genre, pas un film d'auteur' (Peck 1996: 92).[21]

Where Clouzot is suggestive and understated, Chechik is crudely overt; his film does not create anxiety, mystery and suspense but offers a voyeuristic spectacle of sexual and violent confrontation, insistently underscored by extra-diegetic music. Thus an opening sequence shows Adjani (or more probably her body double) nude in the bathroom, being watched by a schoolboy through a conveniently adjacent window. In the refectory scene, as she struggles with the vile food, her bullying husband Guy orders her to 'Swallow it for once in your life', a salacious innuendo reinforced by his remark that 'I'm sure Miss Horner will keep something hot for you'. In case we doubted their relationship, he and Miss Horner are shown humping (with Nicole on top). The drugging and drowning of Guy is a protracted, noisy and splashy affair, which includes the use of an underwater camera to show the drowning man's viewpoint. But the technical skill of such shots often seems purely gratuitous or misplaced. Thus an extreme

21 '*Diabolique* is a genre film, not an auteur's film.' This probably explains why the film was commercially reasonably successful in the USA (Hayward 2005: 95).

close-up shows whisky cascading over ice in his glass (a shot more familiar from commercials than thrillers, particularly as we also see the label on the bottle). Chechik's alterations to the plot and characters often lack coherence. For example, the insipid Mia is supposedly a former nun, but now gives French lessons and sex education classes (she shows a film to her pupils which includes a drawing of an erect penis). In a rather pointless additional scene, Nicole gives a cheque to another of Guy's girlfriends to pay for an abortion. Guy's resuscitation in the bath (the most shocking event in Clouzot's film) is treated summarily, for Chechik is more interested in the protracted battle between Guy and the two women, when finally they drown him in the pristine swimming pool. Here the violence is so protracted that it has the comic impact of an animated cartoon (despite having a garden rake embedded in his head, Guy seems unstoppable).

If *Diabolique* alienates us through its excesses and seems a clumsy travesty of *Les Diaboliques*, Clouzot's own sequel to his film, *Les Espions*, is also alienating. This is partly because it too at times looks like an uninspired pastiche of the director's previous films. The sinister nurses and unscrupulous doctor recall *Le Corbeau*; the sleazy, enclosed clinic invaded by mysterious snoopers recalls both this film and *Les Diaboliques*. While Pierre Larquey reprises his role as a persecuted taxi driver from *Quai des Orfèvres*, there is even a schoolboy called Moinet, who leads the protagonist to a classroom where he is interrogated in a sort of parodic lesson. The main problem with *Les Espions*, however, is a lack of direction and coherence. It makes one aware how Clouzot's successful films invariably depend on tightly controlled plots, skilfully delineated characters, and arresting scenes and images. *Les Espions* evokes a world of mutually assured nuclear destruction, corrupt authority and interchangeable secret agents serving many masters, but it is too diffuse to work as a political or satirical commentary on cold war paranoia. Its décor and characters gesture towards both the absurdist theatre of the 1950s and downbeat spy films more common in the 1960s, but it is too naturalistic to work as a poetic allegory, yet too stylised and verbose to engage us as an action thriller.

Les Espions derives from a novel by Egon Hostovsky translated into French as *Le Vertige de minuit* (1955), which describes how a Czech psychoanalyst based in New York is torn between American spies and their adversaries. Clouzot's adaptation drops the Czech element (which is central to the book), along with Dr Malik's fiancée and mother, relocating the setting in the Paris suburbs. His Dr Malic (played by Gérard Séty) is a Frenchman without affective ties or political allegiances, who runs an unsuccessful psychiatric clinic in Maisons-Lafitte. He has only two patients: a drug addict (Louis Seigner) and a hysterical mute, Lucie (Vera Clouzot). The surveillance which he imposes on them through the spy-holes in the doors of their rooms will, in the course of the film, be extended to Malic himself and the entire institution, though from the beginning we are aware that he is under observation from outside by a man in a black car and inside by the obsessive Lucie (who can see his eye behind the spy-hole). Called out on a false visit to a slaughterhouse at Argenteuil, Malic encounters Colonel Howard of the 'Institut de guerre pyschologique des Etats-Unis'. Though they are observed by everybody else in the café where they meet, Malic accepts one million francs in cash to hospitalise an agent called Alex in his clinic.

This decision radically disrupts Malic's routine, since his previously deserted clinic is now invaded by a strange band of newcomers, some of them played by internationally celebrated actors. His nurse Mme André is replaced by the bullying American Conny (Martita Hunt), the slatternly cook Clotilde by the Beckettian duo Léon and Pierre (they doff their hats mockingly in a piece of business that recalls *Waiting for Godot*), the café waiter Louis by the nosily whinging Victor. Two new patients demand Malic's services: the Lithuanian kleptomaniac Kaminsky (Peter Ustinov) and the schoolmasterly spymaster Cooper (Sam Jaffe). In addition, a group of ocarina players who know only one tune take up residence in the café, and innumerable other anonymous spies invade the neighbourhood. Nevertheless, Alex manages to take refuge unseen in the clinic in a darkened room, where he retains his gun, gloves and dark glasses (Curd Jürgens was dismayed to discover that he would have to perform behind sunglasses throughout the film: Cournot 2003).

The film oscillates awkwardly between comically absurd scenes (Malic attempting to make a confidential telephone call while surrounded by spies in the café), scenes involving rather ponderous exposition of plot or ideas about espionage and loyalty (all the central characters are called upon to deliver self-justifying or menacing speeches which seem theatrical or melodramatic rather than cinematic), and occasional moments of violence (suggested indirectly, since they occur off-screen). While the less important agents Léon and Victor are liquidated for undisclosed offences and Alex keeps intruders at bay by shooting through his door, we learn that the latter is supposedly the nuclear scientist Hugo Vogel, who is on the run from both the East Germans and the Americans. Malic, despite being shown as a weak-willed, mercenary drunkard, decides to protect his new 'patient' by taking a photograph of the drug addict and pretending it is Alex when he gives it to Cooper. But since Alex reveals that he is not Vogel, this ploy only exposes the scientist to greater danger. After bribing Conny with the million francs, Malic tracks down Howard (who commits suicide) and finally encounters the real Vogel on the overnight sleeper train from Paris to Marseille. As the spies close in, Vogel either jumps or is thrown from the compartment window, leaving the impotent Malic with no proof or witnesses to combat his adversaries. On returning to the clinic, he discovers that Lucie has regained the power of speech and will support him. As she says 'Je dirai tout' ('I'll tell everything'), the telephone rings menacingly: they are still under surveillance as the film closes on the piercing ringing.

Malic's relationship with the mute, childlike Lucie may seem irrelevant to the film's main storyline, but at least it shows that amid death and betrayal he succeeds in protecting and curing one patient. Perhaps her obsessive hysteria and muteness are an understandable reaction to the oppressive atmosphere and odious characters who surround her. In one scene that again seems gratuitous in terms of plot but is visually impressive, we see her trashing her room in frustrated rage, surrounded by a cloud of feathers as a pillow bursts open. Another cinematically pleasing scene shows Malic advancing down interminable lines of washing in an attic as he seeks out the dying Howard, suggesting how Malic is unable to escape from such banal domestic constraints and fulfil his role as a saviour. Such moments when form and ambition cohere are all too rare, however. As François Truffaut remarked in his caustic dismissal of *Les Espions*, Clouzot's film pays far too much attention to appearances and sordid details, while failing to convey wider truths about behaviour and feelings (Truffaut 2000: 345). Unlike *Les Diaboliques*, it aspires to enlighten and to discomfort us, rather than to entertain and to impress with technical virtuosity; but in practice these ambitions fall short of the director's aspirations. We may well conclude that as a metaphysical fable, *Les Espions* is self-defeatingly cynical and nihilistic, and that as a thriller it is pointlessly dislocated and pretentious.

Bibliography

Andrew, Dudley (1984), *Concepts in Film Theory*, New York, Oxford University Press

L'Avant-Scène Cinéma (1997), 463, June, script and reviews of *Les Diaboliques*

Barbey d'Aurevilly, Jules (1967), *Les Diaboliques*, Paris, Garnier-Flammarion

Bertin-Maghit, Jean-Pierre (1996), 'Les Diaboliques ou le discours de la terreur', in Pierre Glaudes, ed., *Terreur et représentation*, Grenoble, ELLUG, 271–86

Boileau-Narcejac (1986), *Tandem ou 35 ans de suspense*, Paris, Denoël

Boileau-Narcejac (1988), *Quarante ans de suspense*, vol. 1, ed. Francis Lacassin, Paris, Laffont, Bouquins

Bocquet, José Louis and Marc Godin (1993), *Henri-Georges Clouzot cinéaste*, Paris, La Sirène

Bondy, Jacques-André (1996), 'Pouquoi *Diabolique* n'ira pas à Cannes', *Première*, May, 73–4

Buss, Robin (1994), *French Film Noir*, London/New York, Boyars

Cournot, Michel (2003), *Le Premier Spectateur*, Paris, Gallimard

Dacbert, Sophie and Patrick Lamassoure (1996), 'Inès Clouzot contre Morgan Creek: un conflit diablement médiatique', *Le Film français*, 2600, 1 March, 8

Derry, Charles (1988), *The Suspense Thriller: Films in the Shadow of Alfred Hitchcock*, Jefferson, McFarland

Floc'hlay, Yvon (1987), *Noël Roquevert, l'éternel rouspéteur*, Paris, Editions France-Empire

Freud, Sigmund (1990), 'The Uncanny', in *Art and Literature*, ed. Albert Dickson, London, Penguin

Gauteur, Claude (1997), 'Variations critiques autour de Henri-Georges Clouzot', *L'Avant-Scène Cinéma*, 463, June, 1–13

Gorrara, Claire (2003), *The Roman Noir in Post-War French Culture: Dark Fictions*, Oxford, Oxford University Press

Gow, Gordon (1968), *Suspense in the Cinema*, London, Zwemmer/New York, Barnes

Hayward, Susan (2003), 'Literary Adaptations of the 1950s: *Thérèse Raquin* (1953) and *Les Diaboliques* (1955)', *Studies in French Cinema*, 3, 1, 5–14

Hayward, Susan (2005), *Les Diaboliques*, London, Tauris

Hostovsky, Egon (1955), *Le Vertige de minuit*, trans. Michel Manoll, Laffont

Hottell, Ruth A. (1996), 'The Diabolic Dialogic: *Les Diaboliques* by H.-G. Clouzot', *Literature/Film Quarterly*, 24, 3, 255–60

Lacourbe, Roland (1977), 'Henri-Georges Clouzot', *L'Avant-Scène Cinéma*, 186, 94–124

Lloyd, Christopher (2000), 'Eliminating the Detective: Boileau-Narcejac, Clouzot and *Les Diaboliques*', in Anne Mullen and Emer O'Beirne, eds, *Crime Scenes: Detective Narratives in European Culture since 1945*, Amsterdam/Atlanta, Rodopi, 37–47

Mayne, Judith (2000), *Framed: Lesbians, Feminists and Mediaculture*, Minneapolis, University of Minnesota Press

McGilligan, Patrick (2003), *Alfred Hitchcock; a Life in Darkness and Light*, Chichester, Wiley

Meurisse, Paul (1979), *Les Eperons de la liberté*, Paris, Laffont

Moskowitz, Gene (1955), '*Les Diaboliques*', *Sight and Sound*, 24, 172

Neale, Steve (2000), *Genre and Hollywood*, London, Routledge

Newman, Kim (1996), '*Diabolique*', *Sight and Sound*, September, 39

Peck, Cecilia (1996), 'Isabelle la diabolique', *Première*, May, 88–93

Pizzello, Chris (1996), 'Bringing the Dark Side of Character to Light in *Diabolique*', *American Cinematographer*, 77, 4, April, 36–44

Signoret, Simone (1978), *La Nostalgie n'est plus ce qu'elle était*, Paris, Seuil

Todorov, Tzvetan (1976), *Introduction à la littérature fantastique*, Paris, Seuil

Truffaut, François (2000), *Le Plaisir des yeux: écrits sur le cinéma*, ed. Jean Narboni and Serge Toubiana, Paris, Petite Bibliothèque Cahiers du Cinéma

Truffaut, François and Helen Scott (1985), *Hitchcock*, New York, Simon & Schuster

Wiel, Ophélie (2005), 'Ces messieurs de la famille', *Télérama*, 12 January, 120

Young, Jane (2000), 'A Continuous Spiral: Boileau-Narcejac's *Sueurs froides* and Hitchcock's *Vertigo*', in Anne Mullen and Emer O'Beirne, eds, *Crime Scenes: Detective Narratives in European Culture since 1945*, Amsterdam/Atlanta, Rodopi, 48–58

6

Filming Picasso and Karajan

This chapter deviates from the chronological sequence followed hitherto in order to consider the documentary films which Clouzot made with Pablo Picasso and Herbert von Karajan. *Le Mystère Picasso* was filmed at La Victorine studios in Nice from June to September 1955 and first shown at the Cannes festival in 1956, where it was awarded a special jury prize. Following the popular success of *Le Salaire de la peur* and *Les Diaboliques* (and the critical reservations which the second film had attracted), Clouzot was able to afford to undertake a project that was quite different from such commercial feature films derived from thrillers and adventure stories. *Le Mystère Picasso* attempts to probe the mystery of artistic creation, as Clouzot and his cameraman Claude Renoir film the painter at work on a series of sketches and canvases which appear and disappear in a multiplicity of forms before our gaze. While most of the paintings are shot in bright colour, the transitional studio scenes where director, cinematographer and painter discuss their progress are filmed in high-contrast black and white. Colour (which Clouzot was using for the first time in his career) thus has the obvious aesthetic function of highlighting the act of artistic creation. While professional critics viewed the film with respect, praising its technical innovations, its performative zest and archival interest (despite reservations about Clouzot's packaging of Picasso), cinema audiences proved less enthusiastic about a highbrow enterprise that evidently interested only an intellectual élite. The film was commercially unsuccessful despite, or more probably because of, its prestigious subject (Picasso's acceptance of a percentage of the receipts in lieu of a flat fee therefore proving financially disadvantageous).

Nevertheless, viewed fifty years on, *Le Mystère Picasso* remains an extraordinarily appealing and ambitious document of the greatest artist of the twentieth century and his dialogue with a brilliant film-maker. Ten years later, when he made five films for the Austrian conductor Herbert von Karajan between 1965 and 1967, sponsored by a television production company, Clouzot's career appeared to be in terminal decline. His extravagant behaviour when filming the aptly named *L'Enfer* in 1964 had been followed by serious illness, the abandonment of further shooting, and the impossibility of continuing the film or funding any major project in the foreseeable future. His successful work with Karajan did at least demonstrate Clouzot's durability and versatility, also allowing him to produce his last feature film, *La Prisonnière* in 1968 (and its highly aestheticised manner and artistic milieu clearly owe something to the encounters with high art recorded by the documentaries). But the music films are no more than technically skilful records of the maestro and his musicians in performance: Karajan is at their centre, and we have little sense of the film-maker's presence other than as one of the conductor's facilita-tors. In fact, Karajan carefully used his sessions with Clouzot in order to learn about film-making, subsequently launching his own produc-tions of his performances and directing them himself.

Karajan (1989) was impressed not only by Clouzot's cinematic expertise but also by his musical sensibility and ability to learn a complex score. It is worth recalling that at an early stage of his career the director had worked as a song lyricist (writing the text for Maurice Yvain's operetta *La Belle Histoire*, performed in 1934); he was also a keen amateur painter and collector. He had met Picasso briefly in the 1920s, but got to know him better after moving to Saint-Paul-de-Vence in the early 1950s, near the painter's villa at Vallauris. Bocquet and Godin (1993: 98) note that the Belgian Paul Heasaerts, in his film *Visite à Picasso* (1950), 'est le premier, avant Clouzot, à utiliser le principe de la transparence en interposant une vitre entre Picasso au travail et la caméra'.[1] Picasso's discovery of felt-tip pens made in the USA in 1955 gave him the idea of filming the reverse of a transparent sheet of paper, although in fact he uses special ink and brushes visible on the back of the paper in Clouzot's film. This has the advantage of filling the entire screen with the work in progress, which emerges on

1 'Was the first person before Clouzot to use the principle of transparency, by placing a sheet of glass between Picasso as he worked and the camera.'

the sheet seemingly without human agency; what the viewer sees is a mirror image of what the artist (who is no longer visible) is drawing on the front of the picture. The large canvases painted in oil which conclude the film were filmed conventionally from his side of the canvas, with the painter pausing and withdrawing to allow the camera to record each stage.

Given his world-wide celebrity, it is unsurprising that Picasso was frequently the subject of documentaries. The catalogue of an exhibition held at the Picasso museum in Paris in 1992 lists 170 films devoted to the artist (Clouzot's is twenty-seventh in order of appearance: Bernadec and Breteau-Skira 1992). What distinguishes *Le Mystère Picasso* from most films about painters and painting, however, is its relentless concentration on the act of painting, the creation and transformation of the work of art. Apart from very brief contextualising glimpses of the artist and Clouzot's team in the studio, all that we see on the screen is a succession of sketches and paintings created as the film proceeds. Apart from a few exchanges between Picasso and Clouzot, there is no commentary; in most cases, the soundtrack is filled with the music composed by Georges Auric to accompany the paintings. In other words, we experience the paintings and music as a sort of unfolding performance, full of unexpected deviations and variations. Hence André Chastel's judgement in *Le Monde* in May 1956 that

> Avec un mauvais titre et un départ inutilement pédant, en dépit de la musique d'Auric trop appuyée et parfois franchement encombrante, le film d'H. Clouzot dépasse tout ce que le cinéma a fait jusqu'ici pour la peinture. (Quoted by Bernadec and Breteau-Skira 1992: 62)[2]

Like other critics, Chastel pointed out the 'suspense' generated by the unexpected transformations of what appears on screen. These can be so extensive that they are hard to grasp. For example, among the

> Métamorphoses successives: une fleur est née. Elle devient poisson, qu'accapare et engloutit l'image d'une sirène. La sirène se mue en coq. Le terme? Un faune diable que l'artiste se met à colorer. (Verdet 1956)[3]

2 'With its bad title and unnecessarily pedantic opening, in spite of Auric's music, which is overstated and sometimes unduly intrusive, Clouzot's film far exceeds anything the cinema has done before now for painting.'

3 'Successive metamorphoses: a flower is born. It becomes a fish, which is overtaken and swallowed by the image of a mermaid. The mermaid turns into a cock. The end product? A devil faun which the artist starts to colour in.'

All this could hardly be farther from the static, pedagogic manner adopted by most documentaries about artists, where typically more screen time is occupied by the talking heads of art historians or media celebrities than by the artist's works, which are often shown in the most summary fashion in order simply to illustrate a commentary largely focused on biographical and anecdotal elements. Before offering a fuller descriptive analysis of *Le Mystère Picasso*, however, it is useful to recall some of the critical responses to the film, since they effectively set the terms for any discussion. For all their enthusiasm, the remarks by Chastel just quoted also reveal how ambivalent and grudging was the attitude of many contemporary reviewers towards Clouzot, a film director whom they associated more with popular genre films than with high art. Hence the dislike of the title, with its echoes of the thriller, and the need to see 'suspense' as a linking motif with Clouzot's previous films. Clouzot's introductory comments state somewhat portentously that the film will probe the mystery of artistic creation, revealing the mind behind the artist's hand. Writing in *Cahiers du cinéma* (June 1956), André Bazin objected that, in practice, Clouzot explains nothing; he appears to think that showing the pictures suffices to make them comprehensible. He has rejected didacticism, biography and variety, other than in his soundtrack: 'L'inadmissible musique d'Auric constitue ... évidemment la concession que le réalisateur a cru pouvoir faire à l'anecdote et au pittoresque' (Bazin 1959: 142).[4]

On the other hand, Bazin hailed *Le Mystère Picasso* as a 'Bergsonian' film, in the sense that it shows 'the very duration' of painting as a process:

> les stades intermédiaires ne sont pas des réalités subordonnées et inférieures, comme serait un acheminement vers une plénitude finale, ils sont déjà l'œuvre même, mais destinée à se dévorer ou plutôt à se métamorphoser jusqu'à l'instant où le peintre voudra s'arrêter.

The film has the advantage of preserving, or at least recording, these 'stades recouverts ou surchargés [qui] étaient également des tableaux mais qu'il fallait sacrifier au tableau suivant' (Bazin 1959: 136).[5] He

4 'Auric's intolerable music obviously constitutes the one concession which the director believed he could make towards the anecdotal and picturesque.'

5 'The intermediate stages are not subordinate and inferior realities, as would be a movement towards a final plenitude; they are already the work itself, which is destined to be devoured or metamorphosed until the painter decides to stop.'

noted too that Clouzot's editing accelerates the tempo of Picasso's painting, giving the film a resemblance to Norman McLaren's experiments with animation (though these often involve painting directly on to film). François Truffaut also observed the parallel with animated film, though he predicted that Clouzot's technical wizardry would pass unnoticed by the public (this self-effacement on behalf of Picasso's work was seen as praiseworthy). He too dismissed Auric's music as 'ce pot-pourri d'opéras-comiques qui nous assourdit', and complained that the lack of background commentary denies the spectator a point of comparison with other works by Picasso. Furthermore, the rapidity with which the canvases are filmed (or rather with which the final version of the film is cut) unfortunately recalls 'un caricaturiste de music-hall', particularly in the sequence when Picasso is challenged to work against the clock to finish a sketch before the film runs out (Truffaut 1975: 226).[6]

The chapter devoted to Clouzot in Pierre Cabanne's voluminous study of *Le Siècle de Picasso* (1992) is entitled somewhat dismissively 'Il n'y a pas de mystère Picasso', for 'en insistant sur le côté virtuose de Pablo [le film] dévoile les secrets en les travestissant, en faisant d'eux des tours de passe-passe ou des exercices d'acrobatie gestuelle'. It shows only the appearance and a few stages of the creative process and turns Picasso into an illusionist and an actor, in a demeaning fashion: '*Le Mystère Picasso* c'est la revanche inconsciente du peintre raté qu'est Clouzot sur le génie de don Pablo' (Cabanne 1992: 404–5).[7] Picasso emerges as an artisan, like the rest of the crew, devoid of mystery. Nevertheless, despite this negative evaluation, Cabanne provides detailed and positive descriptions of the paintings shown in the film, which effectively contradict his carping remarks about Clouzot's enterprise, since they show the film works, in the sense that it communicates a powerful sense of Picasso's art and artistry to the viewer. Presenting Clouzot as a failed painter is a strangely self-defeating tactic, particularly as this is the sort of snide criticism usually aimed at art critics; it invites the riposte that, whereas a written

---

'Concealed or over-painted stages which were also paintings but which had to be sacrificed to the following painting.'

6 'A medley of comic operas which deafens us.' 'A music-hall caricaturist.'

7 'There is no Picasso mystery.' 'By emphasising Pablo's virtuosity, the film exposes secrets by travestying them, making them into conjuring tricks and acrobatic gestures.' '*Le Mystère Picasso* is the unconscious revenge of Clouzot the failed painter on the genius of Don Pablo.'

account like Cabanne's book is limited to verbal paraphrase, the film is far more compelling and evocative both as a visual document and in showing the temporal process of creation.

Nor is the suggestion that Clouzot had manipulated the artist really justified if one examines the wider context of Picasso's career, for maintaining and recording the multifarious stages of creation and elaborating his mythic image were long-standing concerns. Clouzot was one of many agents used to further these goals. For example, Picasso's mistress, the Yugoslav photographer Dora Maar, made a record of his drawings and work on the canvas of *Guernica* in 1937, to fulfil his wish 'to fix photographically not the successive stages of a painting but its successive changes' in order to 'understand the mental processes leading to the embodiment of the artist's dream' (Hilton 1976: 234). Similarly, Brassaï took progressive photographs of *The Charnel House* (1944–45, left unfinished) and quoted Picasso's desire to transfer each more advanced state of a painting to another canvas, to conserve the 'different states of a single painting' and perpetually postpone finishing, with its connotations of death and finality (quoted by Hilton 1976: 261). Clouzot's film allows Picasso to enact his myth of creation and destruction with startling rapidity, and to also to display himself as part virtuoso genius and part showman, appearing before 'a shamelessly voyeuristic public as a man of unfailing potency: a compulsively, feverishly productive artist wholly immersed in his work' (Warncke and Walther 2002: 678).

Le Mystère Picasso thus merits more detailed investigation for its technical innovations, its presentation of Picasso and his work, its use of music instead of a more conventional explanatory commentary. The films runs for about seventy-five minutes, during which it shows the creation of twenty-one separate works. The last seven are large canvases painted with oils (measuring approximately 80 x 190 cm), which take up twenty minutes and are filmed in widescreen ratio. If projected in a cinema, this would mean that this concluding transition to the most ambitious and demanding works would be clearly marked by virtually doubling the surface area of the screen visible to spectators (in other words, from the standard ratio of 1.33:1 to 2.35:1), making these large works look twice as big. Unfortunately, if one watches the film on video or DVD on a standard television screen, one experiences the opposite effect to that intended, since the widescreen sequences are letterboxed and occupy half the area of the smaller sketches. On the other hand, there are disadvantages to watching the film in a movie theatre, the most obvious being the impossibility of pausing or repeating viewing of segments whose multiple transformations can be hard to grasp when first seen. Although the average time during which each work is shown is 3.5 minutes (which might seem intolerably long if one were watching a static shot of a finished work), this represents only a fraction of the time actually taken by Picasso. For example, the four minutes devoted to the evolution of the goat's head are compressed from five hours' work (that is, screen time is 1.33 per cent of real time); the second version of *La Plage à La Garoupe* gets less than a minute on screen but took fourteen hours to paint. What one sees, in other words, is a highly accelerated version of selected stages of the creative process, somewhat similar to the use of time-lapse filming in natural history to reveal the development of plants and organisms which otherwise remains invisible to the human eye.

The transitions between the twenty-one works are also marked very clearly by wipes or comparable editing devices in nearly all cases. These boundaries may appear somewhat artificial at times, for example when the succeeding work proves to be another variation on its predecessor (witness the sets of reclining nudes, bullfights, beaches). But they give the film a clear structure and rhythm, effectively dividing it into a series of movements, of themes and variations, shaped visually and musically, oscillating between repetition and diversity in both subject and manner, between accumulation and effacement. Roland Lacourbe (1977: 107) praises Clouzot for achieving a 'Summum de la technique qui permet à la technique de disparaître'[8] (citing the example of the painted sheets which are literally transparent). In fact, the film-maker's mastery includes revelatory glimpses of the filming process (there is no 'mystère Clouzot'), even if these are not ponderously or narcissistically laboured. Many of the complaints which reviewers mixed in with their praise amount to an uneasy recognition that the film is not a conventional documentary, but rather a subtly mannered aesthetic composition, a set of performances linking painting, film and music. Seen (or heard) in this light, Auric's music perhaps ceases to be the noisy irrelevance dismissed by film and art critics.

Le Mystère Picasso gradually shifts from a documentary to an aesthetic manner, as it becomes clear that its subject is not so much

8 'A mastery of technique which allows to technique to disappear.'

Picasso's life and work as the presentation of his compositions as an expressive filmic spectacle. The film begins by irising in on Picasso, seen in long shot in the studio facing an easel. While the commentary announces the intention to explore the mystery of artistic creation, a cloud of cigarette smoke precedes Picasso's closer appearance on screen. A face turns into the familiar image of a dove as he sketches. Both the smoke and transformation suggest he is a sort of magician. The credits run, accompanied by Auric's insistent orchestral music. With the first sketch, we see Picasso drawing; with the second sketch, the lines appear on the screen as if by magic, without human agency, slightly faster than in real time. We hear only the sound of the pen scratching over the paper, as the figure of a nude artist emerges, drawing a reclining female nude (a favourite self-reflective reference, germane to the subject of the film). There is a wipe to a blank screen after seven minutes and forty-eight seconds, and a third sketch appears, set to music, of three nude figures; three minutes later the background is filled in in blue, green, and brown (the first appearance of colour), but no flesh tones are added to the figures. This sequence is shown much faster than real time and wiped after eight minutes. Over these fifteen minutes, we have thus witnessed a graduated progression from Picasso to his work, an acceleration in tempo, the introduction of music and colour. There is no camera movement: only the emergence of line and colours, defining and transforming a subject.

With the fourth and fifth sketches, thicker, coloured lines are used. With its schematic outlines and blocks of colour, the fifth sketch becomes recognisable as a bullfight after two minutes. The music in many sketches recalls the accompaniment to silent films; it is functional, in the sense of occupying a soundtrack that would otherwise be discomfortingly empty, but has no obvious thematic link to what we see on the screen. This objection is countered in the sixth sketch, where a flamenco-style guitar solo matches the visual subject, a bull tossing a matador. The drama of the figures' emergence is also formally supported by the use of stop-motion photography to block in successive colours (red, yellow, grey). This sketch lasts two minutes and, with its more adroit equivalence of subject, form and sound, overcomes the sense of monotony engendered by the apparent randomness of previous sketches. New variations are introduced with the seventh and eighth sketches, with more complex, abstract patterning of geometric shapes (though some are recognisable as heads, a horse, a boat). The seventh is much speeded up, whole lines appearing with abrupt cuts, to the sound of a percussive drumbeat. After ninety seconds, the music pauses; the film then reruns backwards and the whole sketch is erased section by section until a blank screen remains. The eighth sketch adds a jazz trumpet to the drums, and ends by an abrupt cut to show the camera and a voice saying 'coupez'. The sketch is lifted off its supporting frame, revealing Picasso behind it.

An interlude lasting seven minutes now reveals Picasso and the film crew at work. Claude Renoir is seen at the camera positioned behind the artist's easel, while a separate camera films from the front of the painting, over Picasso's right shoulder. (Renoir's brief cameo acknowledges the fact that not only was he the grandson of the Impressionist painter and nephew of the film director, but he was celebrated in his own right for the innovative use of colour cinematography.) Clouzot and Picasso discuss what to do next (using the familiar 'tu', suggesting the camaraderie of equals). Picasso accepts the challenge to finish a sketch using the five minutes of film left in the camera. He is filmed working against the clock, mostly in real time, with the film cutting between the cameras at the front and the back of the sheet; we hear Clouzot shouting out the time and extraneous background noises (a passing aircraft). The camera shooting the sketch is stopped while Picasso prepares his colours. We return to the sketch, intercut with shots of Picasso (working feverishly stripped to the waist), Clouzot, Renoir, and the meter on his camera as the film runs out. Perhaps the drama of this rapid-action painting seems a little forced (the choice not to reload the camera is obviously arbitrary). Nevertheless, this sequence is entertaining and informative, emphasising both the ludic and competitive nature of the whole enterprise.

The performance of drawing and painting in sequence then resumes, as five more sketches set to music are filmed over fourteen minutes: matadors, still lifes, a circus, a goat's head. These are the familiar images of Picasso's personal mythology, endlessly recycled; as Warncke and Walther observe (2002: 565), from 1954, as he entered his seventies, the artist made paraphrase 'his new working principle' (though repetition may ultimately betray an underlying sterility). The first three of these sketches are edited down to only one minute each, which perhaps suggests a law of diminishing returns is operating. The fourth sketch is interrupted by the artist's voice off screen, stating 'je le laisse comme ça' ('I'll leave it like that'). Clouzot and Picasso study the painting, the artist explaining his urge to show the pictures under his pictures; while his over-painting and erasure emphasise 'the contingent, temporary status of an individual work' (Warncke and Walther 2002: 621), the medium of film allows him to fulfil this archaeological aspiration. The final sketch shows an extraordinary series of changes to the modelling and colour of a goat's head, making metamorphosis of form itself the subject of the work.

The seven large oil paintings shot in Cinemascope which conclude the film rehearse now familiar subjects and devices on a more grandiose scale. Only two are seen for more than three minutes, making endless transformation the main theme of these final sequences. A still life combines oil painting and collage, the added pieces appearing to jump into place. The outline, shading and modelling of a reclining nude all change; the figure is overlaid with coloured patches. The intermediate stages of the work are more appealing than the busier, 'finished' version. In any case, the third painting offers us a more abstract version. A similar procedure follows with the fourth and fifth paintings of the matador tossed on a bull's horns (with more flamenco accompaniment). Far subtler gradations of colour and shading are achieved than in the earlier sketches; the massive bull's head becomes progressively less naturalistic, with the second painting reducing man and animal to geometrical forms. The two versions of the beach at La Garoupe also undergo a process of simplification and abstraction, as the details that frantically crowd the canvas (while Picasso expresses his dissatisfaction with the work) are finally stripped away. These final minutes effectively sum up Picasso's contribution to modern art: whereas his images, 'however startling, always have their origins in the real world and in past art' (Hilton 1976: 168), he abandoned the academic study of painting at a very early stage in order to explore the 'representational values of form' (Warncke and Walther 2002: 674). In this sense, he is both revolutionary and traditionalist, remote from the non-figurative, abstract artists who were much in vogue in the mid-twentieth century; one can see why he appeals to a classically minded film-maker like Clouzot.

The final painting is wiped blank and, in the closing minute, Picasso appears before another blank canvas, on which he signs his name and announces the film is over; he walks into the middle distance of the darkened studio past his paintings, seen once more in black and white. Even in these valedictory gestures, the painter puts his stamp on the enterprise. But while celebrating and perpetuating the myth of the artist's indomitable creative vitality, *Le Mystère Picasso* also reveals Clouzot as an impressive innovator in a genre remote from his previous work. The successive commercial failure of this film and the metaphysical espionage thriller *Les Espions* doubtless explains Clouzot's return to a more familiar and safer product with the courtroom melodrama *La Vérité* (1960). Nevertheless, he did not abandon the search for renewal: subsequent films like *L'Enfer* and *La Prisonnière* would attempt to invigorate familiar fictional narratives by placing much more emphasis on formal features.

As has already been suggested, the films made with Herbert von Karajan are much less interesting, since they are essentially competent, documentary records of music-making. The films were commissioned for a television series on the art of conducting, with Armand Thirard as cinematographer. The first two, shot in Vienna in November 1965, show Karajan and the Vienna Symphony orchestra performing Mozart's fifth violin concerto (soloist Yehudi Menuhin), and rehearsing Schumann's fourth symphony. The collaboration continued in January 1966 with the filming of the Berlin Philharmonic orchestra playing Beethoven's fifth symphony and Dvořák's ninth symphony. It concluded with Verdi's requiem, filmed in the empty auditorium of La Scala, Milan, on 14 and 15 January 1967. Clouzot and Karajan had met in 1963; both had the reputation of being domineering perfectionists, and had suffered similar accusations of unscrupulous careerism for their compromises with Nazism during the war. But their partnership was hardly one of equals. Although Karajan speaks sympathetically of Clouzot in his memoirs, the filmmaker is perceived as a superior technician, whose main function is to enshrine the conductor's glory, his belief that his performance is 'a creative act', that a musical work 'does not begin to live until it is in an interpreter's creative hands' (Karajan 1989: 108, 144). Filming was both time-consuming and costly. It took thirty-six hours' work using multiple cameras to shoot one symphony; in the Vienna studio recordings, the orchestra had to mime their performance to a playback of the soundtrack, with inevitable loss of spontaneity. His experience of working with Clouzot taught Karajan that it would be more cost-effective to plan and direct his own films.

Richard Osborne (1998: 537) describes the film of the Schumann rehearsal as 'a visual exploration of the inner stuff of an orchestral performance'. It is certainly a fascinating record of the mechanics of rehearsal and the relationship between conductor, players and music. Visually, however, it seems rather static and predictable: the camera is focused almost entirely on Karajan seen in mid or long-shot, typically from behind the heads and shoulders of the violinists. The conductor is the creator or inspirer coaxing the music from his orchestra; he talks interminably, while the players are glimpsed only occasionally and are silently obedient to his demands. The film of Mozart's violin concerto is set in an elegant rococo salon and strives for a less workmanlike and more dynamic, polished manner. It begins, for example, with a close-up of a candelabra and the orchestra seen reflected in a mirror, returning to the candelabra in conclusion. Close-ups of Menuhin's violin and Karajan's hands and baton are often dominant, though we also see an elaborate high-angle shot of the whole orchestra. Karajan derides the programmatic use of music in his memoirs (1989), that is music used illustratively to accompany arresting visual spectacles (tumbling waterfalls or brooding steel mills). Yet the sight of the camera roaming between conductor, soloist and orchestra is equally programmatic, in that these images are doing little more than illustrate the movements of the score and dominant performers. As Osborne (1998: 543) remarks of the Verdi requiem, what we have is 'a piece of finely crafted musical reportage' rather than memorable film-making. But the films show at least that music was perhaps less dispensable than it might have seemed in the evolution of Clouzot's work. It is worth recalling that Clouzot had virtually stripped extra-diegetic music out of the feature films he made in the 1950s, evidently seeing its conventional background presence as clichéd and redundant (in *Le Salaire de la peur*, *Les Diaboliques*, *Les Espions*); the murder victim in *La Vérité* is actually an over-ambitious young conductor. After his encounter with Karajan, however, he was willing to restore a more significant function to classical music in *La Prisonnière*.

Bibliography

Bazin, André (1959), *Qu'est-ce que le cinéma?*, vol. 2, *Le Cinéma et les autres arts*, Paris, Editions du cerf
Bernadac, Marie-Laure and Gisèle Breteau-Skira (1992), *Picasso à l'écran*, Paris, Centre Georges Pompidou

Bocquet, José Louis and Marc Godin (1993), *Henri-Georges Clouzot cinéaste*, Paris, La Sirène

Cabanne, Pierre (1992), *Le Siècle de Picasso*, vol. 3, *Guernica et la guerre (1937–1955)*, Paris, Gallimard Folio

Hilton, Tim (1976), *Picasso*, London, Thames & Hudson

Karajan, Herbert von (1989), *My Autobiography*, as told to Franz Endler, trans. Stewart Spencer, London, Sidgwick & Jackson

Lacourbe, Roland (1977), 'Henri-Georges Clouzot', *L'Avant-Scène Cinéma*, 186, 94–124

Osborne, Richard (1998), *Herbert von Karajan: A Life in Music*, London, Chatto & Windus

Pilard, Philippe (1969), *Henri-Georges Clouzot*, Paris, Seghers

Truffaut, François (1975), *Les Films de ma vie*, Paris, Flammarion

Verdet, André (1956), *Picasso à son image*, Nice, Galerie H. Matarasso

Warncke, Carsten-Peter and Ingo F. Walther (ed.) (2002), *Pablo Picasso*, Cologne, Taschen

7

The final films

Le Mystère Picasso and *Les Espions* both showed Clouzot attempting to renew himself, with an experimental documentary and an absurdist thriller. Though critics noted these innovations with varying degrees of approval, neither film drew the large audiences to which he had become accustomed over the previous decade. *La Vérité*, released in November 1960, returns to a more familiar, conventional manner. This well-crafted courtroom melodrama, starring Brigitte Bardot, ably supported by the director's stalwarts Paul Meurisse, Charles Vanel and Louis Seigner, proved to be the second most popular French film of the year, attracting 5.6 million spectators. It was awarded the Grand prix du cinéma français, and an Oscar for best foreign film in 1961. Michel Marie (2003: 86) notes that *La Vérité* achieved one of the highest ever first-run attendance figures of over half a million viewers (whereas the first run of *Le Mystère Picasso* had attracted only 37,000 people). The film was a French–Italian co-production, whose budget of 1.5 million dollars was five times higher than the average cost of a French film for the period (though a significant amount of the budget was absorbed by Bardot's fee). No fewer than six writers are credited for the screenplay: the familiar family team of Clouzot, his brother Jérôme Geronimi and wife Vera, were assisted by Michèle Perrein, Simone Drieu and the novelist Christiane Rochefort (whose reputation was built on a series of sometimes controversial works recounting the sexual and social struggles of young women; her novel *Le Repos du guerrier* was filmed by Roger Vadim in 1962, with Bardot in the central role).

The contribution of these four female writers no doubt explains in part *La Vérité*'s sympathetic and sensitive treatment of the character played by Bardot, driven to commit murder and then suicide in her quest for sexual freedom and love, and condemned by a patriarchal and prurient legal system. But Bardot's equivocal screen persona and the film's narrative structure hardly justify a proto-feminist interpretation of *La Vérité*, as we shall see. Themes of sexual oppression and obsession are central to the other two feature films which Clouzot undertook in the 1960s (*L'Enfer* and *La Prisonnière*). The director took advantage of the more permissive, anti-authoritarian climate of the decade to explore (hetero)sexual relationships more explicitly, although they are seen as tragic and tormented rather than as a source of uninhibited pleasure. More significantly, he made another considerable attempt at formal innovation, particularly with the use of colour and sound. Laurent Terzieff recalled that the enormous budget which Clouzot obtained in the deal he struck with Columbia to produce a multi-lingual version of *L'Enfer* proved to be a logistical nightmare. What survived of the film, after the director's extravagance and subsequent heart attack led to cancellation of the project, was 'un catalogue d'effets assez impressionnants. Mais aucune scène. Pas la moindre' (cited in Mauriac 1980: 176).[1] Four years later, Clouzot was at least able to retrieve some of these effects for *La Prisonnière* and graft them on to a reasonably coherent story. Here again, however, he was thwarted by unforgiving circumstances. Filming began in September 1967, but was halted in December 1967 by the director's illness, and subsequently by the events of May 1968; work resumed only in August and the film was released on Clouzot's sixty-first birthday in November 1968. Its reception was lukewarm at best (a showing of *Le Corbeau* at the Cinémathèque in December attracted more favourable attention). The last eight years of Clouzot's life were marked by failing health and an involuntary retirement from film-making, as projects foundered and critics and colleagues dismissed him as a relic of a bygone era.

Yet neither *La Vérité* nor *La Prisonnière* looks like the work of a faltering director. While the first film shows Clouzot's customary mastery of dramatic narrative and psychological engagement, even if stylistically and ideologically it may seem cautiously conservative, the second abandons many of the generic conventions of the well-made melodramatic thriller in favour of the elliptical narrative, subjective realism and stylistic mannerisms more commonly associated with

1 'A catalogue of rather impressive effects. But no scene. Not the slightest.' See chapter one for more details on *L'Enfer*.

1960s art films. As a result, *La Prisonnière* is often visually arresting, even if its plot and characterisation seem at times painfully contrived, and its eroticism excruciatingly misjudged. *La Vérité*'s popular success is due to the combination of Clouzot's storytelling, excellent ensemble playing, its modish subject and of course the sulphurous presence of its star player. As we have already seen, Clouzot made brilliant use of successive generations of top-ranking actors in his three decades as a fully fledged film-maker (Fresnay and Jouvet in the 1940s, Montand and Signoret, Vanel and Meurisse in the 1950s, Terzieff and Bardot in the 1960s). Yet though Brigitte Bardot was a magnificent prize in the late 1950s and early 1960s, she belongs to a different category from Clouzot's other leading players. Whereas their defining characteristics might be summed up as professionalism, durability, charisma and versatility, primarily displayed within the national market, she was an international movie star, whose peculiar brilliance merits special attention.

André Malraux trenchantly encapsulated the distinction:

> Une grande actrice est une femme capable d'incarner un grand nombre de rôles différents, une star est une femme capable de faire naître un grand nombre de scénarios convergents. (Cited by Pilard 1969b: 61 n.3)[2]

While the great actor is hidden beneath the range of parts across which his or her talents are dispersed, to the point of being unrecognisable at times, the star is instantly identifiable because his or her parts are always vehicles for the same iconic role. This is because, as Colin Crisp argues (1997: 216), the star system 'serves to construct specific actors and actresses as cult objects, usually though not always of an erotic nature. The cult objects condense audience fantasies.' Understanding this cult or retrieving such fantasies may prove difficult for subsequent generations of filmgoers and commentators, when social fashions and taboos have changed sufficiently to make the star's appeal or desirability seem rather mysterious or simply non-existent. The evolution of taste and passage of time create barriers which necessitate a form of archaeological reconstruction if one is to analyse such faded charm. How else can one rediscover the allure of comic actors like Jerry Lewis, suave seducers like Maurice

2 'A great actress is a woman capable of embodying a large number of different roles; a star is a woman capable of inspiring a large number of similar scripts.'

Chevalier, or the pouting sex kitten Brigitte Bardot (to cite a trio who, to a dispassionate twenty-first-century viewer, may seem respectively to be prodigiously unfunny, ludicrously unsophisticated, or strangely unerotic)? As Ginette Vincendeau (2000) observes, Bardot's screen sexuality depended to a very large extent on censorship and restraint for its appeal and waned rapidly as the permissive age made nudity, promiscuity and indecorous behaviour commonplace rather than shocking in films of the late 1960s and 1970s. Simone de Beauvoir praised Bardot as an initiator, as a rebel resisting the sexual and domestic restraints imposed on women in the 1950s and 1960s. Fifty years on, in the light of her well-publicised self-destructive tendencies, her early retirement from films in 1973, her subsequent role as an eccentric, disgracefully ageing recluse given to pontificating about animal welfare and national identity, we are likely to see Bardot as a far more equivocal figure. The shameless wild child whose monotonous acting style enraged her detractors seems to be an entity as manufactured and artificial as the over-dressed and over-coiffured female stars of the 1950s whom she displaced.

Unlike Clouzot's previous features, *La Vérité* did not derive from a script, play or novel already written by another author, but was created intentionally for Bardot after her producer Raoul Lévy solicited the director's collaboration. Although Clouzot undertook his habitual background research by attending courtroom trials, the personality and tribulations of Dominique Marceau in *La Vérité* are to a considerable extent derived from Bardot's own experience (just as Louis Malle would thinly fictionalise the perils of stardom when she appeared in *Vie privée* two years later). But while such parallels give the film added resonance (for example, the multiple suicide attempts of both character and star, their exhibitionism, the consequent mixture of adoration and opprobrium they suffer), Clouzot's great success was to make Bardot subservient to the fictional world of his film and to invest her character with genuine pathos. In this respect at least his film diverges from the ephemeral, formulaic productions which exploited Bardot's bankability and stereotyped persona. Bardot herself acknowledged in her memoirs that

Je n'ai jamais été une comédienne … Je ne me suis jamais mise dans la peau d'un personnage, mais j'ai toujours mis les personnages dans ma peau. La différence est d'importance. (Bardot 1996: 274)[3]

Recalling her tormented marital and extra-marital relationships (which included Sami Frey, who plays the lover she kills in *La Vérité*), the suicide attempts which preceded and followed the film, she recognises how the fiction echoes personal experience. With the courtroom scenes, 'Il me semblait que se déroulait mon propre procès' (Bardot, 1996: 272).[4] But since Bardot was never put on trial for murder, what she means is that she was beguiled by the plausibility of Clouzot's invention of an imaginary character and situation to which she could so readily adapt; even if the process of embodiment was involuntary, the character seems sufficiently complex and autonomous for Bardot to be consecrated as a actress rather than patronised as a narcissistic exhibitionist (Bardot 1996: 237).

La Vérité begins in a women's prison, guarded by nuns, where we discover the twenty-two-year-old Dominique Marceau defiantly smoking in her shared cell as she studies her face in a broken mirror. The remainder of the film then takes place either in the courtroom scenes set in the present, or in the recent past, through a series of flashbacks which re-enact the events leading to her shooting of Gilbert Tellier in 1958. Although this narrative reconstruction appears to be objective (that is, there is no deliberate distortion of events by biased witnesses in the fashion of Kurasawa's *Rashomon* (1950), despite the prosecution's claim to the contrary), the truth which emerges invites a variety of interpretations and makes it far from evident that Dominique will be convicted. Nevertheless, she slashes her wrists in her cell on the night before the verdict and dies in hospital after a failed blood transfusion. Such are 'Les aléas du métier', as the defence lawyer (Vanel) remarks to the prosecutor (Meurisse), cynically dismissing Dominique's tragic demise as an occupational hazard which denied the rival lawyers the chance to play their ritual game to the last. The spectator is evidently meant to interpret this dismissive and inadequate judgement as a caustic comment by the film on the failings of justice and the vanity of its proponents. Like Camus's Meursault in *L'Etranger* (1942), Dominique is the alienated observer of her own trial, although unlike Meursault she makes far more effort to justify

3 'I have never been an actress. I have never put myself into the skin of a character, but always put the characters into my skin. The difference is important.'

4 'It seemed to me that my own trial was taking place.'

herself and prefers self-destruction to passively awaiting the judgement of others.

Jean-Pierre Jeancolas (1992: 93) has argued that while a film like *Les Espions* has little interest as a cold-war thriller, it is more appealing when it recycles and parodies elements from Clouzot's earlier films (sinister nurses, dysfunctional classrooms, train corridors packed with menacing strangers). The shattered mirror which shows Dominique her distorted image and serves as a weapon for suicide evidently recalls the mirrors in *Le Corbeau* and *Quai des Orfèvres* which similarly reflect Marie Corbin and Maurice (innocents persecuted for their social ineptitude and frustrated love rather than genuine guilt), not to mention Maurice's failed suicide attempt. On the whole, however, such self-reflexive pastiche looks more like a failure of narrative inspiration in films which otherwise make no attempt to subvert conventional storytelling. Although *La Vérité* overlaps chronologically with New Wave films (and shares some of their favourite themes: sexual adventure, juvenile delinquency, critique of adult authoritarianism and puritanism), films in which Bardot also appeared, it has none of their low-budget formal insouciance. Clouzot fills the void which makes *Les Espions* seem indecipherably or meanderingly self-indulgent by returning to a rigorously organised, logical narrative, a clear (if reasonably complex) thematic argument, and a central character who is both feckless and alluring, and also complemented by adversaries whose antagonism helps define and deepen her dilemma and the audience's sympathy for her.

The initial scenes of *La Vérité* establish the ritual of the court and the regular insertion of flashbacks which replay selected episodes from Dominique's past as part of the process of retrieving and comprehending her motivation. Much is made of the self-glorifying, rhetorical duel between defence and prosecution counsels (with the implication that this is unlikely to allow a very subtle version of the truth to emerge), with the judge (Louis Seigner) acting as a paternalistic arbiter. Though filmographies list Meurisse as playing the *avocat général* (the deputy state prosecutor), he actually plays the counsel for the plaintiff (that is, he acts for Gilbert's mother), while the official public prosecutor is given only a few lines in a combat which is deliberately personalised by Meurisse and Vanel's sparring. As the jurors are selected by lottery and journalists speculate about Dominique's likely sentence, we see a close-up of the defence lawyer drawing an insect in a web (which might be interpreted as showing Dominique either as prey or predator). The first flashback shows the discovery of the body and reveals that Dominique tried to gas herself afterwards. The court then tries to re-establish the causal chain leading to these events, largely by rehearsing aspects of Dominique's biography and implying judgements about her behaviour. Given the film's ostensible anti-authoritarian posture, the viewer is not meant to share the official perception of Dominique (which can be summed up as authoritarian, condescending and uncomprehending).

Rather like Meursault, Dominique is cast as an anti-social rebel or outsider, when in fact her non-conformist behaviour derives from hedonism, indolence and resentment rather than more active, ideological opposition. That her father is a military officer and her sister Annie (Marie-José Nat) a prissy model student only makes Dominique's mutinous outbursts more appealing. The satire of reactionary bourgeois philistinism may seem rather ponderous at times. We learn that Dominique wantonly destroyed her sister's doll when she was eight (a detail relevant only if melodramatically over-interpreted as the first stage on the road to murder: she eventually seduces and kills her sister's boyfriend). Simone de Beauvoir is cited as an immoral author read by Dominique (although it is hard to imagine her having the patience to peruse Beauvoir's earnest tomes), while her attendance at the cinema is absurdly taken as another sign of 'dissipation' (a mocking echo of Raimu's paternalist courtroom tirade in *Les Inconnus dans la maison*). A flashback shows the family arguing over Dominique's urge to move to Paris; after her first suicide attempt, her wish is conceded, and both sisters leave home. While Annie studies to be a professional violinist, Dominique leads a life of depravity; at least according to the judge's voice-over, although his commentary accompanies a flashback montage which shows Dominique wearing a duffel coat and headscarf and loitering hopefully in cafés.

While Annie does the shopping and complains about Dominique's irresponsibility, Dominique finally unleashes her sensuality. She is seen in bed with her lover Michel, then alone, lounging nude in bed, or dancing nude in the apartment. In fact we see only Bardot's legs, shoulders or lower buttocks in this discreetly titillating scene (or possibly those of her body double Dany). In this scene there clearly ceases to be a disjunction between the moralising commentary of the court and the more open-minded perspective offered to the spectator,

since the camera here becomes an instrument of the court's pruri-
ence and the spectator a complaisant voyeur of the teasing display
and concealment of Dominique's body. As Vincendeau (2000)
observes, the narrative may be sympathetic to Bardot's character,
but the *mise en scène* of this solitary exotic dance reveals her more
immediate function is to become an object of desire. Annie's friend,
the aspiring conductor Gilbert, arrives to discover Dominique still
naked in bed; his contrasting sexual inhibition is displayed by the
fact that even indoors he wears a raincoat buttoned up to the chin.
When Dominique dismisses him as 'un conard pontifiant' ('a self-
important twat'), Annie drives her out of the flat; she leaves with her
possessions in a wicker trunk that bounces down the stairs like its
predecessor in *Les Diaboliques*. After a brief fling with Michel, she
shares a hotel room with Daisy. The brevity of her relationship with
Michel surprises the judge. We might take his opinion as an inappro-
priate expectation of bourgeois permanence in relationships based
more on sensual freedom. Yet Dominique's behaviour seems increasingly provocative and destructive. Gilbert's attempts to seduce her are
thwarted by the constant presence of friends in the shared room and
his sense of decorum; thus he politely shakes hands with Daisy when
she interrupts a failed tussle with Dominique, who then takes up with
a biker in order to spite him. The disconsolate Gilbert spends the
night on the streets waiting in vain for her to return.

Many of the scenes portraying the relationship between this
unlikely couple are acidly comic. Gilbert earns money by playing
the organ at church ceremonies; we see him playing while jealously
nagging Dominique, hitting false notes in both ways. They become
lovers while Daisy waits outside in the corridor for them to finish; these
unpromising surroundings silently subvert their urge to view this as
a deeply transforming experience. For a while, however, Dominique
tries to adapt to Gilbert's world, observing him in a training session
for conductors. We discover that as a musician he is passionate and
ambitious: he wants to create his own orchestra and marry Dominique
(ambitions soon revealed as incompatible). Annie too exhibits jealous
rage when she realises that she has been displaced. Another comic
scene shows Gilbert playing the piano while his landlady knits and
Dominique, wearing a demure dress, turns the pages of his music.
But she has no feeling for classical music and is oppressed by his
possessiveness. The landlady overhears their violent quarrels (as she

testifies at the trial). Dominique gets a job at a night club, where she dances to beat music and is the centre of lustful attention; when she dutifully attends Gilbert's rehearsal, she falls asleep. Their mutual goading soon drives them apart. Dominique loses her job and room, then sleeps with an American tourist, seemingly drifting into semi-prostitution. Her father dies; Gilbert and Annie get engaged.

As Dominique's behaviour becomes more openly self-destructive, the overstated moralising courtroom commentary becomes redundant. Her social and emotional world founders (loss of partner, father, job). Her sexual provocation actually isolates her from others, in that she can arouse and satisfy desire, but at the cost of betraying friendship and love. Having separated Gilbert and Annie, she brings them back together by loosening their inhibitions and demonstrating their compatibility. What intrigues the court and spectator in the final sequences of the film is why she killed Gilbert, six months after their relationship ended. Does she shoot him out of frustrated passion or to spite her sister? Does Gilbert abandon Dominique when he realises she is a liability to his career? The prosecution (and Annie) assert that the version of events we see in the final flashbacks, which cast Dominique as a victim rather than a heartless villain, represents her distorted, self-justifying interpretation. Since the preceding flashbacks have been presented as objective accounts and there are no psychological or stylistic cues to suggest a sudden shift to a more subjective perspective, the spectator has far less reason to doubt Dominique's veracity. Gilbert's professional and emotional security is contrasted with her marginalised vulnerability. Now she is the one seen loitering in the street, watching a broadcast of Gilbert conducting his orchestra on a bank of televisions in a shop window. After they spend the night together, it is clear that he wants rid of her; we see him pushing her head down to avoid the concierge spotting her as they leave. Dominique acquires a pistol, ostensibly to shoot herself, shooting Gilbert instead, several times, after he coldly advises her to commit suicide; the bullets run out before she can do so.

The narrative of *La Vérité*, with its tormented heroine, crimes of passion and heightened emotionalism may suggest that it is a skilfully melodramatic 'woman's picture'; we could explain its popular appeal by surmising that female spectators may sympathise with Dominique's dilemma as an emotional and sexual misfit in a very patriarchal society, while male viewers are enticed by the carefully staged exhibition of Bardot's body. Some critics object to what is effectively a double standard that subverts the film's air of moral superiority over its characters. As Jean-Michel Frodon complains, 'le cinéaste prend prétexte du regard des autres, prétendument dénoncé par le film, pour émoustiller le public' (quoted by Gauteur 1997: 12).[5] The voyeurism which is a latent or incidental aspect of *La Vérité* becomes formally and thematically central in *La Prisonnière*. Clouzot's final film explicitly addresses what he had defined as the defining feature of the medium, when he posed the rhetorical question: 'Qu'est-ce qu'il y a de plus voyeur qu'une caméra? Le cinéma est essentiellement un art de voyeur' (quoted by Bocquet and Godin 1993: 81).[6] His main character in *La Prisonnière* asserts the point even more forcefully by claiming that 'tout le monde est voyeur'; if voyeurism is an inherent characteristic of humanity, the cinema allows us to practise it on an imaginary level by letting us watch a representation of others' most intimate moments. Such a broad definition however elides the negative features usually associated with voyeurism (more typically seen as a form of sexual perversion, which violates the dignity of what it observes and makes those who contemplate what it records into accomplices in an oppressive contract). Stan's defence by generalisation or his pose of clear-sighted immoralism are in any case subverted in the film by his female partner José's riposte that he is 'un gamin égoïste et vicieux', 'un voyeur, mais aveugle';[7] his recourse to the camera makes him blind, in that he is incapable of seeing the true value of adult relationships.

La Prisonnière borrows its title from Proust's posthumous novel (published in 1923), which recounts how its neurotic narrator seeks and ultimately fails to capture the elusive Albertine. Although Proust and Clouzot have in common an interest in sexual obsession and compulsive spying, the film otherwise bears no resemblance to the novel, apart perhaps from its aesthetic referencing of experience. The

5 'The film-maker uses the gaze of others (which the film ostensibly denounces), as a pretext for titillating the public.'

6 'What could be more voyeuristic than a movie camera? Cinema is essentially a voyeur's art.' Dudley Andrew (1984: 150–1) suggests that viewing cinema 'is a special type of symbolic behavior distinguished by its essentially regressive character', in that it recalls the moment in early childhood when the subject experienced the narcissistic, pleasurable mastery which sight gave it over itself and its environment.

7 'A selfish, perverted kid. A voyeur, but a blind one.'

screenplay was written by Clouzot, Monique Lange and Marcel Moussy, and describes how José (Elisabeth Wiener) becomes captivated by the wealthy gallery owner Stanislas Hassler (Laurent Terzieff) when she discovers his hobby of photographing female nudes in masochistic postures. (Clouzot himself had worked on a photographic book of female nudes, a project which he decided not to publish separately, recycling certain images in the film.) After posing for Stan, José has a brief love affair with him, but when he rejects her offer of conventional love, she crashes her car and is seriously injured. Although José supposedly has an open relationship with her regular boyfriend Gilbert (a former adman and aspiring kinetic artist who exhibits in Stan's gallery), Gilbert becomes obsessively jealous of both José and Stan. Despite her rejection, José remains emotionally bonded to Stan at the end of the film, while Gilbert forlornly watches over her as she lies swathed in bandages and plaster in her hospital bed.

Much has been made of the potent nature of the gaze in film studies over recent decades. Laura Mulvey argued in her oft-cited essay on 'Visual Pleasure and Narrative Cinema' (published in 1975) that women typically are shown as erotic objects within film narratives and experienced as such by spectators. Her objection is that this 'sexualised image of women says little or nothing about women's reality, but is symptomatic of male fantasy and anxiety that are projected on to the female image' (Mulvey 1989: xiii). Like many films of the permissive era which tried to show sexual behaviour more explicitly (but actually just flaunted actresses' naked bodies), Clouzot's film might easily be taken as offering a politically incorrect object lesson in the dangers of sado-masochistic voyeurism. While Stan supposedly degrades women through his camera lens and trunkful of bondage kit, José submits to her inherent urge to abase herself and Gilbert impotently pursues both of them; all this involves bombarding the spectator with a variety of erotic images and scenes. Clouzot offered a quasi-philosophical thesis evidently meant to provide a moral justification for his film: *La Prisonnière*

> est la description d'un échec: la perversion (c'est-à-dire que l'une des personnes du couple traite l'autre en objet) est la négation de l'amour,

puisque l'amour c'est précisément la communion de deux libertés. (Quoted by Bocquet and Godin 1993: 151)[8]

He also defined sin as 'la désunion de l'homme et de la femme dans la sexualité' (cited by Pilard 1969a, 75),[9] implying a rather bleak perception that the failure of love is a given in a fallen universe. While this argument about perversion and sin may be persuasive enough as far as the characters in *La Prisonnière* are concerned, it ignores the film's complicity with voyeurism, the fact that its narrative and *mise en scène* practise and promote what it feigns to condemn.

Claude Gauteur (1997: 12) sums up the tepid critical reception of the film on the grounds that it was 'jugé trop sulfureux (fond) par les uns, trop vieillot (forme) par les autres'.[10] Few contemporary viewers are likely to agree with this judgement. By today's criteria of acceptability, where explicit sadistic violence (torture, dismemberment, mutilation) is quite common in mainstream films and explicit, unsimulated sexual acts are less common but tend to pass uncensored in art-house films, *La Prisonnière* seems quaintly decorous, no more than mildly titillating or disturbing. In consequence, Clouzot's censorious message about the metaphysics of perversion neither matches what he shows us happening on screen (which amounts largely to topless ladies writhing gracefully under Stan's stern commands) nor the aesthetic charm of these bodies and their magnificently photographed surroundings. Jean-Louis Bory remarked dismissively that *La Prisonnière* was interesting only for 'Dix minutes de documentaire éblouissant sur l'art cinétique' (quoted by Pilard 1969b: 162).[11] In fact, while the film's love triangle may seem banally formulaic, its characters rather less interesting than Stan's kinky dolls, and its supposed boldness tiresomely puerile and sexist, it has to be said that when perceived as an extended demonstration of kinetic art, its display of shape, colour, texture and movement is often visually remarkable. As an aesthetic spectacle where forms dominate figures, where art direction and cinematography (due respectively to Andreas Winding and Jacques Saulnier) overwhelm plot and charac-

---

8 'Is the description of a failure: perversion (that is, the fact that one person in a couple treats the other as an object) is the negation of love, since love is precisely the communion of two liberties.'
9 'The disunion of man and woman in sexuality.'
10 'Judged to be too sulphurous by some (content), and too old-fashioned by others (form).'
11 'Ten minutes of dazzling documentary about kinetic art.'

ter, *La Prisonnière* moves towards an expressive abstractionism quite unlike Clouzot's previous films.

Taking *La Prisonnière* as a rather ponderous study in sado-masochism awkwardly grafted on to an unhappy love story, Jacqueline Lajeunesse compared the film unfavourably to Buñuel's *Belle de jour* (1967), which blurs the boundary between its heroine's fantasies and reality far more provocatively and inventively (cited in *La Revue du cinéma* 1978). But since Clouzot's film is essentially about forms and colour, and the power of photography to distort perception and to enslave or destroy its objects, more appropriate comparisons can be made with other 1960s films which present the camera as an intrusive, destructive force, such as Antonioni's *Blow Up* (1967) (where a hedonistic photographer's exploration of abstract forms and sexual gratification in swinging London unwittingly uncovers an enigmatic murder plot), or Michael Powell's *Peeping Tom* (1960). Released in France as *Le Voyeur*, this film is about a young cameraman, whose ambition is to record on film the ultimate expression of terror; he attempts to achieve this by murdering women as he films them, using a spike concealed in his camera tripod, and forcing them to observe their agony in a distorting mirror also fitted to the camera. His victims are prostitutes, or uninhibited models and actresses; when he meets a librarian who has written a book, he turns his lethal equipment on himself rather than harm her. Though this summary may suggest otherwise, the film is neither exploitative nor prurient; the protagonist is himself shown to be the victim of psychological abuse practised on him by his father (played by Michael Powell himself, in one of many instances of self-directed humour). Although *La Prisonnière* offers no comparable deterministic backstory to explain Stan's behaviour, it borrows several other features from *Peeping Tom*, whether by accident or design. These include: the contrast between 'loose' model and inhibited middle-class woman (though it is José who is punished when she ceases to be the 'petite bourgeoise' whose inhibitions Stan derides); the contrasting use of colour and black-and-white cinematography (in each case, films about disturbed sexual behaviour recorded within the narrative are watched in monochrome);[12] and most notably, the fetishisation of the camera, as monstrous eye, mirror, substitute phallus and weapon of destruction. Stan too unleashes the metallic legs of his tripod with slow deliberation, and positions a mirror to allow his models to observe their abasement. But Clouzot shows the camera's destructive potential metaphorically rather than literally; apart from the car accident, he eschews the physical violence which marks the climactic moments of most of his films.

As these comments and comparisons suggest, *La Prisonnière* adopts many of the expressive and thematic conventions associated with 1960s arts cinema. Pierre Sorlin (1994: 168–9) asserts that

> Broadly speaking, the main novelties of the 1960s were, on the one hand, that the continuity of narration was made less rigid and, on the other hand, that films tended to present themselves as artificial creations rather than as windows opened onto reality.

Whereas *Les Diaboliques*, *Les Espions* and *La Vérité* all pose an enigma, and largely follow the dramatic structure of the thriller, in that the process of disclosure is logical and causal (though often involves concealment and surprise), *La Prisonnière* makes far less attempt to construct a coherent narrative sequence revealing plot or motivation. What we see is fragments of behaviour, and desires whose psychological roots are left unexplored. The previous films also place their characters in a plausibly detailed social world (usually involving the construction of elaborate, naturalistic studio sets), so that the bohemian left-bank milieu of middle-class Parisian students is painstakingly documented in *La Vérité*, for example. *La Prisonnière* again reverses this process. Despite its proliferation of exterior sequences apparently documenting Paris and Brittany, all the locations are made

12 Clouzot's switch from filming *La Vérité* in black and white to using colour in *La Prisonnière* corresponds entirely to evolving norms in the French industry (with only 9 per cent of films shot in colour in 1960, compared to 92 per cent in 1968: Hayward 1993). That said, following his partial use of colour in *Le Mystère Picasso* with Claude Renoir, the exploitation of colour was primary rather than incidental, in line with Colin Crisp's observation that 'Drawing on the cubist and abstract heritage of modern painting, cinematographers such as Alekan and Renoir began a campaign to use color structurally, as a signifying element rather than a crutch for realism' (Crisp 1997: 389).

into aesthetic artefacts. Scenes or shots which seem gratuitous or irritatingly mannered if taken as (unsuccessfully) revealing character or assisting narrative continuity make more sense when seen as exploring form, pattern, colour and movement.

The pre-credits sequence of *La Prisonnière* shows a male hand manipulating a series of dolls, to the sound of strident modern classical music. Unlike the faceless wooden puppets in *L'Assassin habite au 21*, these are exquisitely individuated miniature females; one is nude, one wears a black plastic mac, another has her arms tied behind her back; the hand exposes the breasts of another from inside her white dress. We see extreme close-ups of Stan's spectacled gaze and pursed lips, as he makes a nude rubbery doll writhe sensually on the richly coloured pattern of the table carpet. As an introductory scene, this establishes both Stan's fetishisation[13] of female bodies and the film's disrupted narrative. Since these dolls never appear again, we are inclined to interpret them retrospectively as symbolising his urge to reify women, or their perversely alluring movements as anticipating the performances with live models that are staged later. We cut from Stan's gaze to multi-coloured bottles aligned on the side of a milk float driving through suburbia; on an initial viewing, this spatial (and possibly temporal) transition is of course disorientating, even if the narrative logic is to introduce the contrasting domestic activities of José and Gilbert. An establishing exterior shot of their apartment building is also used to display the credits, with the actors' names being symmetrically superimposed in white capitals over the orange blinds on the windows; Clouzot's name appears over the side of a yellow post-office van. Although the vehicle might arguably be motivated as part of the morning routine, it mainly functions to provide a pleasing colour contrast (in fact this is the only reason one is likely to notice its otherwise insignificant presence). Gilbert and José rush through their preparations for the complicated daily journey into Paris; we glimpse José's nude reflection in the bathroom mirror, though she spurns Gilbert's half-hearted sexual overture. Such details pass too rapidly to acquire much significance on an initial viewing, though retrospectively again they can be taken as signs that this relationship

13 The Freudian castration anxiety and phallic substitution which commentators like Mulvey use to theorise fetishism tends to imply a normative condemnation of imagery which, as Richard Dyer has remarked (1979: 58), offers a pleasurable, sensual heightening of erotic surfaces and forms.

has lost its excitement, that José will be drawn to a man more interested in capturing images of women than one who pursues abstract shapes and pure colours.

Much of what we see on their journey from the suburbs into Paris can be explained as reflecting Gilbert's point of view, as he studies colour (women's coats), patterns of movement (the shifting configurations of railway lines) and shape (hence the close-up of the black-and-white squares of a crossword puzzle); the kinetic artist seeks inspiration in the forms thrown up by the everyday world (while his partner expresses irritation at his aesthetic absorption). Yet the camera lingers over spaces and objects that are patently outside his viewpoint. Thus we see their orange 2CV car reflected in a puddle, with a cut to a striped object being whipped across the river (possibly a float on a fishing rod), before the camera tilts up to capture the 2CV crossing the bridge above. Unlike the shot of the 2CV van crushing the paper boat in the puddle at the beginning of *Les Diaboliques*, these two shots are spatially and temporally discontinuous and redundant in terms of supplying narrative information; we are therefore more likely to read their lack of functionality as markers of the art film which is unconstrained by the denotative clarity of classical narration (see Bordwell 1985).

The first of three sequences intercalated throughout the film shows José working at an editing table at the ORTF (state broadcasting organisation); she is editing interviews with dejected women who talk about being sexually abused and enslaved by men they are unable or unwilling to leave. José is at first surprised by their masochistic submissiveness, then fascinated. Much of the second sequence consists of a long reaction shot of her watching and listening to another interview. With the third, non-diegetic music (Mahler's fourth symphony) is heard and overlaps on to a sequence showing Stan watching the slides he took of José and Maguy posing. The sound bridge and juxtaposition suggest that, like the abused women whom she now resembles, José has discovered her need for abasement; Mahler's lush, romantic music is used as a leitmotif for Stan and José's ephemeral love affair. No doubt the thesis implied by these parallels and indeed by the film's title (that is, women are the captives of their desire to be sexually humiliated and dominated) will seem offensive and false to many spectators. One might object too that it looks dangerously close to Stan's perverted sexuality, which Clouzot ostensibly condemns. Also that the material differences (of class, race, age, education, and so on) between the deprived women in the documentary footage and socially privileged José are actually so great that they are barely comparable; unlike the interviewees, José voluntarily chooses her compact with Stan.

The complex sequence presenting the exhibition preview at Stan's gallery shows José's growing estrangement from Gilbert and how she is beguiled by Stan and the hypnotically pulsating kinetic art objects and psychedelic sounds that surround the visitors. The crowd includes actors and celebrities ('la fine fleur du Tout-Paris': Bocquet and Godin 1993: 157), artists, and glamorous women. Pretentious or faltering critical appreciation is interspersed with more libidinous exchanges. Each object is overlaid by a different type of electronic music. Entering a labyrinth, José lapses into a semi-hallucinatory state. She sees multiple, distorted reflections of Gilbert and a woman journalist; as she watches them kissing, José's reflection is fragmented in a kaleidoscope. The journalist caresses an enormous rotating screw as Gilbert tries to sell himself to her and derides traditional figurative art; in fact, he gets screwed in another sense when she writes a mocking review of the exhibition. Stan gives a rather pompous speech about 'l'art cinétique', claiming that by manufacturing multiple limited copies of artworks he is launching 'le supermarché artistique' and democratising art. Neither the dandyish Stan nor the affluent crowd looks as though they have any interest at all in reaching the masses; as he admits, this is just a sales pitch.

Using distorted imagery or avant-garde sets and décor designed by celebrated artists in order to provide objective correlatives for characters' fantasies or delirium is of course a relatively common cinematic device. One thinks, for example, of the famous episode set in a hall of mirrors in Orson Welles's *The Lady from Shanghai* (1948), or Salvador Dalí's designs for the dream sequences in Hitchcock's *Spellbound* (1945). Psychedelic episodes feature in many quite conventional 1960s films (for example Stanley Donen's comedy thriller *Arabesque*, 1966). What distinguishes Clouzot is his genuine interest in the expressive possibilities of geometric abstract art, which extends beyond a purely illustrative function. Rather than arguing that the labyrinth scenes enact José's mental state in some problematic metaphorical fashion, it is simpler to say that the character is literally absorbed into the art, as her image fragments and she becomes part of the kinetic spectacle.

Clouzot's acquaintance with the Hungarian-born artist Victor Vasarely (1908–97) introduced him to Op-art and gave him access to the works featured in *La Prisonnière*. Best known for his 'kinematic images' – superimposed panes creating dynamic, moving impressions depending on the viewpoint of the observer – and his permutations of geometric forms using a strictly defined palette of colours, Vasarely aimed to create a 'perpetual mobile of optical illusion', or visual kinetics (Wikipedia 2005). The design and cinematography of *La Prisonnière* often seem to be applying these or similar processes to the film (for example with the colour and pattern of characters' dress or background objects, their spatial positioning).

With her brightly patterned clothes, frequent costume changes and richly textured auburn hair, José herself often becomes a gaudy object moving across the screen. When she enters a newsagent, visually at least our attention is focused on the bold contrasts of her orange bag overlaid with pink circles and dark blue shirt. Invited after the preview to enter Stan's private apartment, where he is attended to by a white-coated manservant (played by Dario Moreno, last seen as the bar-owner in *Le Salaire de la peur*), she discovers a treasure trove of objets d'art. Stan's pastime ostensibly involves photographing fragments of famous writers' handwriting, an arcane and austere pursuit which is a flimsy cover for his interest in women's bodies – women's bodies contorted into unnatural postures, as a glimpse of a slide interpolated among the calligraphic specimens showing a nude woman in chains, or the presence of one of Hans Bellmer's dolls suggest (these are life-like assemblages of female limbs, torsos and orifices combined in surreal shapes).

While the hunchback Brignon, the voyeur who pays Dora to photograph nude prostitutes in *Quai des Orfèvres*, is presented as a dirty old man who deserves to be murdered, the coldly elegant Stan, who controls both the camera and the elaborate ritual of the photographic sessions, inspires fascination rather than repulsion.[14] Though Gilbert uncomprehendingly denounces him as 'complètement siphonné',[15]

14 Laurent Terzieff reports that while Clouzot and Elisabeth Wiener came to blows during the filming of *La Prisonnière*, 'il me ménageait, il m'aimait comme cet autre lui-même que j'étais, alors' ('he spared me, he loved me like the other version of himself which I was playing': cited in Mauriac 1980: 184). Showing Stan smoking a pipe like the elderly director during the idyll in Brittany was doubtless taking their doubling too far.
15 'Completely crazy.'

José is enthralled by the spectacle, first watching the amateur model Maguy, then posing with her. José expresses some shame at her own voyeurism and submissive exhibitionism, but what we see is a rather tasteful erotic performance (whose failure to be either explicit or excessive makes it seem camply comic rather than shocking). The climax of the first session involves Maguy (Dany Carrel), stripped down to black knickers and a transparent plastic mac, gyrating sweatily as Stan frenziedly fires off his cameras; he finally rips open the coat and plunges his face into Maguy's breasts. This rather contradicts his claim that he avoids sexual contact with his models, as does his subsequent conventional love-making with José. Unlike the voyeurs of *Psycho* and *Peeping Tom*, whom parental tyranny and sexual dysfunction have turned into psychopathic killers, it would seem that Stan the aesthetic dandy consciously chooses to abstain from relationships based on equality or mutual affection. Thus he brusquely cuts short the idyllic honeymoon with José on the Brittany coast when he discovers that she has had a tourist photograph developed showing them as an amorous couple and is sending a sentimental postcard to a girlfriend; Stan cannot bear to be the object of another photographer's banal gaze or of schoolgirlish admiration.

Stan's relationship with José is in fact entirely consensual (unlike those in the TV film she is editing). His domination over her is curiously stylised; thus they enact an imaginary photographic session where he makes her walk with a limp by wearing only her right shoe (we recall the sulky temptress Denise's limping gait in *Le Corbeau*). But this playacting seems to release hidden self-destructive impulses in both of them. After witnessing a car accident on her way to a session, José later has a flashback to this incident and crashes her own car, apparently at the same place. A high-angle shot shows Stan crawling precariously along the edge of the roof top above his apartment. After knocking José down in a jealous rage, Gilbert confronts him on the roof, but Stan dominates the scene both spatially and psychologically. The roof becomes another labyrinth, through which Stan teasingly dodges Gilbert's pursuit, while whistling mockingly (the whistling boosted with amplified echoes which are impossible in the ambient environment). Stan is seen in long shot, silhouetted at the end of a diagonal line of chimney blocks or vents (no doubt matching Gilbert's geometric obsession), then teetering on the edge above the long drop to the street. Far from pushing him over, Gilbert pulls him back twice. The red blinds on the windows of the building opposite (which multiply between cuts) and the Eiffel tower thrusting up in the background jokingly emphasise the emotional, homoerotic intensity of the confrontation, where Gilbert behaves less like a vengeful rival than a would-be lover. But Stan has no claims on José, Gilbert or even life.

This roof-top pursuit also replicates the more playful game of hide-and-seek enjoyed by Stan and José on the beach in Brittany, although this is primarily an exercise in framing and composing colours, textures and movements: Stan's bright red jacket, José's yellow coat, the geometric lines of boats and mooring ropes through which they pass. For all its apparent charm as a found object, the seaweed necklace wrapped round José's neck nonetheless re-asserts her bondage, just as Stan's red jacket (replacing his habitual black or charcoal) can be taken as symbolising the destructive course of this relationship. That nature itself is potently destructive is suggested by the stupendous shot of the couple perched on a rock in the ocean, drenched by vast breakers; a slow zoom out makes it clear that this is no back projection, but that they are literally surrounded by the raging sea. Some of these rather wilfully artistic compositions are less effective: when we see the couple standing next to Stan's orange sports car, elegantly profiled against a cloudy seascape, we seem nearer the artful kitsch of the car commercial than the sublime. After she is abandoned, José tearfully telephones Stan to warn him of Gilbert's impending visit. As we hear Mahler's music on the soundtrack (presumably marking the end of the affair: Stan says 'Adieu'), for a few seconds we are shown the telephone wires and circuitry that transmit the call. This shot echoes one similarly showing the sending of a letter by pneumatic tube in *Baisers volés* (1968), though *La Prisonnière* has little of the playful charm of Truffaut or the whimsical self-referentiality of earlier New Wave films like Truffaut's *Tirez sur le pianiste* (1960).

Laurent Terzieff claimed that Clouzot had in fact adopted a more improvised style when making *La Prisonnière*: 'Il ne composait pas du tout, il souhait voler des plans à la vie mais sa formation s'y opposait un peu' (quoted by Bocquet and Godin 1993: 144).[16] Though this may explain the presence of certain shots which seem thematically empty, the overall impression created by the film in its final, edited form is

16 'He did not compose at all; he wanted to capture shots spontaneously from life, but his training hindered this a bit.'

of a meticulously composed aesthetic spectacle. This is demonstrated by the film's climactic conclusion, for example, where two complex montages involving hundreds of shots (some subliminal) and elaborate special effects present first José's car crash, then her delirium as she lies in hospital suspended between life and death. The first sequence lasts fifty seconds. A high-pitched buzz cues José's flashback, represented by a series of images each lasting a fraction of a second (viewed frame by frame, we discover these alternate black, red, blue and green screens with shots of Gilbert's, Stan's and José's faces). We shift to an objective viewpoint as her car hits the level-crossing barrier, stalls on the tracks, and is pulverised by a train; we end with her body sprawled across the rails. The crash itself was filmed by the assistant director Robert Ménegoz (it took three weeks to shoot and six Renault 4s: Pilard, 1969b).

The second sequence, lasting three and a half minutes and involving hundreds of images and sounds, is far more intricate. What we see and hear in grossly distorted, fragmented form effectively summarises much of the film, as though José were reliving her experiences at a frantically accelerated pace. Thus we hear camera shutters clattering, echoing electronic music, José's moaning, car tyres screeching, Mahler's music. We see Stan with his camera, José in chains, Maguy and Bellmer's doll; Stan and Gilbert's faces meld into one face; Gilbert beats Stan with a door; multiple eyes and cameras cover the screen; Stan's ripping-up of the holiday photo is run backwards, as though the relationship might be rebuilt. When José awakens, she sees Gilbert by the bed but thinks he's Stan. As Mahler's music swells up over a shot of her bandaged head, she jumps out of focus and the film ends. José has lost her grip on reality and remains trapped in the labyrinth of her fantasies. But we are unlikely to be moved by her plight: the barrage of sounds and images relaying her disturbed mental state is technically impressive, but emotionally alienating. La Prisonnière takes us into a world of cinematic abstraction unlike any of Clouzot's previous films; whether this journey is likely to please his habitual viewers and where it leaves him as a film-maker are questions to be considered in conclusion.

Bibliography

Andrew, Dudley (1984), *Concepts in Film Theory*, New York, Oxford University Press

Bardot, Brigitte (1996), *Initiales B.B. Mémoires*, Paris, Le Grand Livre du Mois

Bocquet, José Louis and Marc Godin (1993), *Henri-Georges Clouzot cinéaste*, Paris, La Sirène

Bordwell, David (1985), *Narration in the Fiction Film*, Madison, University of Wisconsin Press

Carrel, Dany (1991), *L'Annamite*, Paris, Laffont

Crisp, Colin (1997), *The Classic French Cinema 1930–1960*, Bloomington, Indiana University Press/London, I.B. Tauris

Dyer, Richard (1979), *Stars*, London, British Film Institute

Gauteur, Claude (1997), 'Variations critiques autour de Henri-Georges Clouzot', *L'Avant-Scène Cinéma*, 463, June, 1–13

Hayward, Susan (1993), *French National Cinema*, London, Routledge

Jeancolas, Jean-Pierre (1992), 'Clouzot en 1991', *Positif*, 374, April, 92–5

Marie, Michel (2003), *The French New Wave: An Artistic School*, trans. Richard Neupert, Oxford, Blackwell

Mauriac, Claude (1980), *Laurent Terzieff*, Paris, Stock

Mulvey, Laura (1989), *Visual and Other Pleasures*, Bloomington and Indianapolis, Indiana University Press

Pilard, Philippe (1969a), 'A propos d'Henri-Georges Clouzot', *La Revue du cinéma*, 232, November, 69–77

Pilard, Philippe (1969b), *Henri-Georges Clouzot*, Paris, Seghers

La Revue du cinéma (1978), various authors on Clouzot, 331b, September, 205–14

Sorlin, Pierre (1994), *European Cinemas, European Societies 1939–1990*, London, Routledge

Vincendeau, Ginette (2000), *Stars and Stardom in French Cinema*, London/New York, Continuum

Wikipedia (2005), http://en.wikipedia.org/wiki/Victor_Vasarely

Conclusion

Summing up Clouzot's achievement in the year of his death, Roland Lacourbe wrote that his films reveal 'le souci permanent du détail vrai, la volonté obstinée d'ancrer son œuvre dans le réel le plus concret', but also 'une certaine forme de cinéma "à l'ancienne mode"' (Lacourbe 1977: 95).[1] This is Clouzot as meticulous realist and author of well-made films; though ostensibly complimentary, the appraisal is subtly dismissive, recalling Truffaut's attacks on Clouzot's outmoded literary manner, his obsession with sordid detail and futile perfectionism (Truffaut 2000). It is certainly true that all Clouzot's feature films offer us painstaking reconstructions of a recognisable social world, ranging from Paris and provincial France in the late nineteenth century and mid-twentieth century to Palestine and Central America. In some cases, the background is sufficiently detailed and accurate for the films to acquire a genuine documentary value, insofar as they offer spectators historical insights into past customs, institutions and periods (such as the music hall in *Quai des Orfèvres*). Indeed, it is tempting to reverse Truffaut's critique, by arguing that Clouzot's command of detail validates his films as social documents. For instance, Clouzot's version of the occupation and liberation in *Manon* seems far more wide-ranging, authentic and persuasive (precisely because its cynical bleakness captures the spirit of the time) than the romantic melodrama and simplistic heroism offered thirty years later in Truffaut's *Le Dernier Métro*.

But the documentary manner is also part of a strategy of illusion,

---

1 'A continuing concern for true details, the obstinate will to anchor his work in the most concrete reality.' 'A certain form of old-style cinema.'

whose aim is to integrate imaginary characters and a fictional narrative into a three-dimensional social world (a world invented as part
of the film-making process: Clouzot's Palestine and Central America
were manufactured by the director and his team). Clouzot's sets, locations and props may well seduce us into believing in their fictional
reality, but this is surely an incidental achievement and certainly
not in itself a mark of great originality. His aim, as he said, was to
make the unbelievable seem plausible (see Jeancolas 1992: 92). This
is most evidently achieved in *Les Diaboliques*, since if one analyses
the plot and characters dispassionately, they seem ridiculously far-
fetched; yet actually watching the film remains a strangely beguiling
experience, even after repeated viewings. On the other hand, for all
its metaphysical ambitions, a film like *Les Espions* (the main object of
Truffaut's derision) demonstrates that assembling a group of eccentric characters in a series of sinister locales, making them vehicles
for an absurdist message, and filming them skilfully may still fail to
engage us emotionally, intellectually or aesthetically.

The final chapters of this study have shown how Clouzot made
considerable effort at the end of his career to renew both his style and
subjects as a film-maker. Complaining, as his more hostile critics do,
that he clung to outmoded formulas and conventions suggests either
wilful ignorance or at least undue attention to works like *Le Mystère
Picasso* and *La Prisonnière*. In the first film, Clouzot goes beyond the
didactic and predictable conventions of the art documentary; in the
process, he manages to tell us a great deal about Picasso as a creative
figure and to create an innovative aesthetic spectacle. *La Prisonnière*
again displays a visually dazzling engagement with abstract art; as a
fictional narrative, it does however resemble a pastiche of 1960s art
films. Although features like disrupted narration, thematically unmotivated shots, insistence on abstract forms, hallucinatory sequences,
and eroticism all reflect a conscious effort to move beyond the formal
and moral constraints imposed on mainstream films in the preceding
decades, Clouzot in his last film is an imitator rather than an innovator, even if he is not merely reduced to imitating his own obses-
sions and mannerisms.

Clouzot's career, films and reception can all be conveniently
divided into three contrasting parts. His career can be traced as a sym-
metrical parabola, since his lengthy apprenticeship as a screenwriter
and assistant director, extending through the 1930s until 1942, is

matched by the dozen years from 1964 till his death, which mark his professional and personal decline. Clouzot's success, whether measured in creative or commercial terms, occurred in the middle two decades between *Le Corbeau* in 1943 and *La Vérité* in 1960. The films from the beginning and end of his career can be categorised respectively either as entertainments (most notably the features adopted from popular literary sources, like *L'Assassin habite au 21* or *Miquette et sa mère*, which are relatively uncontroversial in subject and conventional in style) or as experiments, conscious but not always successful attempts at renewal (*Les Espions, La Prisonnière*). Between these two extremes we find the films for which Clouzot is now remembered. A further contrast is provided by Clouzot's success in drawing mass audiences and the far more ambivalent reactions of critics. While some commentators see his popular appeal as a virtue, more hostile reviewers have drawn attention to supposedly reactionary features (their disapproval gradually shifting from moral objections in the 1940s and early 1950s to complaints from New Wave supporters in the later 1950s that Clouzot's aesthetic was outdated).

Clouzot's enduring popular appeal is demonstrated by the ready availability of most of his films, which in the three decades since his death have been regularly shown on French television and in art-house cinemas in France (and even occasionally in the UK, for instance at the Edinburgh Festival in 2003). At the time of writing, nearly all Clouzot's major films are commercially available in video or DVD format (with the exception of *Miquette, Manon* and *La Vérité*), and many are available in sub-titled versions. If there is no great difficulty in gaining access to his films (so Clouzot remains a recognised and marketable figure), how one evaluates his achievement as a film-maker is evidently more problematic, since this raises questions not only about Clouzot but about film studies as an academic discipline, a critical discourse, or arbiter of changing tastes and fashions. A lot depends on how one reacts to terms like well-made film, classic French cinema, or tradition of quality. Films that seemed tiresomely outmoded thirty or forty years ago, when formal and ideological radicalism and aggressive theorising were much in vogue, usually benefit when viewed more dispassionately from the longer-term historical perspective of the twenty-first century. That Clouzot is an exemplary member of a mainstream tradition of film-making (as defined by Colin Crisp in his magisterial study of *The Classic French Cinema*,

1997) now seems incontrovertible. Yet few critics since his death have felt the urge to re-examine Clouzot's output within this tradition, other than in the format of essays devoted to a few individual films (notably, *Le Corbeau*, *Quai des Orfèvres*, *Les Diaboliques*).

David Bordwell notes that 'Godard raises as does no other director the possibility of a sheerly capricious or arbitrary use of technique'. Consequently, 'Those who dislike Godard's films may well find the works' resistance to large-scale coherence intolerably frustrating; those who admire the films have probably learned to savor a movie as a string of vivid, somewhat isolated effects' (Bordwell 1985: 312, 321). Clouzot's films demonstrate the process in reverse: technique almost invariably underpins narrative coherence and psychological consistency. His most dated films are arguably those like *Les Espions* and *La Prisonnière* where causal relationships are loosened, since their gratuitous and fragmented treatment of character and story owes too much to artistic fashions (1950s absurdism, 1960s eroticism and abstract art) that are alien to Clouzot. His boldest films, on the other hand, with their logical narrative sequence and unambiguous spatio-temporal clarity, are those which seek to 'break down the boundaries between high art and low art' (Mayne 2000: 45) by working *within* the conventions of literary adaptation and recognised genres (the thriller, adventure story or film noir). While avant-garde mannerism may be granted an unmerited importance in critical discourse, artistry which is self-effacing or serves the cause of popular entertainment is too easily overlooked (or subsumed into broader discussions of generic features which pay little attention to the specificity of individual works).

Yet Clouzot is evidently more than an entertainer, particularly if entertainment is taken to mean the production of formulaic fantasies that offer banal or consoling simplifications of life's problems. His most potent films are rarely consoling, since they dwell relentlessly on mental and physical suffering, human duplicity, social injustice and hypocrisy, and the indifference or absence of providence. They offer not escapism but a rather grim morality, as indeed titles like *Le Corbeau*, *Le Salaire de la peur* and *Les Diaboliques* explicitly suggest. Those who seek to imitate Clouzot while shunning or ignoring his moral perspective have never succeeded. Even when remade by respected directors, the US versions of his films are bland dilutions, which eschew Clouzot's provocative pessimism (while denying American audiences access to the original). William Friedkin's adaptation of *Le Salaire de la peur* as *Sorcerer* (1977) was a flop, while Otto Preminger's adaptation of *Le Corbeau* as *The Thirteenth Letter* (1951) led to the blockage of US exhibition of *Le Corbeau* and the destruction of most copies until the late 1950s. Neither film has been commercially available in Europe for decades, to the best of my knowledge. Though Preminger's film (which can be viewed at the BFI film archive in London) rather skilfully transposes *Le Corbeau* to French Canada, it has none of the wit and venom of the original. Dr Pearson (the equivalent of Germain) is a bland charmer, while the anonymous letter-writer is much more polite than the 'corbeau'; all the references to abortion and corruption are deleted, so that a caustic social satire becomes a much blander thriller. (For a fuller discussion, see Williams 2002.)

In 1959, the weekly magazine *L'Express* organised a debate on French cinema between Clouzot, Jacques Becker, Louis Malle and Claude Chabrol, taken as representing the older and younger generations of film-makers. Although the discussion ranges somewhat inconclusively over sundry topics (the cinema's expressive strengths and limitations compared with other art forms, the importance of budgets and audiences, the status of Hitchcock, the star system), there is little significant dissent between the generations. While acknowledging Hitchcock as a master entertainer, Clouzot doubts that he has anything to say; Becker finds the younger generation's over-interpretation of Hitchcock incomprehensible; Malle perceives 'toute une épaisseur' behind Hitchcock's showmanship (without explaining what this extra dimension involves); Chabrol concedes that *Cahiers du cinéma*'s promotion of Hitchcock was initially fabricated, but then acquired its own momentum; Becker adds that Hitchcock is a phenomenon partly because of his sheer productivity. But all four agree that the film director's goal should be to stamp his own creative personality on his work and to extend the cinema's means of expression (by way of example, Clouzot describes his abortive attempt, in collaboration with Sartre, to write a screenplay presenting a character's stream of consciousness). Three of the four had their careers prematurely cut short: like Clouzot, Becker produced only a dozen films, dying aged fifty-four in 1960, the year after this encounter, while Malle died at sixty-three in 1995. Only Chabrol, now in his mid-seventies, continues to be phenomenally productive. Yet all four brilliantly illustrate a certain tendency of French cinema: to make films that are popular but not banal, innovative and provocative but not hermetic, intelligent and serious but not pretentious and dull. Cinema as consummate craftsmanship, cinema as caustic commentary, whose enduring artistry beguiles and disturbs.

Bibliography

Bordwell, David (1985), *Narration in the Fiction Film*, Madison, University of Wisconsin Press

Crisp, Colin (1997), *The Classic French Cinema*, Bloomington, Indiana University Press/London, I.B. Tauris

L'Express (1959), 'Pourquoi font-ils des films (Clouzot, Becker, Malle Chabrol)?', 7 May, 33–6

Jeancolas, Jean-Pierre (1992), 'Clouzot en 1991', *Positif*, April, 374, 92–5

Lacourbe, Roland (1977), 'Henri-Georges Clouzot', *L'Avant-Scène Cinéma*, 186, 94–124

Truffaut, François (2000), *Le Plaisir des yeux: écrits sur le cinéma*, ed. Jean Narboni and Serge Toubiana, Paris, Petite Bibliothèque des Cahiers du cinéma

Williams, Alan (2002), 'The Raven and the Nanny: The Remake as Crosscultural Encounter', in J. Forrest and L.R. Koos, eds, *Dead Ringers: The Remake in Theory and Practice*, New York, State University of New York, 151–68

Filmography

Clouzot as director *(dates are of initial release in France)*

La Terreur des Batignolles 1931, 15 mins, b/w

Production: Osso
Script: Jacques de Baroncelli
Photography: Louis Chaix
Sound: Bugnon
Art director: Wilke
Music: D.E. Inghelbrecht
Actors: Louis-Jacques Boucaut (burglar), Germaine Aussey (Marianne), Jean Wall (Robert)

L'Assassin habite au 21 1942 (*The Murderer Lives at No 21*), 84 mins, b/w

Production: Continental Films
Script: H.-G. Clouzot and S.-A. Steeman (from Steeman's novel)
Photography: Armand Thirard
Sound: W.R. Sivel
Art director: André Andrejew
Music: Maurice Yvain
Editor: Christian Gaudin
Principal actors: Pierre Fresnay (Commissaire Wens), Suzy Delair (Mila Malou), Pierre Larquey (Colin), Noël Roquevert (Linz), Jean Tissier (Lalah-Poor)

Le Corbeau 1943 (*The Raven*), 92 mins, b/w

Production: Continental Films
Script: Louis Chavance and H.-G. Clouzot
Photography: Nicolas Hayer
Sound: W.R. Sivel
Art director: André Andrejew
Music: Tony Aubin
Editor: Marguerite Beaugé
Principal actors: Pierre Fresnay (Dr Germain), Ginette Leclerc (Denise), Pierre Larquey (Dr Vorzet), Héléna Manson (Marie Corbin), Micheline Francey (Laura Vorzet), Noël Roquevert (Saillens), Liliane Maigné (Rolande), Roger Blin (cancer patient), Sylvie (his mother)

Quai des Orfèvres 1947 (*Jenny Lamour*), 105 mins, b/w

Production: Majestic Films
Script: Jean Ferry and H.-G. Clouzot (based on Steeman's novel *Légitime défense*)
Photography: A. Thirard
Sound: W.R. Sivel
Art director: Max Douy
Music: Francis Lopez
Editor: Charles Bretoneiche
Principal actors: Louis Jouvet (Inspecteur Antoine), Suzy Delair (Jenny Lamour), Bernard Blier (Maurice Martineau), Simone Renant (Dora), Pierre Larquey (taxi driver), Charles Dullin (Brignon), Robert Dalban (Paulo)

Manon 1949, 96 mins, b/w

Production: Alcina
Script: Jean Ferry and H.-G. Clouzot (updated from Abbé Prévost's novel)
Photography: A. Thirard
Sound: W.R. Sivel
Art director: Max Douy
Music: Paul Misraki
Editor: Monique Kirsanoff
Principal actors: Cécile Aubry (Manon), Michel Auclair (Robert Desgrieux), Serge Reggiani (Léon Lescaut)

Le Retour de Jean 1949, 28 mins, b/w

Episode in *Retour à la vie*
Production: Films Marceau
Script: J. Ferry and H.-G. Clouzot
Photography: Louis Page
Sound: Roger Biard
Art director: Max Douy
Music: P. Misraki
Editor: M. Kirsanoff
Principal actors: Louis Jouvet (Jean Girard), Bernard (Léo Lapara), Jo
    Dest (escaped German)

Miquette et sa mère 1950, 96 mins, b/w

Production: Alcina, CICC, Silver Films
Script: J. Ferry and H.-G. Clouzot (from play by Robert de Flers and
    G.-A. de Caillavet)
Photography: A. Thirard
Sound: W.R. Sivel
Art director: Georges Wakhewitch
Music: Albert Lasry
Principal actors: Danièle Delorme (Miquette), Louis Jouvet (Monch-
    ablon), Bourvil (Urbain), Saturnin Fabre (Marquis), Mireille Perrey
    (Mme Grandier)

Le Salaire de la peur 1953 (*The Wages of Fear*), 142 mins, b/w

Production: CICC, Filmsonor, Vera Films, Fono Roma
Script: Jérôme Geronimi and H.-G. Clouzot (from G. Arnaud's
    novel)
Photography: A. Thirard
Sound: W.R. Sivel
Art director: René Renoux
Music: Georges Auric
Editor: Henri Rust
Principal actors: Yves Montand (Mario), Charles Vanel (Jo), Folco Lulli
    (Luigi), Peter Van Eyck (Bimba), Vera Clouzot (Linda), William
    Tubbs (O'Brien), Dario Moreno (Hernandez), Jo Dest (Smerloff)

Les Diaboliques 1955 (*The Fiends*), 114 mins, b/w

Production: Filmsonor, Vera Films
Script: J. Geronimi, H.-G. Clouzot, René Masson and Frédéric Grendel
(based on Boileau-Narcejac's *Celle qui n'était plus*)
Photography: A. Thirard
Sound: W.R. Sivel
Art director: Léon Barsacq
Music: Georges Van Parys
Editor: Madeleine Gug
Principal actors: Paul Meurisse (Michel Delasalle), Simone Signoret
(Nicole Horner), Vera Clouzot (Christina Delasalle), Jean Brochard
(Plantiveau), Pierre Larquey (Drain), Michel Serrault (Raymond),
Charles Vanel (Fichet), Yves-Marie Maurin (Moinet)

Le Mystère Picasso 1956 (*The Picasso Mystery*), 75 mins, b/w and
colour

Production: Filmsonor
Script: H.-G. Clouzot and P. Picasso
Photography: Claude Renoir
Sound: Jo de Bretagne
Music: G. Auric
Editor: Henri Colpi
With Clouzot and Picasso

Les Espions 1957 (*The Spies*), 137 mins, b/w

Production: Filmsonor, Vera Films, Pretoria Film
Script: J. Geronimi and H.-G. Clouzot (from Egon Hostovsky's novel
Le Vertige de minuit)
Photography: C. Matras
Sound: W.R. Sivel
Art director: R. Renoux
Music: G. Auric
Editor: M. Gug
Principal actors: Gérard Séty (Dr Malic), Vera Clouzot (Lucie), Curd Jür-
gens (Alex), Paul Carpenter (Howard), Peter Ustinov (Kaminsky),
Sam Jaffe (Cooper), Martita Hunt (Conny)

La Vérité 1960 (*The Truth*), 124 mins, b/w

Production: Iéna, CEIAP
Script: H.-G. Clouzot, J. Geronimi, S. Drieu, M. Perrein, C. Rochefort
Photography: A. Thirard
Sound: W.R. Sivel
Art director: J. André
Editor: Albert Jurgenson
Principal actors: Brigitte Bardot (Dominique Marceau), Marie-José Nat (Annie Marceau), Sami Frey (Gilbert Tellier), Paul Meurisse (prosecuting counsel), Charles Vanel (defence counsel), Louis Seigner (judge)

La Quatrième Symphonie de Schumann 1966 Production: Cosmotel

Performed by the Vienna Symphony Orchestra, conductor Herbert von Karajan

Le Cinquième Concerto pour violon de Mozart 1966 Production: Cosmotel

Performed by Yehudi Menuhin and the Vienna Symphony Orchestra, conductor Herbert von Karajan

La Cinquième Symphonie de Beethoven 1966 Production: Cosmotel

Performed by the Berlin Philharmonic Orchestra, conductor Herbert von Karajan

La Neuvième Symphonie de Dvořák 1966 Production: Cosmotel

Performed by the Berlin Philharmonic Orchestra, conductor Herbert von Karajan

Le Requiem de Verdi 1967 Production: Cosmotel

Performed by the chorus and orchestra of La Scala, Milan, conducted by Herbert von Karajan

La Prisonnière 1968 (*The Prisoner*), 105 mins, colour

Production: Films Corona, Vera Films, Fono Roma
Script: H.-G. Clouzot, M. Lange, M. Moussy
Photography: A. Winding
Sound: L. Ducarme and W.R. Sivel

Art director: J. Saulnier
Music: G. Amy
Editor: Noëlle Balenci
Principal actors: Elisabeth Wiener (José), Laurent Terzieff (Stan), Bernard Fresson (Gilbert), Dany Carrel (Maguy), Dario Moreno (Salah)

Clouzot as scriptwriter

Clouzot is credited as contributing to the script, dialogue, lyrics or adaptation of the following films (directors shown in brackets):

Je serai seule apres minuit (Jacques de Baroncelli, 1931)
Le Chanteur inconnu (Victor Tourjansky, 1931)
Ma cousine de Varsovie (Carmine Gallone, 1931)
Un soir de rafle (Carmine Gallone, 1931)
Faut-il les marier? (Carl Lamac and Pierre Billon, 1932)
La Chanson d'une nuit (Anatole Litvak, 1932)
Le Dernier Choc (Jacques de Baroncelli, 1932)
Le Roi des palaces (Carmine Gallone, 1932)
Caprice de princesse (Karl Hartl, 1933)
Château de rêve (Geza von Bolvary, 1933)
Tout pour l'amour (Joe May, 1933)
Itto (Jean Benoît-Lévy and Marie Epstein, 1935)
Education de prince (Alexandre Esway, 1938)
Le Révolté (Léon Mathot and Rober Bibal, 1938)
Le Duel (Pierre Fresnay, 1939)
Le Monde tremblera (Richard Pottier, 1939)
Le Dernier des six (Georges Lacombe, 1941)
Les Inconnus dans la maison (Henri Decoin, 1941)
Si tous les gars du monde (Christian-Jaque, 1955)
L'Enfer (Claude Chabrol, 1994)

Select bibliography

Archives and screenplays

Apart from the archival material held at the Bibliothèque du Film in Paris and the critical essays on separate films already cited in the references to the chapters of this book, the most useful sources of information and ideas about Clouzot are provided by *L'Avant-Scène Cinéma*, which has published screenplays and selected reviews of the following films:

Le Corbeau (1977, 186)
Quai des Orfèvres (1963, 29; reprinted 1999, 487)
Le Salaire de la peur (1962, 17)
Les Diaboliques (1997, 463)

Biography

Bocquet, José-Louis and Marc Godin, (1993, re-issued 2003), *Henri-Georges Clouzot cinéaste*, Paris, La Sirène. (For a well-documented account of Clouzot's life and career, this is the only book that can be recommended.)

French cinema and film studies

Bordwell, David (1985), *Narration in the Fiction Film*, Madison, University of Wisconsin Press. (Excellent analysis of how plot and narrative structure work in film.)

Crisp, Colin (1997), *The Classic French Cinema*, Bloomington, Indiana University Press/London, I.B. Tauris. (Helpfully places Clouzot's work in the wider context of French cinema and classic film.)

Powrie, Phil and Keith Reader (2002), *French Cinema: A Student's Guide*, London, Arnold. (A clear, informative and comprehensive introduction.)

Reference works and online resources

Blandford, Steve, Barry Keith Grant and Jim Hillier (2001), *The Film Studies Dictionary*, London, Arnold. (Clear and comprehensive guide to terminology and concepts.)

Passek, Jean-Loup (1996), *Dictionnaire du cinéma*, 2 vols, Paris, Larousse. (Excellent guide in French to terminology, history, directors and actors.)

Rapp, Bernard and Jean-Claude Lamy (2002), *Dictionnaire des films*, Paris, Larousse. (An equivalent guide in French listing films, with detailed entries for major works.)

Key online resources for information on films and critical material include: Film Index International, International Movie Database, and the MLA bibliography.

Index

Page numbers in *italics* refer to illustrations, and 'n.' after a page number indicates the number of a note on that page.